Educating Ex-Criminal Tribes

Educating Ex-Criminal Tribes

Issues and Concerns

Malli Gandhi

RAWAT PUBLICATIONS
Jaipur • New Delhi • Bangalore • Guwahati • Kolkata

ISBN 978-81-316-0788-6

Published by
Prem Rawat for **Rawat Publications**
Satyam Apts, Sector 3, Jawahar Nagar, Jaipur 302 004 (India)
Phone: 0141 265 1748/7006 Fax: 0141 265 1748
E-mail: info@rawatbooks.com
Website: www.rawatbooks.com

New Delhi Office
4858/24, Ansari Road, Daryaganj, New Delhi 110 002
Phone: 011 2326 3290

Also at *Bangalore, Guwahati* and *Kolkata*

Typeset by Rawat Computers, Jaipur
Printed and bound in India

In memory of

Vennnelakanti Raghavaiah
Palaparti Veeraiah
Devarakonda Hanumantha Rao
Madigani Devadathu
Galeti Venkateswarlu
Chadala Janki Ramarao

for their contribution to the
development of Denotified Communities.

Contents

Acknowledgements

I am very thankful to Professor Hrushikesh Senapaty, Director, NCERT; Professor B.K. Tripathi, Joint Director, NCERT and Professor D.G. Rao, Principal, RIE, Mysore for their constant support and encouragement. I am thankful to Shri Bhiku Ramji Idate, Chairman, NCDNT; Shri H.K. Dash, Member Secretary; Dr. B.L. Meena, Joint Secretary and Dr. B.K. Lodhi, Deputy Secretary, NCDNT, New Delhi for their encouragement. I am also indebted to all the village elders with whom I have interacted at Siddhapuram, Stuartpuram, Kapparallatippa, Sitanagaram and Lingala and whose valuable information has been utilised for the study. I am very grateful to Sri Rafi Ahmad, headmaster, DNT School, Kapparallatippa; Smt. Deta Pabe, headmistress, Salvation Army Aided Primary School, Stuartpuram; Sri D. Hussain, headmaster, Government Denotified Tribal Elementary School, Siddhapuram; Sri N. Peter Smiles, headmaster, Government Upper Primary DNT School, Sitanagaram (Tadepalli) and all the teaching staff working in the five DNT schools for providing me necessary information and helping me in executing research tools. I am equally indebted to all the tribal parents in the DNT colonies, community leaders and children in the selected schools without whose help the present work might not have been completed. I am equally thankful to District Education Authorities, Mandal Education Officers, Mandal Resource Persons and the Managers of the villages for their cooperation, information and timely help. I sincerely thank Professor V. Ramakrishna (University of Hyderabad), Dr V. Lalitha (NIRSA, Hyderabad), Professor P. Venkata Rao (University of Hyderabad), Dr K. Sashidhar Rao (IASE, Hyderabad), Prof M.L.K. Murthy (University of Hyderabad), Professor D. Narasimha Reddy, Professor Haragopal and Prof Sudarshanam (University of Hyderabad), Prof Kalapana Kannabiran, Director, CSD, Hyderabad for their academic help. I sincerely thank Sri K. Ganapathi Bhat for his valuable comments and suggestions. I also thank Dr A.S.N. Rao Sindhe for his timely help. I am thankful to the staff members of National Archives, New Delhi;

Tamil Nadu State Archives, Chennai and Andhra Pradesh State Archives, Hyderabad for providing me necessary records. I am equally thankful to the staff members of various libraries – Sarawatha Niketanam Library, Rajahmundry; Gautami Library, Vetapalem; Jawaharlal Nehru University Library, New Delhi University of Hyderabad Library staff; Bharatiya Adimjati Sevak Sangh, New Delhi; Nehru Memorial Museum and Library, New Delhi and Anthropological Survey of India, Mysore for providing me necessary records and books.

Shri Pranit Rawat shaped this work in many ways. I sincerely thank him for his painstaking effort for accepting and publishing this work. I also thank Sri Ravindra Kumar at Rawat Publications for editing my manuscript.

Malli Gandhi

Preface

India has been the home for many heterogeneous ethnic groups. These groups generally lived in solitude, having no communication with outside world. As a result, they had no civilisation impact. This was mainly responsible for their poverty, backwardness and social alienation. In the case of tribes, listed as 'Criminal' (Denotified/Nomadic/Semi-Nomadic) they have been suffering from a stigma. It is, indeed, very important to know about the educational opportunities available to these communities/tribes in the present habitat known as settlements or villages.

The present work reviews some of the important aspects and issues involved in the primary schooling of the children hailing from the Denotified Tribes (DNT) families of erstwhile Criminal Tribes (CT) settlements of the colonial era. Today, there is a strong objection raised regarding the pathetic conditions of education and educational institutions prevailing in the settlement (colonies) schools. The status of Andhra Pradesh in general, and India in particular, in respect of these tribes stands in unique contrast to the rest of the country. There are social and behavioural changes taking place among the members of the DNT settlement areas in Andhra Pradesh. The DNT settlements such as Stuartpuram, Sitanagaram (Guntur district), Kapparallatippa and Bitragunta (Nellore district), Siddhapuram (Kurnool district) and Lingala (Mahaboobnagar district) in Andhra Pradesh constitute a major segment of the total Scheduled Tribes population in India. In all these settlement areas, Yerukulas, Woddars, Katheras, Chenchus, Sugalis, Yanadis, Dasaris and other nomadic tribes form a major part of the population. Some of the settlers are still having serious problems of crime and illiteracy. On the whole, the scenario in Andhra Pradesh offers a vivid contrast on any comparison. Representatives from the academic research (from University of Hyderabad); senior faculty members of Regional Institute of Education (RIE) Mysore, settlement school headmasters, teachers, Mandal Education Officers (MEOs), Mandal resource persons, parents of the school children, NGOs

(Samskar) and experts from Sarva Shiksha Abhiyan (SSA), Hyderabad have taken part directly and indirectly in the entire course of the work. The present study has focused on the following important issues such as: (1) Profiling the problems of the DNT children – problems of learning and those related to teachers, students, curriculum, administration, etc. (2) Profiles of primary schools (pen pictures of primary schools) in the DNT settlements (colonies), (3) Present status of education among the DNT children, (4) Gaps, strategies, remedies and suggestions, (5) The relation between school, home and community in the DNT settlements, and (6) A vision for the future education of the DNT children.

One of the main problems identified by the field experiences and the field survey in DNT settlements is about the social treatment meted out to the families of these tribes. For generations together, the DNT families and their members have been labelled as criminals and suffered dishonour and social negligence. The reasons are not far to seek here, given the background of the socially despicable avocation as practised by some of the people belonging to these tribes. The children and women, in particular, have suffered ignominy from mainstream society. The stigma of criminality is still one of the major impediments in the smooth running of educational progress of children and youth. Children often face a kind of social alienation in most walks of social life.

Social alienation, particularly at young age, hampers the growth of psycho-social faculties of the children. Social practices of the mainstream society have denied opportunities for the children coming from the so-called CT families residing in the settlement areas. The approaches of the government often remain impersonal with lack of human element and eye on social cohesiveness in its approach. However, there can be education without even the formal modes and methods of schooling. But mere efforts on mainstream socialisation does not open a wide social canvas for the children because there is already a hostile attitude in the outside society. The school or the process of schooling in settlement areas or settlement schools may be used as instruments or tools to impart social culture, feelings of common fraternity, community approach, adjustment mentality, atmosphere of working and learning together and, finally moral dynamics of social and cultural behaviour. The schools in settlement areas are to be treated or perceived from a different angle where they are expected to combine the roles of an instructor, change agent, catalyst and humanist.

The positive aspect in the government schools or those run by private parties is that there is a general schooling atmosphere that best suits the needs of the children from the mainstream society. This kind of atmosphere need not always be congenial to the requirements of social and cultural transformation of the children who are already suffering the social stigma and are alienated. The government is taking care to mainstream the differently-abled children through advocating their admission into general schools so that these children too will have the necessary advantage of 'feel good' factor and forget the physical constraints. The same approach may, perhaps, be extended without any reservations in case of the children who are socially alienated. However, in the present case, efforts shall be directed towards the direction of mingling ordinary children with the children of these tribes in separate schools with residential facilities. Since the DNTs too are considered under the general item of 'tribes' by the planners and policy makers, the scope for public sanctions for the welfare of these relatively ignored tribes is limited and confined.

Among the socially and economically backward classes majority of the families wish to retain some of their children at home without sending them to school. They have their own family and economic reasons for not sending their wards to centres of learning. Barring further discussion on this, the point of reference here is that children from the so-called criminal families (whether reformed or not) have a tendency of not going to school or dropping out of school if already admitted. For, there is an unwritten feeling among these children that they will receive not only education, but also social humiliation from co-learners as well as teachers (sometimes). Secluded, aloof and separated they feel happier than being insulted in the rest of the society. It is very important that the ice be broken. So, special schools or shaping the existing schools/facilities into special schools for an ideal social integration are necessary. Samskar, an NGO in Andhra Pradesh, has already succeeded in using the school as a centre of social integration and mainstreaming in Nizamabad district in Andhra Pradesh, where it is working with a similar problem with Jogini women and children.

The need (both felt and perceived) is that the children in these settlement areas should be exposed to a kind of development education where aspects of social development and mainstreaming is unhindered and healthy socialisation will combine to keep the morale of the learners on a higher pedestal. Along with prescribed and formatted curriculum, realistic or scientific knowledge, social outlook and personality development may be included in the general teaching atmosphere of the schools in settlements. Efforts are to be made to encourage ordinary students from outside the settlement to get admitted into these schools so that the dichotomy between these branded children and the other children may get diluted in the course of time. Lack of census data, absence of policy level discussions on DNTs and their children, seeming that the issues of the DNTs are outside the purview of Planning Commission estimates (always Primitive Tribal Groups other than DNTs are covered), weak community participation in these settlements and lack of need-based training given to teachers teaching in the settlement schools are some of the serious gaps found through the present study in the selected DNT schools of Andhra Pradesh.

The aims and objectives of the present study is to know about the education system prevailing in the DNT schools from origin to the present, to study the educational facilities provided to the children of the DNTs in the schools, to know the perception of children, parents and community members about their education, to analyse the problems or factors affecting the students' achievements, to know the problems of teachers, educational functionaries in providing quality education in the DNT schools and to study the specific qualities of the children in the settlements and finally to suggest the ways and means to bring about meaningful education required in these schools. However, the main aim is to study the factors affecting students' achievements in the selected primary schools of DNT settlements in Andhra Pradesh. The present study also intends to gather information and examine to what extent education has spread among the DNTs of Andhra Pradesh, its implication for the empowerment and development of DNT communities, to review the status of education of the DNTs in the past and present scenario, to suggest the ways and means for better education of the DNT communities, the education dimension of DNTs; finally to study the socio-economic background of the DNTs as a backdrop of education for the DNTs in Andhra Pradesh.

The study makes an endeavour in establishing linkages between the contemporary realities of schooling in the settlements on the one hand and to understand the field situation of schooling, issues and problems that directly or indirectly having a bearing on their educational prospects of the DNT children on the other. The study closely looks into the educational status of the DNT children and their school participation, problems relating to provisions, incentives, infrastructure, teaching transaction, teaching learning conditions, materials, etc.

Due to acute poverty, unemployment, displacement and migration, a small section of these tribes were forced to take to illegal means to eke out their livelihood. In spite of their 'criminal' activities allegedly profitable, they are unable to lead a happy life. Their children are facing social discrimination, stigma and ill-treatment in the public. Due to poverty, ignorance, illiteracy, illness and rising levels of unemployment and stress, the DNT children are unable to develop in a proper atmosphere. These problems are analysed to draw proper conclusions. In addition, the study closely looks into the educational progress, school participation, educational inequalities among the DNT children and the role of the children in the family set-up and their contribution to the family economy is also considered relevant to the present study.

The present study intends to look into the aspects of basic education, residential schooling, primary, secondary and vocational education. For educating the children of the DNTs in every settlement, taluks, there should be residential schools exclusively for them. Therefore, the study looks into adequate special provisions and budgetary allocations to be made. Further, the study also deals with the elimination of child labour practices, protection of children from atrocities, protection of girl children in the settlements/*thandas* and promoting education among the DNT tribal girl children in the selected DNT settlements. It is difficult for the DNTs to send their children to regular schools because their livelihood makes it necessary for them to keep moving. The DNTs include people who move from village to village doing agricultural and labour contract works. The parents of the DNT children move seasonally in search of paid work in cities. These children are found all over the country as rag pickers, etc. Therefore, special mobile schools, residential or ashram schools should be opened for them. The study looks into the following research questions:

- What are the problems faced by the DNT children in primary schools of Andhra Pradesh?
- What are the government initiated programmes to help the DNT children?
- What are the problems hampering the academic growth of the children of the DNT schools in Andhra Pradesh?
- What are the academic achievements of the DNT school children of classes 1 to 5?
- What are the problems related to enrolment, retention of the DNT children of Andhra Pradesh?
- What is the educational system prevailing in the DNT settlements in Andhra Pradesh?
- What are the educational facilities available for the DNT children in Andhra Pradesh?
- What are the specific academic, socio-economic and cultural problems which are affecting the student achievement at primary stage in DNT schools?
- What are the main problems of teachers, head teachers, parents and educational functionaries in providing quality education to DNT children?
- What are the specific socio-economic problems of DNT children studying in settlement schools at primary stage?
- What are the ways and means to bring about a meaningful education in the DNT schools?
- What is the contemporary reality of schooling of children belonging to DNT tribes?
- What is the present field situation of schooling in the DNT settlements or colonies and issues and problems that directly or indirectly are having a bearing on their educational prospects?

- What is the educational status of the DNT children? What is the present scenario of the children in the DNT settlements?
- What are the problems relating to funding, provisions, schools, hostels, incentives, infrastructure, teaching transaction, teaching-learning conditions, teaching-learning materials in the DNT schools?
- What is the strategy of curriculum transaction in the DNT schools?
- What is the language used for the transaction and language barrier for the effective learning among the children of the DNTs and how to enhance teacher competence in DNT schools in Andhra Pradesh?

The study is divided into six chapters as follows: the first chapter titled, 'From Criminal Tribes to Denotified Tribes: A Historical Survey' deals with establishment of CT settlements in Andhra Pradesh and the initiatives taken for the education of the children of the CTs in a historical perspective. The second chapter, 'Reformatory Education for the Children of "Criminal Tribes" in Madras Presidency' deals with the origin and development of Reformatory schools, its aims and objectives, training imparted in the schools, etc. The third chapter, 'Vocational Education for the Children of Criminal Tribes' focuses on the role of the missionaries and the government in introducing vocational training for the children living in the settlements. The fourth chapter, 'Educational Status of the Denotified Tribes in Andhra Pradesh: Attainments and Challenges' focuses on educational status of the children in present existing DNT colonies. The fifth chapter, 'Factors Affecting Literacy of Denotified Tribe Children in the Settlement Schools of Andhra Pradesh' deals with collection of data, field work and research methodology adopted to conduct the study in the selected settlement schools. The sixth chapter, 'Implications' provides broad hints based on the contents covered earlier and also makes certain suggestions, action points relating to the improvement of educational programmes in the DNT schools.

1

From 'Criminal' Tribes to Denotified Tribes

A Historical Survey

The aims and objectives of this chapter is to present: (1) a brief historical background and concept of Criminal Tribes (CT) settlements, (2) role of the Christian Missionaries, (3) official policy, (4) settlement patterns, (5) progress made in the settlements in Andhra Pradesh over a period of time, (6) from 'criminal' tribes to denotified communities and (7) to study the socio-economic background of the DNTs as a backdrop of education. Source materials for this are government records collected from the State Archives Andhra Pradesh (Hyderabad), Tamil Nadu (Chennai) and National Archives (New Delhi). The archival sources like Law (General) Department, Home Department, Revenue Department, Public Works (Labour) Department, Judicial Department, Development Department, Forest Department, Missionary sources, published books and government reports constitute the major source for the present chapter.

Historical Background and Concept of CT Settlements

India is the only country in the world where the British Government in 19th century branded certain tribes as 'criminal' tribes, inferring that they were criminals by birth and crime was their profession.[1] To contain them, one of the programmes implemented by the then government was to gather active criminals belonging to those tribes at one place, like an open air jail, but along with their families. Often, Christian Missionaries were given the management of these 'criminal' settlements with magisterial powers. In such a situation, a culture of crime developed. As crime is anti-social, there has been always a clash with the rest of the society. According to Hindu Varna system, when crime is attributed as a profession of a particular group of people, it becomes a part of design by the divine. It becomes very difficult to make them understand reason and change. Some of the people belonging to other social categories involved in crime do not have the stigma of criminality unlike the Denotified Communities/Tribes in India. When the British Government branded certain castes, communities and tribes as criminals, it meant that those thus branded would become so considered by birth and profession. Perhaps, the Criminal Tribes Act (CTA) had an implicit assertion that a woman from criminal family would necessarily conceive a criminal embryo. The Denotified Tribes (DNTs) have been included in this category, whereas other criminals escaped the branding.

The problem of crime is a major issue faced by mankind, though it varies its form from place to place and period to period, according to the value system of people. Crime on the streets, in towns, banks or on trains have become a common topic for discussion in every part of the country. It is as old as human-failing as the birth of mankind itself. In India or elsewhere in the world, the mass media are filled daily with lurid descriptions of genocide, sensational robberies, gangsterism, police politician collusion in matters associated with corruption, unthinkable embezzlements of public funds by respected financial officers, etc. Y.C. Simhardri stated: 'In any society, the social structure is usually responsible for the confronting and non-confronting behaviour of people'.[2] Clarence Darrow points, 'Crime is an act forbidden by law of the land, and one which is considered sufficiently serious to warrant providing penalties for its commission'.[3]

It is unfortunate to call the whole tribe or a clan or family as criminals. There is no country in the world, to our knowledge, whose people practise crime as their occupation. Biswas stated: 'It is very likely that the present ex-criminal tribes of India are the off-shoots of Thugs, and that after the creation of Thuggee department by the then government of India, the migratory habits of these people were stopped and many of them consequently settled in different provinces of India'.[4]

The idea of CT settlements was first started in 1868. The CT settlements were coincided on the same lines as those attempted by the Thuggee and Dacoity Department in 1931 in North India. J.V. Stephens, the member of the viceroy's council, in charge of law and order, stated: 'The special feature of India is the caste system. A family of carpenters will be carpenters, a century or five centuries, hence, if they last so long. When a man tells you that he is an offender against the law, he has been so from the beginning and will be so to the end. Reform is impossible, for it is his trade, his caste almost I may say his religion to commit crime'.[5]

This was the background for the establishment of 'criminal tribes' settlements in India. The government started this work on two assumptions. First, all persons born in a particular group or caste are criminal by birth and secondly, once a criminal one is always a criminal. These two assumptions led to the idea that the so-called CTs were dangerous elements in the society, should be protected from them.[6] The criminal tribes village writes Booth Tucker, 'is like a rabbit warren. When the ferret appears at one end, they escaped at the other. They will sleep in the open air, in places from which they can observe all comers. They will scatter themselves over a wide area amongst out of the way of villages, where police supervision is impossible'.[7]

The CTA was the handiwork of the British colonialism. By classifying certain social groups as CTs, the British had sought to gain control over them in order to deploy them for vigilance over other groups that were rebelling or conspiring against foreign domination. The Criminal Tribes Act developed the culture of settlements. It is the root cause of the emergence of CT settlements. CTA and CT settlements ruined the culture of civility and sociability. The settlements were islands of slavery in the midst of independent India. The abolition of the CTA and CT settlements is the contribution of the freedom struggle. The freedom struggle was thrust forward to shed the residual chains of the CTA and the abolition of the structures of the settlements.

Role of the Christian Missionaries

Criminal Tribes Settlements were established in such districts where grave crime was prevalent. In order to provide a settled life, government opened settlements. The Salvation Army, London Mission, Canadian Mission and the American Baptist (Telugu) Mission were entrusted with the management of the Criminal settlements.[8] These missions had three main objectives: (1) to implement the CTA effectively and control the inmates of the settlements within the framework of the CTA, which reduced the inmates virtually to slaves of the management; (2) to convert the inmates to Christianity and (3) to provide some opportunities of employment to the adults and education to their children.

The government found the work done by the Missionaries, such as the Salvation Army (SA) successful. The SA was the first organisation that stepped into the activities among the CTs. They started their work with the Doms rehabilitation in Uttar Pradesh.[9] The Madras Government invited the SA to take charge of the CTs and their homes. Dadabhai Naoroji said: 'The Salvation Army's help has been requisitioned from time to time. Whether it is SA or whether it is any other reforming body, the religious zeal is very often a necessary element in pursuing difficult task of people of this kind and winning them from evil ways.'[10] William Booth Tucker, the SA Officer in Andhra, managed successfully two settlements in Guntur District, one at Sitanagaram (1913) and the other at Stuartpuram (1914). The Lieutenant Governor of United Provinces, John Hewett, said: 'The most gratifying feature of the history of criminal tribes has been the success of the Salvation Army Settlements. Booth Tucker and other self-sacrificing members of the organisation were on the way to turn the criminals from hopeless enemies of mankind into useful citizens'.[11]

Conversion to Christianity as a means of controlling crime is doubtless overrated by both missionaries and public officials and underrated by many police officers. Crime among the underprivileged is not so much a problem of a specific group as a disease of the social organism.[12]

It was stated: 'All are convinced that Christianity is true and offers the only salvation to Yerukulas, Woddars, Yanadis and Gollas. Some have worshipped their idols so long it will require a few years to banish them from their minds. Some enjoy their sins too much to give them up all at once. But all will be Christians in five years or ten'.[13] There were four main reasons for the conversion of Yerukulas and Woddars to Christianity. They were: (1) the changed lives of out-caste converts, (2) the loss of faith in Hinduism (3) the influence of the schools and churches and (4) to liberate themselves from the criminal laws.

Official Policy

About the management of the CT settlements there was a debate in Madras Legislative Assembly as to why should Christian Missionaries alone be given the management work of these settlements. Because of the dedication and zeal of the Christian Missionaries, their interest in the reformation, rehabilitation of the depressed classes and, in addition to that, their interest in evangelisation were responsible for handing over the CT settlements to these people.[14]

The different laws on the so-called CT settlements have been influenced by the colonial considerations of political mechanism and economic needs. The colonial administrators believed that maintenance of law and order would be a mere exercise in vacuum, unless a better control could be achieved over the indigenous population. It was then imperative that a stray and shifting population could not be conducive to the so-called 'good' government and the colonial notion of 'pax Britannica'. In order to achieve this, unlike in the West where legislation regulated incidences of crime, in India, interception of crime was attempted. The colonial government here tried to confine the male factors to settlements.[15] Some wandering tribes without any fixed habitat became dubbed as 'criminal' and were set up in settlements. It was stated: 'If the local government has reason to believe that any tribe, gang or class of persons or any part of a tribe gang or class is addicted to the systematic commission of offences it may declare that such tribe, gang or class or part of the tribe, gang or class as a criminal tribe'.[16] A broader economic structure had grown up around the life of the settlements. Stolen-property dealers, corrupt officials, investors in crime and greedy lawyers all exploited the situation. These tribes are found in almost all parts of India. The total population of these tribes in India was estimated in different states totalling approximately more than eight million population.

The primary object of a 'Criminal Settlement' is reformation but not segregation or confinement. Its management has fallen into the hands of the police. The police and the government officers had no training for the reclamation of criminals. Their duty is to inspire trust in the criminal classes. In the non-governmental agencies, the government will get the help of self-sacrificing men. They are prepared to devote their lives to the reformatory work. The government officers who are interested in the reclamation service are transferred sometimes when suitable substitutes may not be found to carry on the work. It is noticed that the work of the non-governmental agency for management has been successful. The consideration is its economy. The government cannot get skilled service for the remuneration actually it pays to the non-official agencies. The manager of a settlement has full freedom to undertake the responsibility of the CTs in the settlements. But the non-official manager enjoys independence and prestige. He refuses to inform unimportant matters to higher authorities for decision. To maintain peace and order, the government officials will take the help of the police. The work of reclamation is more likely to be done effectively by men who make it their main object in life than by public servants. The public servants may not show the necessary interest on the reclamation work.[17] The government opined: 'The experiences gained in other provinces indicate that organisations like Salvation Army carried out the reclamation work with less money and got good results'.[18]

Registration was done for every member of the designated tribe and categorised as a 'Criminal' or as a 'Potential Criminal'. The Criminal Tribes were instructed to register themselves either with the police department or the village administration, the purpose being to locate and keep vigil on them. Every new born child was, thus, forced to be registered to update records. Failure to register was a punishable offence. The CTs were asked to report themselves at the nearest police station at fixed intervals. A surveillance system was built up by making every registered person belonging to a CT or settlement report to the police or to the village administration. The movements of each settler were recorded and each one had to get written permission (passes) from tho authorities to go out of the settlement and when returning to the settlement had to furnish information about the purpose and destination or the movement. Regardless of whether any crime was indulged in, merely belonging to the 'Criminal Tribe or Settlement' provided sufficient legal grounds for total vigilance. Of course, those individuals and families which were really involved in criminal operations never bothered to register themselves or report to the authorities. To exercise effective control and watch over them, active criminals and families were rounded up and sent to special settlements. The management of these settlements was given over to Christian Missionaries, who were given police powers. Some arable land was made available and the settlers were expected to cultivate it and live on its produce. Reporting to the management thrice a day was a routine instruction; night checks and controls were conducted. Some settlements were fenced with barbed wires.[19] In Andhra Pradesh there were five such settlements established between 1908 and 1917. The culture of crime was perpetuated by isolating the members of the settlements who enjoyed independence and prestige.

Settlement Patterns

The colonial government felt that penal, agricultural, industrial and reformatory settlements were the best sources for the reformation work on these criminal classes.[20] The Madras Government felt that agricultural and industrial settlements are the best sources for reclamation work because in the *coolie* work, the labourers do little work. If a man is given a small plot of land, he goes to the land early in the morning and works till late. Even if he has other works to perform, he will spare some time to work in his plot. Hence, the government made it compulsory in all settlements that agriculture should be the main industry. Each family was distributed a block of dry land and a piece of wet land to maintain themselves. If any one is found to neglect his land he was given punishment with harsh work such as breaking stones, digging earth, etc. and the land was taken away from him and given to another. The government considered that, in course of time, a *patta* for his land may be given to the settler.[21]

In industrial settlements, the following piece work was given: (1) Silk worm rearing; (2) Silk reeling, spinning and weaving; (3) Wool spinning or weaving; (4) Carpet-making; (5) Cotton-weaving and warping; (6) Carpentry and Black-smithy; (7) Shoe-making; (8) Tailoring; (9) Mat- and basket-making; (10) Coir-picking; (11) Pottery; (12) Fitting and metal work; (13) Stone-breaking, dressing, quarrying or mining; (14) Gardening; (15) Building and repairing buildings; (16) Making of bags and boxes; (17) Poultry farming and sheep farming and (18) Scavenging, etc.[22]

The government decided to establish the settlements during the year 1910. A total number of 25 tribes living in 20 districts were declared by the government as Criminal Tribes. Seven CT settlements were established under the Act up to the end of the year 1915. Five settlements were managed by the Salvation Army (SA), one by the American Baptist Telugu Mission (ABM) at Kavali and the others were under the official management.[23] The following classes of settlements and institutions have been established by the SA: (1) Agricultural Settlements, (2) Mixed Agro-industrial Settlements, (3) Industrial Settlements, (4) Homes for released prisoners, (5) Homes for juvenile adult released prisoners and (6) Homes for children, etc.

The settlements were equipped with all infrastructural facilities for the administrative staff. The settlements were directly administered by the government. All the infrastructure was kept under its control. The

Missionary management were asked to pay a nominal rent to the government for using the infrastructure and the buildings.[24] The manager was the sole incharge of the settlement where he was appointed. Clerks had to assist the manager for the administrative correspondence and other work. Peons looked after the administrative works. The midwife used to assist the doctor and looked after the delivery cases. The compounder used to supply the required medicines to those who attended the hospital. The agricultural maistries helped the settlers in instructing the unskilled labourers in doing agricultural work. The wardboy assisted the doctors and attended the hospital work regularly. The teachers had to run the school and watchers used to look into the whereabouts of the settlers. The scavengers had to sweep the managers' bungalow, offices, schools, hospital, etc.

Progress Made in the Settlements

CT settlements in Andhra Pradesh were well known. The earliest settlement was Kalichedu settlement established for Dasaris, Dommaras and Yerukulas. This was an *Industrial settlement.* Kavali settlement was an *Agricultural settlement* established by the American Baptist Telugu Mission (ABM). Sitanagaram settlement was an *Industrial settlement* established by SA in 1913. Siddhapuram settlement was a *Voluntary settlement* established in 1913. Bethapudi settlement, known as Stuartpuram, was established in 1914 by SA. Bhumannagadda settlement was an *Agricultural settlement* intended for the Nowabpeta Korachas by the SA in the same year. A *Reformatory settlement* in Guntur was established by SA, intended to be a home for the prisoners undergoing imprisonment in Madras Presidency. Chintal Devi settlement was established by the government for the settlement of Kanjar Bhats who belonged to Bombay presidency.[25]

Kalichedu Settlement: Origin

Kalichedu settlement was started during the year 1911 in Nellore district. Mr Ludwig, who was the then local manager of Messrs H. Brandt Mica Mines Company, opened the 'settlement'. Kalichedu settlement was opened with 200 people belonging to Katheras or Dasaris.[26] They had faced a number of difficulties in the beginning. The government provided a police constable, hospital and school during the year 1915. Mr Ludwig strove hard for the progress of the settlement.[27]

Notification of Katheras and Dasaris

Katheras were not accustomed to hard work in the beginning. They were notified as a 'Criminal Tribe' along with the other people (Dasaris) living in Kurnool, Guntur, Godavari and Krishna districts. Their movements were restricted to Kalichedu settlement. They were identified as CTs with the Dommaras of Nellore district.[28]

Satisfactory Condition of the Colony Until the Outbreak of the War

The settlement worked very well until the outbreak of the European War in 1914. The Company's work on the mines was closed due to the outbreak of the European War. The settlers were thrown out of work. Some of the Dasaris were transferred to Kavali settlement in order to provide them suitable employment during the year 1916. They were provided with unskilled labour. They were given repair works for the government buildings, road construction work and other contract works provided by the Public Works Department.[29] The settlers acquired great skill in mica mines work and there was a great demand for them in the neighbouring villages. Agriculture, mat-making were some of the other industries provided to them.[30]

Employment in Tea Gardens

Some families of Dasaris immigrated to Assam for the sake of employment in the tea gardens. The United Planters' Association of South India recruited some of the Dasaris in their estates on voluntary basis.[31] Coffee-picking, weeding, road-work, etc. were given to them. The turnout of these people was very satisfactory. The Dasaris who were working in the estates complained of ill-treatment by the managers. They escaped from the estates and returned back to Kalichedu.[32]

Agriculture at Kalichedu

The managers often complained about the difficulty of providing employment to Dasaris. They were not self-supporting. During the year 1920, agriculture was taken up by them.[33] Forty acres of dry land was brought under cultivation during the year 1921. Some of them did not know how to cultivate their lands. They were engaged in the works provided by District Boards, Public Works Department, etc. A textile industry was opened in Kalichedu during the year 1921. The Dasaris prepared excellent mats of date palm leaves and sold them in the market.[34]

Kalichedu School

A school was opened in Kalichedu during the year 1917. Competent teachers were employed in the school. During the year 1920, there were 400 children studying in the school out of which 39 bright children were transferred to SA School at Nellore during the year 1921 from the settlement school. The government paid a grant of ₹ 3 per child who were kept under the care of the SA.[35]

The settlement management authorities could not provide sufficient work for the Dasaris for a number of years. There was an increase in the number of absconders from Kalichedu during the year 1930. The inefficient police encouraged the Dasaris to commit crime. Therefore, the government decided to close down the Kalichedu settlement and transferred them to Stuartpuram settlement. The settlement failed due to non-availability of employment for the tribes, weak administration, corrupt police, etc.[36]

Bhumannagadda Settlement (Chittoor District)

The settlement was opened for the Nawabpeta Korachas during the year 1913. The SA took the management of the settlement during the year 1915. The government handed over 855 acres of land to settle the Nawabpeta Korachas. Adjutant Allan the SA Manager took the responsibility of the 550 members of the Korachas. The SA took the control of the settlement from the Police Department during the year 1916. Booth Tucker said: 'The police were interfering in the management of the settlement even after it had been handed over to the Salvation Army'.[37] Adjutant Allan the then manager of the settlement did not understand Telugu. There was a communication gap between the settlers and the manager. The manager was totally ignorant of the nature, manners and customs of the settlers. He did not know how to deal with the settlers. He granted free passes to the settlers. Frequently, there were a number of people absconding from the settlement. The SA authorities were not satisfied with his performance.[38] Captain Swami Das was appointed as the manager of the settlement during the year 1920. Subsequently, Captain Green and Lieutenant Premanandam became the managers of the settlement. They gradually improved the conditions of the settlement. Since 1925, the management of the settlement began to run smoothly.[39]

Women at the Settlement

The women in the settlement were very active. They played a very important role in the settlement. They used to sell *Karivepaaku* (Kalipatta) leaves in the neighbouring villages. It was stated that: Women formed an important factor in the settlement. They generally came and went as they liked and acted as spies and informants to their leaders. They used to go out on the pretext of selling Kadipatta leaves. But really speaking they frequently went to spy on the land and to keep themselves in touch with the absconding members. The women have been formally placed in the settlements and many of them have been registered. 'It was hoped that the industrial training for the tearing women in the settlements will further tends to put down crime'.[40]

Employment

Agriculture was the main occupation of the settlers. During the year 1926, the settlers cultivated 700 acres of land. Dams were constructed in the settlement for the agricultural purpose of the settlers. Booth Tucker, the Salvation Army officer further improved their agricultural activities.

The settlers were also provided with weaving and silk industries to support their income.[41] The Korachas made ropes, baskets, traded sheep, goats, etc. However, the settlement was not self-supporting. The SA provided a special recurring grant of ₹ 5,000 per month for the supervision of the settlement.[42]

School

For the education of the children of the Korachas an elementary school was opened in the settlement. Fifty-seven children attended the school regularly. Weaving and sericulture industries were introduced to the school children. The children carried the sericulture work regularly. Sewing, thread drawing and other activities in the sericulture programme were also taught by the teachers.[43]

Success of the Settlement

The overall progress of the settlement was not satisfactory. Under the management of Adjutant Allen the settlement did not progress much. There were fights among the Korachas and the settlement was disturbed due to the outside influence. There were a number of absconders from the settlement. The managers who succeeded Captain Green and Swami Das did not show much interest in the improvement of the settlement. The settlement remained backward in all respects. The strength of the settlement gradually decreased since 1930. During the year 1931 there were 152 females, 135 children and 161 males in the settlement. Since then the settlement faced a number of obstacles in its progress.[44]

Bitragunta Reformatory Settlement, Kappalla Tippa and Kavali Settlements

Nellore District

Kavali settlement was started for the Yerukulas of Nellore district in October 1912, on voluntary basis with 152 persons. Rev. Bullard of the American Baptist Mission opened the settlement.[45] In 1912, Rev. Bullard, with the permission of the police authorities, took charge of 20 Yerukala families and opened the Industrial Yerukala settlement at Kavali. En route they changed their mind, and wishing to escape and going to Kalichedu the Yerukulas went to Bullard and pretended their desire to conversion to Christianity.[46] This was agreed upon by Bullard. The District Magistrate gave his consent to settle the Yerukulas in Kavali. The ABM readily accepted the proposal to provide as far as possible, the necessary conditions for social, industrial, educational and hygienic improvement of the Kavali settlement.[47] Rev. Bullard wanted to keep all of them under his direct supervision so that he could experiment and rehabilitate them until the mission achieved its goal. He provided them with looms, warping machines and a building to work and store the materials. He also planned to start a silk factory but it did not fructify due to climatic reasons. From the outside, the Kavali settlement had to face enormous problems. None of the Yerukulas were accustomed to any kind of settled labour.[48]

Difficulties in Finding Remunerative and Profitable Work at Kavali

The strength of the settlement increased to 55 families by the end of the year 1913. In January 1914, the settlement was subsequently notified as one established under section 16 of the CT Act.[49] Minor industries such as weaving, fibre work, gardening, stone quarrying mat and basket-making and tile manufacturing were introduced. However, the progress of the 'settlement' was slow. It was difficult to find remunerative and profitable work on account of the nature of the soil; besides, the Yerukulas were found wanting in skilled work. In spite of the best efforts in agriculture, Kavali settlement was unable to develop as a self-supporting unit.

Land for Agriculture

The Yerukulas were provided 950 acres of land for agricultural purpose. The land was located at Kavali and Bitragunta reserve forest. Tools were provided for the Yerukulas to cultivate the land. The efforts made by them was not successful due to the reason that the soil was unfit for cultivation.[50]

Health

The birthrate during the year 1915 was 36 per mille. The settlers complained of the excessive mortality at the settlement. The sub. assistant surgeon Kavali used to pay periodical visits. The government paid him an allowance of ₹ 10 per month. The death rate during the year 1915 was 47 per mille. Black scourge (Euly lostomiasis) was very much prevalent among the settlers during the year 1916. No special efforts were taken to eliminate the disease.

Strength

The strength of the settlement at the end of 1915 was 257 men, 244 women and 330 children, a total of 831 persons of whom 743 were present in the settlement. About 200 people were transferred to the Stuartpuram settlement.

Undertaking to Bear the Net Cost of the Settlement

S.D. Bawden succeeded Bullard. The government was impressed by the efforts made by Bawden. During the year 1915, the Labour Department recruited some of the Yerukulas to work in the estates in the Anamalais.

The Yerukulas were also provided work in the United Planters Association Company of South India.[51] A total number of 72 families of the Yerukulas were given employment in the company. The strength of the Yerukulas in Kavali during the year 1915 was 600. Since then, the strength of the settlement increased gradually.[52]

Progress after 1916

Bullard was an expert in agriculture. The then District Magistrate granted him 100 acres of waste land for the purpose of opening the settlement. Bullard irrigated the land provided to him with deep well water. The district magistrate kept under his supervision 55 families of the Yerukulas who had escaped from Kalichedu.[53] The government sanctioned a non-recurring grant of ₹ 5,000 for the opening of the settlement. During the year 1914, the settlement was notified as a criminal tribe settlement.[54]

Reformatory Work Among the Children

A school was constructed in Kavali during the year 1914. The attendance was made compulsory for all the children (6 to 12 years) in the village.[55] A boarding school was also constructed for the benefit of the school-going children. Boys and girls were separated from their parents in order to protect the children from the influence of their parents.[56] During the year 1920, there were 90 boys and 70 girls attending the school regularly. A night school was opened in the village for the education of the youth (children who were above the age of 12 years) in the Kavali settlement.[57]

The Yerukulas used to attend the religious services conducted by the American Baptist Church in the settlement. A daily morning prayer and a service on Sundays were organised by the manager. The Yerukulas went to the church and showed required respect to the managers, but did not pay attention to the gospels given by the Baptist church fathers. Mr Bullard used to stress the importance of moral discipline to convert the Yerukulas. The Hindu members of the tribe constructed a temple and appointed a priest to conduct regular bhajans in the settlement.[58]

New Settlements at Allur and Bitragunta

During the year 1916, the entire cost for the maintenance of the Yerukulas was met by the government. The net cost of running of the Kavali settlement was ₹ 11,674.[59] The District Magistrate, the Inspector General of Police and the manager felt that there was no further prospects for the settlement as it was not self-supporting. They recommended for shifting over of the Kavali settlement to Allur.[60]

In December 1916, Kavali settlement transferred some of the Yerukulas to Bitragunta where the Bitragunta Reformatory settlement had already commenced in January 1917. The government accepted the proposal of the District Magistrate to transfer 75 families of Yerukulas to the experimental settlement, 50 of whom had to be sent from Kavali and the rest from Kalichedu.[61] The Agricultural settlement at Bitragunta was declared to be a part of Kavali settlement. This was under the supervision of Bawden who worked hard to make the Yerukulas a self-respecting and self-supporting people. The government believed that education of settlers' children would be the best possible way to solve the problem of reclaiming the CTs.[62] With regard to incorrigibles, Mr Bawden wanted a separate settlement subject to certain conditions: (1) Incorrigibles should not be allowed to escape; (2) When a man absconded from Kavali, Bitragunta or Allur settlement for the second or third time, his family should be sent to the penal settlement; and (3) No community food was allowed.[63]

In 1919, the settlement had a strength of 1,860 members of whom 138 were at Allur, 363 at Bitragunta and 1,058 at Kavli. The rest being out of view, in prison or on leave. The process of transferring well-behaved Yerukulas from Kavali to the new settlements continued and in 1920 there were 153 settlers at Allur, 443 at Bitragunta and 916 at Kavali.[64] The Yerukulas at Kavali were subjected to a strict discipline and the wages given to them were inadequate. Kavali settlement was disciplinary and probationary and the work that was available there was almost entirely coolie work. Mr Moir, the then Commissioner of labour, investigated the economic conditions at Kavali in 1921 and reported that the unsatisfactory conditions at Kavali were due to two reasons, namely (1) a far too rapid increase in the strength of the settlement and (2) unjustifiable optimism regarding the agricultural possibilities of the settlement.[65]

According to Moir, reduction in strength is the only solution to the problem. The government decided to convert the settlement at Kavali into a penal or reformatory settlement, the one at Guntur being discontinued. Only incorrigibles were kept at Kavali and the rest were transferred to Allur Swamp area. Rev. Bawden had a serious quarrel with Singapeta people which resulted in a riot, and a serious criminal case was filed against him at the Magistrate Court, Kovur.[66]

During the year 1918, the Yerukulas cultivated 85 acres of land. The crops cultivatod by them were gram and cholam. The health conditions of the Yerukulas were very poor. The birth rate during 1920 was 36 per mille. The Yerukulas complained of the excessive mortality in the settlement. The annual death rate was 29 per mille during the year 1921. The sub-assistant surgeon Kavali visited the settlement periodically to provide medical assistance for them. The death rate during the year 1925 was 47 per mille. Special measures were taken to eliminate the 'black scourge' ankylostomiasis which was rampant in Bitragunta, Allur and Kavali.[67]

Special constables were appointed from the settlers themselves. The settlers discontinued the practice of escaping from the village. The settlement was not having a fence or a compound wall. The night roll call was completely stopped. The special constables were highly respected by the Yerukulas. The strength of the Yerukulas during the year 1925 was 300 men, 290 women and 380 children with a total of 970 persons.[68]

The government proposed for closing down the settlement at Kavali. The settlers were well disciplined and a lot of progress was made by them. The government considered only the future of the Yerukulas. Since there was no scope of making the village an agricultural settlement or making the village self-supporting the government finally decided to close the Kavali settlement.[69]

Why did the government close the Kavali settlement when it was in the flourishing condition? There were conflicting questions among the Yerukulas, Managers, Baptist Mission authorities, the Inspector General of Police and the District Magistrates. They were not happy in selecting Allur as a suitable place to shift the settlement from Kavali. But the government appointed a Committee consisting of Inspector General of Police, the District Magistrate and Mr Bawden. The Committee inspected Allur swamp lands and finally recommended for the shifting of the settlement to the new site. The settlement was shifted to the Eastern part of Bitragunta railway station near the 130th mile stone at the northern road of Madras – Vijayawada highway. The government started the new settlement as an experimental settlement. The settlement was named as Bitragunta reformatory settlement. The settlement was declared as a part of the Kavali settlement. The government had sanctioned an advance of ₹ 7,500 for the purchasing of cattle, seeds, plough, etc. for the settlers.[70] The government also opened a subsidiary settlement at Allur.

The new settlements (one at Allur and the other at Bitragunta) distributed the Yerukulas and Katheras. The cost of expenditure became more on the part of three installments. To reduce the expenditure the government closed Kalichedu settlement.[71] A large number of Yerukulas were brought to Kavali during the year 1929. There were 1,350 people on the rolls. The government increased the maintenance charges of the Yerukulas. One acre of land was given to each family in these villages.[72]

Some of the Yerukulas, who behaved well, were transferred to other settlements. The settlers were subjected to strict discipline. The settlers were paid low wages to the actual quantity of work turned out by them. Men used to be paid 7 annas and women were paid 6 annas per day. The managers adopted a policy to pay according to the turnout of the work done by the poor Yerukulas. The managers often complained that it was very difficult to provide suitable work for them. A large number of Yerukulas absconded from the three places due to strict discipline, lack of employment and low wages paid to them. It was stated: 'In many of the cases the settlers were suspected merely because they happened to be criminal tribe members'.[73]

The villagers started earning their livelihood by their hard work and labour contracts during the year 1928. The juveniles were given training by the managers to earn their living. The concept of boy scouts and girl guides was introduced in the schools. Night schools were regularly organised in the settlement for men and women who could not attend the school during the day time. There were 3,000 Yerukulas in all the three villages during the year 1929. The domestic industries were completely stopped by the villagers (mat-making, weaving, basket-making, etc.) due to the low money they got from them. Mr Moir said, 'Every escape or conviction represents a total failure in that individual case; every return from jail a beginning anew'.[74]

The villagers were paid low wages for the contract works during the year 1930. The workers in each gang were guarded by the maistries and the special constables. The villagers used to camp out for doing the work. Some of the Yerukulas took the opportunity of absconding from the camp. Further, they used to walk a number of miles every day. It caused them physical exertion and low earning due to the wastage of time in walking.[75]

The conditions of the three villages during the year 1931 was very poor. There was no work for them. The lands provided to the villagers were submerged in the water. In order to solve the employment problem of the villagers, a large number of the Yerukulas were transferred to other settlements. The panchayats were organised in the three villages to control their behaviour. The members of the Panchayat were taken from the villagers themselves.[76] The total strength of the three villages during the year 1932 was 3,500. The death rate was 18 per cent, and the birth rate was 45 per cent. Intra-mural industries were started. A weaving maistry was appointed to instruct them in weaving clothes. Bullard had done excellent work for the reformatory work among the children in the villages.[77]

A tractor was purchased by the agricultural department for ploughing the swamp lands. Side drains were dug to divert the flood water in order to protect the lands from submersion. To protect the crops, flood banks were constructed. The superintending engineer visited the lands and installed a pumping plant during the year 1933. In 1934, the management of the settlement was taken over by the police department and the Inspector of Police became the manager of the settlement since then.[78]

During the year 1939, the then Labour Commissioner, Madras, transferred some of the Yerukulas from Kavali to Sitanagaram. They were provided work in the Kistna Cement Works at Tadepalli. The Yerukulas were kept at Kaza. They were provided quarrying and stone breaking works, garden cultivation work, etc.[79] During the year 1940, the settlement was managed by one manager, two clerks, one peon, one midwife, one compounder, two agricultural *maistries*, one ward boy, five teachers, 10 watchmen, two scavengers and one sweeper.[80] With the repeal of the CTA, the inhabitants were left free in September 1948 and the settlement office was abolished and the outpost at Bitragunta was converted into a pucca police station in January 1949.[81]

Sitanagaram Settlement (Guntur District)

The Salvation Army took up the question of the formation of the settlements for the reclamation of CTs during the year 1910. A small settlement was formed at Sitanagaram. In the beginning, some Yerukula women, whose husbands and relatives were in jail, were placed in the settlement. During the year 1912, the then British Government sanctioned an amount of ₹ 5,000 as a special non-recurring grant to the SA to start the settlement.[82] An extent of 87 acres of land was also provided to the SA free of cost with occupancy rights. (It was relinquished by the Madras and Southern Mahratta Railway Company).[83] The government had permitted the SA (1) to adopt persuasive methods to settle the Yerukulas, (2) if the persuasive, methods of the SA failed to apply the provisions of the CT Act to settle down the Yerukulas in Sitanagaram. However, the persuasive methods of the Salvation Army failed. The government declared the Yerukulas living in Godavari and Guntur districts as CTs. Their movements were restricted under Section 12 of the CT Act 1911.

The progress of Sitanagaram Settlement was very fast. It was necessitated to the then British Government for the formation of another settlement to control the overflow of the settlers in Sitanagaram. Thus, the settlement at Bethapudi was opened as an auxiliary settlement.[84]

Location of Sitanagaram

Sitanagaram Settlement is situated in Guntur district. Lying on the south bank of the Krishna that emerges from a corridor in the Palnad hills and empties into the Bay of Bengal in a broad sweeping curve, this is largely a flat, deltaic plain. It is bounded by Prakasam and Nellore districts in the South and in the West by Prakasam and Krishna districts.[85] Guntur is a rich and surplus district. As Robert Eric Frykenberg said, 'Its plain is a luxurious carpet of green all the year round: Sugarcane, rice and other staple crops are interspersed all over the district being fed by irrigation canals. Cash crops like tobacco fetch foreign exchange from Britain, America, Soviet Russia and East European countries. The main line of the railways, joined by subsidiary lines at Vijayawada, connect the district with the leading industrial commercial and other popular centres of India'.[86]

The Grand Trunk road, running from Calcutta (now Kolkata) to Madras (now Chennai) passes through Guntur. Physiographically, Guntur district may be divided into three district regions, viz. the Mainland, the Costal belt and the Delta region. Besides the three principal castes of Brahmins, Kshatriyas and Vaisyas, the Sudras comprise both advanced and backward classes in addition to Scheduled Castes and Scheduled Tribes. Lambadies, Yerukulas, Yanadis, and Chenchus are wandering tribes, all living in their own settlements in close proximity to forests and speaking their own dialects.

Occupation of the 'Settlers'

The main occupation provided for the Yerukulas in the settlement was quarrying. But the settlers were not accustomed to do hard labour. They did not accept to take up the work. The government considered quarrying as a salutary form of employment. This work was introduced to bring discipline and industrious nature among the settlers.[87] The government sanctioned an amount of ₹ 10,000 during the year 1914 for the development of quarrying industry in the settlement. The manager said: 'The work could be done only by the able bodied people. There were in the settlement some men and women who were unfit to do quarrying. There was no other work on which they could be usefully employed'.[88]

The manager, however, provided hand spinning and handloom weaving which were the most suitable occupations for the settlers. Training was given for men and women in hand spinning and handloom weaving. This provided the settlers with sufficient work. Khadi cloth was produced. The Labour Department used to purchase the cloth. The cloth was supplied to the surrounding 'Scheduled Caste' people. The Commissioner of Labour said, 'There will be no difficulty in finding a market for the Khadi produced by the settlers as it can be utilised for the supply of clothing to the Scheduled Caste pupils eligible for the ameliorative work of the Labour Department'.[89] The government found the market for the Khadi cloth produced by the settlers. The government fixed the selling price of the clothing. The manager said: 'It is proposed to introduce spinning and weaving in the settlement for the unregistered settlers. They are at liberty to go anywhere they like in quest of work. Some of them have already left the settlement. 'It is not possible to provide work for others in the settlement itself'.[90]

The industries introduced in Sitanagaram Settlement were (1) sock-making for the police department, (2) mat-making and (3) weaving of Madras handkerchiefs. It was stated: 'The settlers need so much to produce an undefined amount of cloth. The cloth will be sold to the department for a certain amount of rupees. The wages are to be paid by the Department for the unstated amount of cloth. There is no indication of estimated out-turn or the requirement of the department. The scheme was a badly cooked dish of figures heavily spiced, with manipulation which the government was not prepared to serve'.[91]

Land to the extent of 84.06 acres was given at Sitanagaram to the SA, free of charge, for occupancy rights and free of assessment. The government recommended that persuasive methods should be adopted in respect of the Yerukala settlers and in case those methods failed, they could apply the provisions of the CTA. The persuasive methods having failed completely in their case, the CT settlement was established in the year 1913 with the handful of men who were released from jail. Section 12 of the Act restricted the movements of these people. The Yerukulas of Godavari and Guntur were brought under the provisions of the CTA. Their number became unmanageable and, therefore, the British Government established another settlement at Bethapudi which came to be known as Stuartpuram (Bethapudi) settlement subsequently.[92]

Division of Sitanagaram into Two Settlements

In October 1915, the Sitanagaram settlement was divided into two parts, namely, Sainayapuram and Kondapet settlement, each under the management of an European SA Officer.[93] This division was made for the effective supervision of the settlement. It was only an internal arrangement. Agriculture was the chief means of livelihood and other main occupations practised was stone quarrying by the Yeruklas and is so even today. The work was further developed by the SA with the establishment of train links to the quarries. Weaving, silk spinning, carpentry, sewing and other subsidiary industries were provided for the settlers. They also had shown interest in mat and basket-making. In 1914, only 40 acres of land was cultivated due to non-availability of agricultural land. However, during the same year, the government realising the need for more land, handed over a larger tract of fertile land, to SA for the purpose of parcelling it out to the settlers for cultivation.[94]

Escapes and Crime

In the initial stages, there were a large number of absconders from among the settlers. The DIG of Police, Railways and CID were entrusted with the general supervision and control of all the settlements in Madras Presidency. Mr Hannygton, the DIG, Madras, reported that captain Robilliard of the SA at Stuartpuram was a person of a exceptionally high calibre. Since there was demand for more land for the settlers, the government gave more land for agricultural pursuits. Supervision was also strictly enforced. This minimised the number of absconders. The population of the settlement at the end of the year 1915 comprised 301 men, 271 women and 337 children with a total of 909 members.[95] Fear of floods and indolent habits kept the settlers away from taking full advantage of the 130 acres of land granted to them for agricultural purposes. The annual report during the year 1916 showed that they were dependent mainly on the quarry work.[96]

School and Education

An elementary school was started by the SA in April 1913. A night school was also opened. It continued to do commendable work. The weaving section attached to the school possessed five looms. The school provided employment to the pupils who attended the school regularly in the early part of the day. The other cottage industries such as mat-making, smithy and carpentry were also instituted in the settlement.[97]

Progress after 1916

The conditions of the settlement, during the year 1917, was very bad. The settlement had to grapple with two successively serious epidemics during the year 1917. As a result of cholera and small pox, the settlers became restless and began to abscond in large numbers.[98] The government, dissatisfied with the working conditions of the settlement, decided to abolish it during the year 1917. It was decided to slowly deplete the strength of the settlers by periodical transfers of the inmates to other settlements, more favourably to the agricultural settlements. A total number of 100 families were transferred to Stuartpuram settlement.[99]

During the year 1919, the Labour Commissioner took charge of all the CT settlements. There was gradual improvement in the general condition of all the settlements.[100] Availability of employment and a fairly good rainfall were responsible for this improvement. This showed a marked decline in the incidence of crime. This established a notion that wherever there was economic distress the incidence of petty crimes would increase; otherwise; the phenomenon would be the same.

The year 1921–22 was marked for the special efforts of the government to send children to attend the school. There were 70 boys and 57 girls of school-going age, out of which 48 boys and 57 girls attended the school regularly. A night school was also maintained in the settlement.[101] The general behaviour of the settlers was so satisfactory that 14 families were released from the settlement as a reward to their good conduct. This was a good augury, and a good system followed by the government. The released persons were asked to go to their native places. Paradoxically, some people remained in the settlement even after their release. This showed, first, that the settlers developed an emotional attachment for the settlements; secondly, when they were interned, the settlers lost their property and were afraid of going back to their native places; and thirdly, the settlement manager used to provide them with some kind of employment for keeping their body and soul together. Weaving, carpet-making, stone-dressing and other miscellaneous jobs kept them busy throughout the year. The cottage industries were in a flourishing condition and the settlers took real interest in cultivating lands also.[102]

There was an increase in the number of settlers during the year 1925. The Rudrapad Korachas and a few settlers from Bhumannagadda settlement were brought to Sitanagaram settlement. The total number of people during the year 1925 was 1,110 members. All the settlers were provided with work. The total earnings of the settlers was ₹ 28,000. Carpet industry was introduced in the settlement by Mr Moir. A maistry was employed in the settlement to assist the settlers in carpet industry.[103]

The strength of the settlement during the year 1927 was 1,092. There were 41 absconders from the settlement. The total earnings of the settlers were ₹ 37,000. There were 396 children in the settlement. The average attendance of the school was 120. Cholera was prevalent in the settlement and in the neighbouring villages. The settlement was without a doctor. The sub-assistant surgeon, Mangalagiri used to visit the hospital twice in a week to meet the medical needs of the settlers.[104] The behaviour of the settlers was satisfactory. Fourteen families were released from the settlement as a reward of their good conduct. A stone dressing maistry was appointed to teach masonry work in the settlement. This was to develop skilled labour among the settlers. The total strength of the settlers increased to 1,107 during the year 1929–30. Around 200 acres of land was cultivated by the settlers.[105] The settlers extended their cultivation up to Undavalli Lanka during the year 1932. Weaving, carpet-making, stone-dressing kept the settlers busy throughout the year.[106] Their earnings were fairly good. They were successful in carpet industry.[107] They had earned an amount of ₹ 2,700 by selling the carpets in nearby places.[108] The then Commissioner of Labour, T.G. Rutherford, provided work for the settlers in Cement Cos. Ltd., Bombay. They had opened up limestone deposits in Kaza. The settlers in Sitanagaram and Bitragunta were employed on the quarry work in the lime stone deposits. The unfavourable seasonal and economic conditions of the year 1934, contributed to the increased volume of crime.[109]

Hospital: Health Conditions in Sitanagaram Settlement

A dispensary was established during the year 1915. The number of patients who attended the settlement dispensary during the year 1933–34 was 990. The average attendance of the patients was 33. The dispensary was very popular and useful for the settlers. But there was no medical officer working in the settlement. The patients were sent to Mangalagiri hospital. The equipment in the hospital was inadequate. A sub-assistant surgeon used to visit the settlement hospital. The settlement was situated at a distance of 8 miles from Mangalagiri and 2 miles from Bezawada. Much difficulty was felt by the Medical Officer for the treatment of urgent cases such as accidents in quarry work, etc.

During the year 1933, a sub-assistant surgeon and a compounder were appointed in the settlement.[110]

The economic depression was further aggravated by the failure of crops during the year 1934. The carpet industry was closed in the settlement during the year 1933. No provisions were made by the government to purchase the looms and other articles. The materials of the settlers were sold in public auction.[111] In 1937, there was a little improvement in the economic situation. There was considerable amount of employment in most parts of the Presidency. Effective control exercised by the anti-crime measures, the cooperation rendered by the village vigilance committees, the interest showed by the members of the public, the valuable services of the Criminal Intelligence Branch and the concomitant change in the attitude of the CTS, and also the effective work by the rank and file of the police, cumulatively contributed to an appreciable decrease in crime. In addition, the movements of the Yerukulas and some of the Kanjar Bhats was restricted to Sitanagaram settlement.[112]

The then Commissioner of Labour, G.W. Priestly, transferred some of the settlers of Bitragunta to Sitanagaram. The abolition proposals of the Bitragunta settlement was started in 1937. The government proposed to construct a new settlement called Chintaladevi settlement during the year 1937. The government wanted to close the Bitragunta settlement due to two reasons: (1) The expenditure incurred on the settlement was more. (2) The settlers depended heavily on the maintenance cost of the government without doing any hard work.[113]

The next Labour Commissioner was Mr Ramakrishna. During his tenure, the settlers were provided employment in Andhra Cotton Mills, Cement Company, Associated Cement Co. Ltd. etc. on piece work basis.[114] A total number of 100 settlers (50 men and 50 women) were provided work in the settlement. Men used to be paid 5 annas a day and women were paid 3 annas per day.[115] The settlers were provided railway passes to attend to the work daily in neighbouring places. The Assistant Manager of the settlement supervised the settlers efficiently during the year 1940. All the settlers were put within the enclosure of the barbed wire fencing. The settlers were made to work on quarrying, stone dressing, etc. Big stones were transported to the settlement from the adjoining hills on tram line.[116]

Carpentry was introduced in the school and regular classes were held in the carpentry work. Tools and materials were purchased and supplied to the school during the year 1939. During the year 1940, the quarry work in the Public Works Department had become very small. They could not provide work for all the settlers. Private contractors were requested to provide work for the settlers. The work in the quarries was stopped due to the expiry of the lease to the Guntur District Board. Fifty per cent of the settlers suffered without any work. The settlers were provided work in the Kistna Cement Works at Kaza. The settlers were sent to Kaza on temporary 'O' passes issued for 15 days. The police also arranged bandobust during the nights with the help of the maistries appointed in the settlement. (The quarry work in the settlement was actually provided by the companies in Bombay. The mining work in the settlements was taken by these companies for lease and got rich profits out of the labour of the settlers). Some other settlers were sent to Piduguralla for work.[117]

During the year 1941–42, the drainage system in the settlement was improved. The level of the roads was raised to prevent water stagnation. The conditions of the houses were improved. The settlers constructed their houses with stone and mud. The settlers developed in all aspects.[118] The settlers were self-supporting. Due to unsatisfactory monsoons, the agricultural operations made by the settlers was not successful. The settlers cultivated only 83 acres of land.

The managers faced many difficulties to get the work from the settlers in the beginning. Only a small portion of the land was cultivated by the settlers. A cattle pound was constructed in the settlement during the same year. Pumpsets were also provided to keep the wells in the settlement.

During the year 1942, the then Labour Commissioner provided employment to some more settlers in the cement company at Vijayawada. The settlers were transferred to Sitanagaram from Bitragunta settlement. The settlers were provided railway passes to attend the work in the lime-stone quarries. The factory was very near to Tadepalli railway station. The Bitragunta settlers were employed on company's quarries. The managers used to give strict instructions to the settlers before they proceeded to the quarry work. The settlers were paid 8 to 10 annas a day for men and 4 to 5 annas a day for women. A tram line was laid to the settlement. Big lumps of rocks were carried to the settlement. The settlers were asked to break the rocks. The settlers were kept in the barbed wire enclosures. The settlers were also asked to make the transport arrangements in handcarts on the double-shafted carriers managed by two men.[119]

L. Underwood, the Deputy Inspector General of Police, CID and Railways, Madras, requested the then Secretary of the Madras Government to sanction a library for children and supply of other literatures to the settlement school.[120] The school at Sitanagaram was upgraded to an upper primary school in 1946. The DIG of Police also requested for maintenance allowance to the released settlers, which was also conceded by the government during the year 1947.

In 1948, the law and order situation was under control although there was some increase in petty crimes. The abrogation of the CTA in that year in addition to large scale premature release of criminals from prison, deteriorating economic situation, widespread labour and agrarian unrest, better reporting of cases, were considered as the main cause for the slight increase in crime. Dacoity, robbery, house breaking and other petty crimes also slightly increased. This was the sum position in almost all the districts in the province.[121]

Pursuant to the introduction of prohibition, the morals and material well-being of the settlers improved. The health and hygiene of the settlers were considered satisfactory due to the establishment of rural dispensaries. All the internees under the CTA, who did not come under the purview of 'Habitual Offenders' as defined in Section 2(4) of the Habitual Offender's Act 1948, were released from the settlements. However, most of the released settlers continued to stay on in the settlements. Concessions regarding education, free clothing and other facilities were given to all the children of the internees as well as to those of the voluntary settlers as usual.[122]

During the year 1949, there was an increase in the total number of crimes by about 5 per cent in comparison with the figures of 1940. General economic depression, consequent upon the shortage of food stuffs and their soaring prices, abolition of the CTA, campaigning of a free and proper registration of crimes and the preoccupation of the police in dealing with the Communist upsurge in the country in 1948, again led to the upward swing in the crime rate of Habitual Offenders. The Habitual Offenders Act came into force on 29 April 1948 in the Presidency.[123]

During the year 1952, Sitanagaram settlement was managed by four managers, viz. Syed Abdul Gaffar, T. Govindarajulu, K. Sreemantham, and K.V.R. Patnaik. There were 246 settlers in the settlement (71 men, 73 women and 102 children). The strength of the internees under Section 2(4) of the Madras Restriction of Habitual Offenders Act, 1948 was 30 members.[124] Many of the settlers were permanently released from the settlement. The settlers cultivated 203 acres of land. Sixty-four families in the settlement were provided land for cultivation. Each family was given 2 ½ acres. Cholam, hemp, red-gram, sajja and turmeric crops were grown by the settlers. The crops yielded good results. Agricultural officers were recruited for the settlement.[125] There was no organised industry in the settlement during the year 1955. The quarry industry in the settlement was abandoned. The workers were employed as bandy (cart) drivers, and as manual labourers in quarries. Goat and sheep rearing, petty shopping, rearing buffaloes for milk, poultry rearing, shoe-making, employment as watchers and employment in the ferry, etc. were other main sources of income for the Yerukulas in Sitanagaram. The health conditions of the settlers during the year 1960 was satisfactory. There were no epidemics in the settlement. An Ayurvedic Rural Dispensary was opened in the settlement. One regular doctor was appointed in the hospital. He was assisted by a midwife and a ward boy. They worked satisfactorily in the settlement. The school in Sitanagaram worked with six standards during the year 1965. The strength of the school was 78 children. A total number of eight children studied in the outside schools, three were given training in midwifery. One boy studied MBBS in the Medical College, Guntur. One person was selected as a sub-inspector of police from the settlement. The Sitanagaram Settlement Tenants Co-operative Society worked in the settlement satisfactorily.[126] The settlers were given cows, bulls, buffaloes, goats and sheep by the government. Agricultural advances were also provided to the settlers. The economic conditions of the settlers from 1970 onwards was quite satisfactory. The settlers were engaged in different kinds of employment. They managed to earn their livelihood. The general behaviour of the settlers was very good. Pumpsets were installed on the Krishna river bund, on the main canal bund, on either side to provide wet cultivation in the settlement. The Superintending Engineer, Vijayawada provided regular water for the settlers' lands. The settlers cultivated their lands located at Tadepalli, Gundimedu Lanka and Undavalli Lanka. The District Collector, Guntur, leased out these lands to the settlers. A police station was also established at Tadepalli. The police station was situated 1 km from the settlement. The District Superintendent of Police, Guntur, and the Incharge Sub-inspector of Sitanagaram settlements used to visit the settlement regularly to prevent crime among the settlers. The government did not chalk out any programme as there were no industries in the settlement and the settlement was converted into a free colony.[127] However, the registration of persons in the settlement continued under the Madras Restriction of Habitual Offenders Act, 1948.

The special feature of Sitanagaram settlement was that it was a penal settlement. Mr Bawden, the Manager of Bitragunta Reformatory settlement, scheduled it as a penal settlement for the incorrigible members of the CTs. When Sir Harold Stuart visited the Sitanagaram settlement, he was asked by the Manager, Mr Duboulay – 'Do you advocate the starting of another settlement where the reformed men will be provided for?' It was a penal settlement, so many settlers were transferred to Stuartpuram from Sitanagaram settlement.[128]

As a settlement, which was converted into a free colony after the repeal of the CTA, was very near to the city of Vijayawada it was exposed to many employment potentialities for the settlers. The equipment, workshops, and other appliances were simply rusting under a roof for a long time. Thanks to the work of Lavanam and Hemalatha Lavanam who did lot of work and due to this a significant change could be seen among them today.

The major problem faced by the settlers and non-settlers was their living in the same settlement, side by side. The settlers were given land for cultivation, whereas the non-settlers did not have even a piece of land, though their ancestors lived in the settlement under the management of the SA. It was because of their good conduct they were released and denied any land. In other words, the non-settlers were punished for their good conduct. However, they maintain close contact with the settlers. The government, in all fairness, should have taken a sympathetic stand for these helpless non-settlers and provided them with pattas for cultivation and house-building. There are 49 families of the settlers constituting a total population of 1,071 people in Sitanagaram settlement.

Among the 150 families who were interned in Sitanagaram settlement, the government discharged them from the purview of the CTA and asked them to leave the settlement. Out of a total number of 1,205 members, 44 acres of land was leased out to the settlement management. Further, another 66.77 acres of land was leased out to the settlement management and allotted to Ramakrishna Vidyalaya High School, Maganti Annapurna Devi Primary School, Sri Venkateswara Swami Temple, for formation of the Krishna Bundh and also for an assignment to three political sufferers.[129]

Agriculture is the main occupation of the settlers of the Sitanagaram settlement even today. The government extended full remission of fees to the children of the notified tribes and sanctioned grant of residential and industrial scholarships. Irrigation facilities were provided by erecting two lift irrigation-pumpsets on the northern side of the Buckingham Canal. Crops, such as paddy, turmeric, chillies and groundnut were raised on the land here. A rural dispensary which was running in the settlement was very useful to the settlers. Small scale industries, such as, carpentry, smithy, mat-making, basket-making, weaving existed in the settlement previously, but these are now defunct. Even in quarry work, individual exploitation is prevalent. Instead of giving the right of the management of the quarry work to an individual, if it is entrusted to the society, this evil can be eradicated. The Tribal Welfare Department, Guntur District, conducted a detailed survey of the settlement in June 1986. The survey covered 45 families. We are able to collect data for 40 families, as the remaining families have left the settlement. There are no habitual offenders at present in the colony. All the colonists have sprung up with voluntary settlers.[130]

Stuartpuram Settlement (Guntur Dist)

Stuartpuram is in between Bapatla (Guntur district) and Chirala (Prakasam District) on the Madras – New Delhi Grand Trunk Rail Road. Stuartpuram settlement was called as a good conduct settlement. It means, men who behaved well at Sitanagaram were sent to this place and the misbehaved were taken to Sitanagaram. The strength in the beginning of the settlement was 691 consisting of 200 males, 196 females and 295 children. It was named after Stuart, the then Home member for the Madras Government.[131]

Origin of Stuartpuram Settlement

The Yerukulas of Guntur district used to camp near the village of Bethapudi, Bapatla Taluk, Guntur district, from December to August every year. They carried grain for the ryots of Ongole, Bapatla and Tenali Taluks during the months. They grazed their cattle at Vinukonda in Guntur district from August to December. The Yerukulas used to commit petty offences when they had no work. But the police became more active and attentive to the offences which the Yerukulas committed during the year 1913. The Yerukulas took shelter under the SA in order to escape the punishment given by the local police.[132] The government in order to settle the Yerukulas in the beginning gave 1,860 acres of land and money grants to the SA during the year 1915. There was a good amount of unallotted sandy soil in Bapatla. The government had allotted a portion of land to the Salvation Army in order to settle Yerukulas. The Salvation Army reclaimed the land and brought it under cultivation. During the year 1915, the number of the Yerukulas increased due to the reason that some of the Yerukulas were brought from Sitanagaram and Kalichedu. But the Yerukulas were suspected without any reason. The neighbouring villagers complained to the police repeatedly about their 'criminal' behaviour. The police took the complaints made by the neighbouring *ryots* of Bapatla very seriously and notified the Yerukulas as one of the CTs. Their movements were restricted to the surrounding places of Bapatla.[133] The then Inspector General of Police stated: 'the government had reason to believe that crime had on the whole increased in the vicinity of Bapatla and that some of the increase was due to the propensity of the Bethapudi settlement of the Salvation Army and the Bapatla Yanadi settlement, a small concern under the management of the Bapatla Church Panchayat.'[134]

Agitation in 1915

Every year, the inhabitants of Bapatla and the neighbouring villagers agitated and protested against the government to remove the settlements from Betapudi. They often complained against the Yerukulas living silently in the settlement. They were unhappy due to the reason that the land was provided to the settlers. They wanted to grab the land from the government. On careful enquiry, the government was convinced that the Yerukulas were not responsible for any offence in the neighbourhood. The agitation was set up by certain rich landlords due to unworthy and selfish motives. Adequate protection was provided to the settlers by the government.

Notification of Stuartpuram Settlement Under CT Act

In 1915, the Bethapudi settlement was declared as one of the CT settlements established under the Criminal Tribes Act.[135] In the beginning, the Yerukulas were not under anybody's control. They used to come from different places to the settlement.[136]

Occupation of the Yerukulas

Agriculture was the chief occupation of the Yerukulas in Stuartpuram. A large extent of land was brought under cultivation by them. The government provided irrigation facilities to improve their cultivation. Coconut and mulberry trees were planted by the SA. The Yerukulas got money from the sale of mats, coolie labour and trading of cattle. The inmates, whose conduct was good, were appointed as watchmen. They used to give regular information about the Yerukulas to the managers. The Yerukulas considered the post of watchman very honourable. The watchman maintained good discipline among the settlers.[137]

The Manager

The first manager of the settlement was captain Robilliard. Robilliard was an intelligent person. He was an expert in agricultural activities in gardening. He had gained a lot of experience in rubber plantation work in the East. He developed the settlement on admirable lines. The government congratulated him for the useful work he had done in the settlement.[138]

Strength

The strength of the Stuartpuram during the year 1915 was 302 men, 323 women, 243 boys and 238 girls. The total strength of the Yerukulas was 1,106 members. There was plenty of work and space for the other Yerukulas in the settlement. The government, in order to maintain discipline among the Yerukulas, enforced strict rules. The number of the strength in the settlement did not increase. However, the settlement suffered with bureaucratic measures, application of CTA, rapid influx of turbulent elements, bad character of the managers, police and the surrounding people. The government also transferred some of the Yerukula members from Kavali settlement.[139]

Self-supporting Stage of Stuartpuram

The settlement flourished with agriculture. All the Yerukulas were self-contended. The settlement was self-supporting. The SA received the recurring grant made by the government very late to run the settlement. The SA also suffered severe financial constraints to run the settlements due to lack of proper grants. The settlement was outstanding in its administration in Guntur District. The features of the settlement was remarkable. There were also many defects in the administration of the settlement. There were many defects in the registration of the Yerukulas under the CTA.[140]

The Yerukulas, who were innocent and could not commit even a single crime and who did not have any relation or association with the Yerukulas who were registered, were also registered under the CTA.

Except being Yerukulas they were branded as CTs and were placed in the settlements. This made the Stuartpuram settlement very crowded. The settlement was beyond the capacity of the SA to properly administer it. The good conduct of Yerukulas were mixed up with other bad characters such as professional robbers and dacoits in the settlement. Though this mistake was noticed by the government nothing was done to improve the conditions of the settlement and the entire responsibility was handed over to the SA to set right the conditions of the settlement.

The strength of the Yerukulas gradually increased in the settlement. The strength of the settlement during the year 1925 was 1,500. The SA had given land pattas to 140 Yerukulas. The Yerukulas got the right to cultivate the allotted portion of the land without anybody's interference. The land was allotted on the condition that the settlers have to behave on the satisfactory lines under the guidance of the SA.

Extension of the Stuartpuram

Paddy cultivation was the main occupation of the settlers. The Yerukulas extended the cultivation on satisfactory lines. During the year 1920, the settlers cultivated 500 acres of land. 'Settlement pattas' were provided to them. Water supply was plentiful. The crops were successful. The settlement was filled with coconut, eucalyptus, mulberry, etc. The settlers' achievements were very encouraging. Food crops such as ragi and paddy were cultivated by the Yerukulas. Steady progress was maintained by the Yerukulas every year. During good seasons, the Yerukulas cultivated their lands without fail.[141]

Irrigation Difficulties

The Yerukulas had faced many difficulties during the year 1925. Owing to the bad season and lack of timely rains the Yerukulas did not cultivate their lands. The settlement did not have proper irrigation facilities. The water from Krishna canal was not released. The Yerukulas did not irrigate their lands because of lack of water in the Romperu drain. A dam was constructed across the Romperu.[142] The government promised the Yerukulas for the continuous supply of water during the cultivation periods. But the settlers experienced the false promises of the government. The government later constructed the Perali dam. But the Executive engineer did not take proper interest to complete the construction of the dam on time. Thus, Yerukulas faced many problems to cultivate their lands.

Plantation Work Industry

The primary objective of the settlement was to make the Yerukulas into self-supporting cultivators. The plantation work was started by the government with the help of the Yerukulas. They had worked hard to develop the plants. It was stated: 'The Salvation Army should be directed to the primary objective of the settlement. Instead of developing the land already placed at their disposal, the Salvation Army seems to have fallen a victim to the experimental enterprise of Mr Robilliard, whose enthusiasm as a planter has outrun the objects of his appointment'.[143]

The government had developed the plantation industry in the settlement in order to boost up the income of the Yerukulas. The following plantation work was developed in Stuartpurm: (1) Plantation of forest trees, (2) Casuarina plantation, (3) Coconut plantation, (4) Rubber estates, (5) The Mulberries, (6) the Eucalyptus plantation, etc.[144] Davis, the then Collector of Guntur inspected the settlement and said: 'We would like to open 100 acres of land by the sea for the purpose of planting forest trees'.[145] The land was free from any kind of revenue. The government constructed roads for carting the timber. The trees were cut by the forest department. The Yerukulas were not allowed to take the forest wood and products. The government auctioned the forest trees to private contractors. The then District Forest Officer said: 'The axe men to fell trees in the reserves often have to be brought from a distance. I see no reason why the Yerukulas should not be trained in this branch of forestry and in any case the plantation work attached to the settlement would afford some means of employment in the case of bad seasons'.[146]

A lot of waste land was available in the settlement. The government planted another 100 acres of land with coconut plants. It was suggested to plant 50 plants per acre. The plant was grown in an area of 40 x 40m. The coconut palms yielded well. It was reported that: 'while travelling from Madras to Bapatla if any one notices outside the view near Stuartpuram the coconut palms used to attract the viewers.' Mr Gordon Brown, the then expert in coconut industry and inspector of Federated Malay, stated: 'Having a large space I suggest casuarinas planting as a cash crop between the coconuts. We can plant the same number and at the end of three years we could clear a space around each tree'.[147]

R.W. Davis, the then collector of Guntur, handed over the Vedullapalli forest reserve to the SA for the casuarina plantation work. Money was also sanctioned to the SA to develop the plantation work in the settlement. The government asked the SA not to collect any money from the Yerukulas. But the SA regarded the forest reserve and the casuarina plants as its property. The SA contracted the lands and casuarina plants to the private landholders to bring the plants to maturity. The forest department leased out some portion of the land to the private owners. The forest department favoured eucalyptus and coconut plantation in Stuartpuram. The government understood that the SA and the forest department leased out the lands to private contractors. The produce of the land was taken away by the SA. The casuarina plantation work was a commercial enterprise for the Yerukulas in Stuartpuram.[148]

Extension of Dry Cultivation

Mr Moir, another Labour Commissioner, suggested for the dry cultivation in Stuartpuram. Advances were given to the Yerukulas for the purchase of cattle for the purpose of manure. The coconut plants brought the profit of ₹ 1 per tree every day. It gave a profit of ₹ 5,000 per year from the 100 acres. There was considerable amount of land for the plantation work in Stuartpuram. The plantation work was undertaken seriously by the Yerukulas.[149]

The government also planted a portion of land with casuarina plants, coconut plants, rubber plants and eucalyptus plants in Stuartpuram. The casuarina plants were planted three years ahead of the coconut plants. The government realised the successfulness of the plantations. The casuarina plants work was made in Stuartpuram as a cash crop.[150] The casuarina plants were used as wind breakers on the rubber estate. The rubber plantations did very well. The mulberries were intermixed with the casuarina plants. Brunter, the then officer from the Federated Malay, said: 'The whole settlement was fermented with rubber, coconut, mulberry and casuarina plants'.[151] The Salvation Army planted eucalyptus plants in the settlement. Booth Tucker, the then Commissioner of the Salvation Army, said: 'I advise you to go for eucalyptus and mulberries as these are trees with a great future and they have as you know a great advantage of cropping so that you can cut them at intervals of ten to fifteen years and they spring up from the same roots without the necessity of replanting'.[152] Eucalyptus plants do not require so much watering. The cost of growing eucalyptus was met by the government. The government got profits from the plantation work in the settlement. During the year 1916, the government undertook the work of planting the cash crops and plantation work in the settlement.[153]

The fertile land was not inexhaustible in the settlement. The bad seasons had a disastrous effect on the economic conditions of the Yerukulas. There was a lot of demand for fuel in the north-east states. The settlers supplied the required fuel. The plantation work was taken up by the Yerukulas on a large scale in the sandy area around Bapatla. The Yerukulas got accustomed to the plantation work, watering and filling. The Yerukulas were provided with sufficient work as a means of employment during the bad seasons. The burden of supporting the settlement during the bad seasons was wholly on the SA. One-way plantation work provided regular employment. Only new settlers got benefited out of the work. However, the plantation industry was taken up by the SA and the government as a temporary measure only.[154]

A block of 360 acres of dryland and 1,500 acres in the Romperu Swamp were placed at the disposal of the SA in 1914. The SA employed agricultural maistries from old settlers. They used to instruct the new settlers on the techniques of cultivation. The settlers cultivated paddy, ragi, and groundnut. They got money from mats, ropes, baskets, curry leaf, tomato and green gram cultivation. They were also given road work, stone quarrying, drain digging and other works by the Public Works Department. Their income during the year 1915 was ₹ 19,520.08. The manager leased out lands to the settlers. Harold Stuart noted: 'The case of Stuartpuram settlement is unfairly. This settlement was most successful having the best land. Its progress appeared fast'. Bazlulla, the agricultural officer, set up a scheme for casuarinas and for tomato canning. Robilliard favoured planting coconut and eucalyptus. In order to ensure a better supply of water, a dam across the river Romperu was built in 1919. There was an increase of the settlers income from ₹ 84,189,05 to ₹ 1,03,109.08 (sic) during the year 1923–24.

Progress of the Settlement Since 1925

George Paddison proposed to build a bund in order to protect the fields from submersion of water from the swamp. The cyclone in November 1927 ruined the whole crop of paddy. Robilliard, in his record, showed that some of the settlers resorted to begging. A number of settlers had given evidence that they were regularly cultivating the land. The Tahsildar of Bapatla visited the settlement and issued permanent pattas to the settlers who had been regularly cultivating for a period of three years and against whom there was no complaint of crime.[155]

A Karnam (village officer) was appointed on full time basis to look after the land records, measurements, allotments and supervision of the cattle. The government gave up land cess over the settlers lands to encourage cultivation. When they were asked to go to work they refused. Then an order was given that no kind of passes were to be given to the settlers, not even for purchasing rice. Thus, they were made to go to work. The cases of escapes and of overstays of leave were more in number in the settlement. Marjori Banks suggested the construction of a lock-up at the settlement during the year 1916. Absconders were rigorously prosecuted. The practice of issuing passes made some of the settlers to abscond from the settlement.[156]

A store was opened in the settlement during the year 1919. There were many ways to cheat the settlers. In the store, two kinds of rice were available – broken rice (nukalu) and whole rice. The Yerukulas were cheated many times by giving poor quality rice with dust and stones in the store rice. The SA was also responsible for the opening of a railway station in 1921. The opening of the railway station extended their income by introducing the cultivation of tomato growing.[157]

In addition to agricultural activity and labour work, the Yerukulas were also provided work in an industry by the name of Indian Leaf Tobacco Department (ILTD), opened at nearby village Ramanagar (Epurupalem) in 1915.[158] Men used to be paid wages at the rate of 8 annas per day, 48 annas per week, i.e. ₹ 3 (16 annas made a rupee in those days) and women used to be paid 7 annas per day (42 per week, ₹ 2.62).[159] The Yerukulas were employed in pounding paddy belonging to the Komatis at Chirala, Perala, Epurupalem, Bapatla and in carting stones from Karamchedu during the year 1920. Some settlers worked in settlement gardens. The manager engaged them in filling up of pits. Every year the tobacco cultivation expanded on the sandy area.

A co-operative society was organised with 290 shareholders before 1927. The main purpose for which co-operative societies were organised were: (1) acquisition of house sites on the easy payment system, (2) loans for agricultural purposes, (3) cultivation and reclamation of land, etc.[160] During the year 1930, the settlers were sent on 'O' passes to the Kodandla Rama Mica Mines in the Rapur taluk of Nellore district for employment.[161]

A beat post was opened prior to 1956 to check the physical presence of the criminals in the settlement. C.B. Cunningham, the then Inspector General of Police, Madras, wrote: 'Many habitual criminals have been reformed and are being reformed here. The police should come to the manager with their problems and difficulties as a fellow worker and colleague'.[162]

New forms were introduced in the settlement to facilitate the identification of unregistered persons. There were lapses and infighting amongst the settlers. This was largely due to the sale of toddy in neighbouring villages. Old men and women received subsistence allowance under two categories: (1) widows with children and (2) women whose husbands had absconded or were in jail.[163] The Administration Report for the year 1933–34 stated: 'the cash given at present may be misused. The certainty of getting food would be appreciated by those in real need'.[164] During the year 1936, nearly 168 families were released on 'O' passes and permitted to live in a newly formed colony near Chirala adjoining the premises of the ILTD company.[165]

The Salvation Army thought that education was essential for the Yerukulas of this settlement and, therefore, started an elementary school in 1916. Out of 481 children in the settlement, 250 children were school-going during the year 1916. Class books, maps, slates and slated pencils, pictures of animals and plants, a globe, Ananda primer and Ananda readers for standards I, II and III and garden implements were purchased by the manager. A boarding school was established for the sake of orphan children, children whose parents were in jail and children of parents who had just returned from jails. The SA dissuaded the parents from meeting their children.

The SA appointed peons for the reformation of the children of ex-settlers. The headmaster was with a certificate of higher grade training. Mackenzie, the Salvation Army official, wanted to change the structure of the building to create a new atmosphere in the settlement. The closing down of the Stuartpuram Boarding School (1926) was a severe blow on the settler's children. The Salvation Army constructed a church in the year 1915. Dowson, the then Deputy Inspector General of Police, Madras, said: 'The Kiddies looked fat and happy. The settlement is in a most flourishing condition'.[166]

The SA opened a new girls' school for women's education during the year 1921. During the year 1926, few girls were transferred to Nellore Industrial School. The settlers had a brigade of scouts since 1923. A small bugle band had been formed and equipment supplied. A post office was opened in the settlement during the year 1934. The supply of mid-day meals was started from December 1947. Separate hostels were also being maintained by the SA for these children. There are nearly 155 students in these hostels today. In the hostels, there are 101 boys and 54 girls studying in classes I to 10th (the SSC). In the year 1958, the Salvation Army, combined with the Inspector General of Police, opened a new high school for children of the settlers. The strength of the high school as per the annual record of the year 2005 is 277.

Death rate was high during the year 1915 due to influenza. A new hospital was built by the government. Cooked food was distributed to the settlers up to 30 September 1919. During the year 1920, there was great effect of Malaria in Stuartpuram. The sub-assistant surgeon was called bi-weekly from Bapatla and medicines were supplied for diseases like dysentery, cholera, malaria, fever, small pox, beriberi, boils, heart diseases, stomach ache, etc.[167] The National Health Week was celebrated for the first time during the year 1927. V. Sitarama Ayyar took a keen interest in the well-being of the settlers. G.R. Premayya, a non-official visitor, made the following remarks: 'It is a great blessing to the settlers to have an experienced compounder and a midwife living in the settlement'.[168]

Records were maintained for the births and deaths in the settlement. There was a serious attack of small pox in the settlement during the year 1950. In the beginning, the police used to consult the SA for the whereabouts of the settlers.[169] The police could not enter the settlement without the permission of the manager of the SA. In spite of the manager and local police, there used to be constant fights between the settlers. Maintenance of peace and order was a very big problem. Those settlers who found themselves criminally active and uncontrollable were brought under restrictions and Penalties of Section 10 of the Madras Habitual Offenders Act 1948.[170] The then Commissioner of Labour stated: 'The settlers were not incorrigibles and they were not confined behind barbed wires. No special police staff was employed to watch the settlers'.[171]

After Independence, Indian government removed all the powers of the SA. The authority of the management was shifted to the Tribal Welfare Department. There has been an overall change in the settlement at present. More than 200 members received even university education. This is obviously due to the awareness among the youth. In addition to the SA, other social workers namely Gora, Lavanam, Hemalatha Lavanam and M.V. Thomas endeavoured hard to reform these people.[172] During the years 1983–85, the Andhra Pradesh government implemented a scheme to improve these settlers economically. It is noteworthy that there were freedom fighters in the settlement. Mention may be made of Madigani Dattu, Devarakonda Hanumantha Rao who inspired the settlers with the spirit of nationalism and introduced Gandhian ideology to them. In the modern period, during the freedom struggle, the British Government tried to humiliate the educated upper middle-class Congress leaders by placing them in the prison cells along with the criminals of Denotified Tribes. This sent an indirect message to the freedom fighters that their act too was an act of crime and that they did not get any better treatment in jails. Deverakonda Raju was identified as the most notorious criminal in the eyes of the colonial government. He was famously called Sardar as he was believed to have perfected the art of crime and the art of stealing. When in jail, he could meet and interact with the leaders of freedom struggle when the latter were placed in his cell. Some of the leaders took advantage, interacted with the habitual criminals and promised them that they would help in repealing of the CTA after Independence. Devarakonda Raju was one of those many who was attracted towards freedom struggle and freedom fighters like Gandhiji. Raju soon developed a different attitude and he was the first person in Stuartpuram who shaped himself as a nationalist while in jail. After his release from the jail he changed his dress into khadi and wore a Gandhi cap. He started enlightening the Stuartpuram inhabitants on the nature of freedom struggle and leaders like Gandhiji. He even unsuccessfully tried to organise a meeting of leaders of freedom struggle in Stuartpuram. This kind of exposure to the freedom struggle for some of the inmates of DNT settlements generated a new ethos among them. But the managers of the settlement nipped it in the bud. Under the influence of freedom struggle, Raju took a pledge that he would not commit crime again. Also, he took a resolve to educate his children. His son Devarakonda Hanumantha Rao later became a convenor of ST Cell in the provincial Congress Committee.

Political consciousness in the settlement has increased over the years and a number of them are active political workers today. In the year 1975, the panchayat system was introduced in Stuartpuram. This was under Murukonda Padu Panchayat. From the year 1981–82, it is under Betapudi Panchayat. There are nearly 10,000 voters. The

Stuartpuram ex-settlers are trying to have a separate constituency but this is yet to come into existence. The youth who are working in various private and public employment are very keen on the development of Stuartpuram. They organised 'Yerukula Ekalavya Samithi' an organisation which is the centre for many activities.[173]

Siddhapuram Settlement (Kurnool Dist): Origin and Progress till 1927

Siddhapuram settlement is in between Atmakur and Srisailam road. The settlement is situated in the midst of Nallamalai forest of Andhra Pradesh. Siddhapuram was a voluntary settlement. The site of the settlement was shifted to the interior village in the forest area about 13 km east of Venkatapuram village (which is on Atmakur – Srisailam road). It is in Atmakur police station limits and about 12 km east of Atmakur town. The change of the settlement to the new site contributed to the health and comfort of the Woddars. In January 1927, the site of the settlement was shifted to the present place.[174] The strength of Siddhapuram in the beginning was 112 (30 men, 40 women and 42 children).[175]

Occupations

Before coming to Siddhapuram, the Woddars had a meagre income. They led a hand-to-mouth existence in the surrounding areas. Their earnings from agricultural operations were insufficient to maintain their families. The British Government constructed a huge water reservoir to cultivate the lands attached to the settlement. Every year the crop yield has been dismally low. The manual work is not fetching more than ₹ 15 per day. The primary occupations of the Woddars of Siddhapuram were: (1) agriculture, (2) manual work, (3) cutting wood and processing it, (4) daily labour work, (5) basket and mat-making, (6) petty business and (7) quarrying.[176] The settlement was kept under the charge of a sub-inspector of police assisted by a constable. The sub-inspector was a key person to manage the settlement. The items of work suitable for employment of Woddars in Siddhapuram were: (1) earth work in connection with the clearance, (2) earth work for excavating distributary channels.[177]

Apart from the subsidiary industries, the main source of livelihood for the Woddars was agriculture. Thousand and sixty-six acres of land was distributed to the settlers in the beginning.[178] In addition to these settlers, some other Woddars belonging to Guntur, Hyderabad, Krishna, East and West Godavari districts, Lingala, Chittoor, Nellore, Hubli and Betamcharla were transferred to this settlement. They were also provided more than 175 acres of land and labour works.[179] They were provided with bullocks, horse gram and cholum were cultivated among other crops and some vegetables like brinjals, green chillies, etc. were grown by the Woddars. The tamarind crop gave them encouragement to get more money.[180] Implements were provided for repairs. They were given seeds for their crops. Fodder was supplied to the cattle. Maistries were appointed to instruct them about the value of land and the knowledge of the production of various crops.[181] Agricultural loans were granted to the Woddars by the then Labour Commissioner Moir.[182] The loans were used for purchase of cattle and carts. A survey was conducted by the Revenue Department. According to it, temporary pattas were sanctioned for a period of five years to the settlers.[183] Later on, permanent pattas were provided. The government supplied Ongole breeding bulls in 1932 to the Woddars to improve the livestock. Cows were given as gifts to the Woddars who showed interest in agriculture.[184] As the bulk of the Woddars were highly ignorant of farm practices, two farm servants were appointed to help them in addition to the agricultural maistries.

Till January 1942, Woddars maintained themselves by doing coolie work such as road repairs, improvements to schools and managers' quarters, tank revetment, and repairs to the police lines. The average earning of a male was 3 annas per day (18 paise) and that of a female was 2½ annas per day (15 paise).[185] They had sufficient scope to earn a living by doing: (1) coolie work, (2) cultivation of their own lands and also of the ryots, (3) ploughing and weeding operations, (4) re-ploughing of land after harvest, clearing of lands overgrown with grass, (5) cutting fuel and selling it in head loads, (6) cutting grass and selling it as fodder, (7) cutting 'tangedu' wood and removing its bark and (8) repairs of roads, etc.[186]

In addition to this, they were given daily labour such as breaking clods, spreading earth, supply of water to the machinery, pushing empties and loaded wagons at the site of the Navy, etc.[187] The settlers earned money from various heads of the public works department such as: construction work, forest contract work, cultivation, spinning, weaving, clearance of jungle, sale of cattle, etc.[188]

During the year 1954, about 1,300 Woddars were employed during the tobacco season. The Siddhapuram tank is one of the biggest tanks in Kurnool district with a tank bed of 504.06 acres with abundant facilities for fishing.[189] Mr Turner of the Krishna Cement Works, Mangalagiri, had kindly consented to provide work for some Woddars in the limestone quarries at Kaza in Krishna district. Thus, some families of Woddars were sent to Kaza.[190]

Cottage Industries

During the year 1920, the Siddhapuram colony's advisory committee resolved to provide a match factory on cottage industries scale in the colony to provide subsidiary occupation to the Woddars. The settlers had a large airy wool shed with 12 looms and prepared cumbles (blankets). The looms were all locally made. During the year 1920, the Woddars made 182 cumblies.[191]

Progress of the Wool Industry

The weaving industry was vital to the success of the settlement which supplied guaze cloth for hospitals. There was no demand for the cumblies produced here.[192] Due to the following reasons weaving industry was closed:[193] (1) Because of unfavourable fluctuation in the yarn market. (2) The cloth of finer counts was available in market at cheaper rate. There was difficulty in finding a market for the coarse cloth manufactured in the settlement. (3) There was no scope for unlimited expenditure. (4) The settlers were not evincing much interest in the industry because of low wages.[194]

Sericulture programme was developed but failed. The men at Siddhapuram draw a hill allowance at the rate of 3/10th of their pay. During the year 1925, a co-operative society was also formed in the settlement.[195] It can be observed that every year a few member of the settlers used to abandon the settlement. The causes of such an action was the periodic outbreak of famines in neighbouring regions accentuated by the consequent steep rise in prices and lack of work during this period which forced some of them to leave the settlement. Added to this, lack of irrigation facilities resulted in the failure of crops. It had become a recurring feature and, hence, they quit the area in quest of some work outside their place of residence. Above all, some of them willfully left the settlement since they found themselves unfit for any manual work which was nothing but drudgery to them. They had been inclined towards the practice of crime which almost became their second nature by the time they were brought to Siddhapuram settlement. Though such a tendency was not rampant among settlers, we cannot totally rule out the existence of this tendency in any one of the Criminal Tribes settlement.

For the education of the Woddar children, a school was constructed during the year 1915. Education was imparted in the three Rs (reading, writing and arithmetic) and no attempt had been made to give them industrial training. The attendance was fairly regular. Taylor, the then labour commissioner, said: 'The children look well-cared-for and show satisfactory knowledge of their subjects.'[196]

The educated Woddars were sent to teachers' training institute in Kurnool and were appointed as teachers in the school. The girls were taught sewing. They had the proficiency in making their own jackets. During the year 1938, the school was developed into a first grade elementary school.[197] The government sanctioned to open the sixth standard in the settlement school at Siddhapuram during 1947–48 and to convert one higher elementary grade teacher's post into a secondary grade post.[198] The strength of the high school as per the annual record of the year 2007 was 158. At present, the location and condition of the school at Siddhapuram is deplorable. There are only two graduates in the settlement who are still unemployed.

A medical officer was appointed on Siddhapuram tank project and all the sick Woddars were treated by him. Malaria was a common disease in forest areas and, hence, also in Siddhapuram. The sub-assistant surgeon of Atmakur used to visit the settlement four times in a month. A dispensary with a compounder was opened in April 1929. The common diseases treated in the settlement were bronchitis, fever, pneumonia, dyspepsia, small pox, common cold, digestive disorders, throat complaints, ulcers and skin diseases, etc.[199] Here, we want to cite one interesting factor. In those days, 'health week' was celebrated every year and the manager awarded prizes for the cleanest house; ₹ 6 as 1st prize and for the healthiest baby ₹ 2 as 1st prize.[200] The prizes were an incentive to the settlers to keep their huts and surroundings clean and to devote attention to the health of their babies. The condition of the village at present is really pathetic. The only hospital established in 1929 became dysfunctional and women die at the time of delivery. For medical help, at present they have to rush to Atmakur. They pleaded for a hospital.

It is an interesting factor that the manager of Siddhapuram settlement was instructed to keep a record of all the settlers living in the settlement with a brief note of their history, associations, avocations, movements, conduct and behaviour with a view to help the police to have a proper control and watch over them. Police patrol in the night regularly and check the settlers, to find out whether they go out in the night for committing crimes.[201] The managers of the settlement reposed confidence in the settlers and made them understand that they were ryots and not criminals. The then Labour Commissioner, Mr Moir, said: 'The success of this settlement was due to the efficient and tactful management of K. Subramana Ayyar the then Inspector General of Police'.[202]

Until March 1937, it was a voluntary settlement. In 1937, the government declared the settlement as a regular CT settlement. Up to 1941, the administration of the settlement was under the control of the Commissioner of Labour. From 1943 onwards the administration was taken over by the DIG of Police. The administrative control of the settlement was transferred to the Harijan Welfare Department in June 1954. In 1955, the management was handed over to the social welfare department. In 1965 it was brought under revenue department in the cadre of Deputy Tahsildar. Finally, in 1976, it was declared as a free colony.

In Siddhapuram, there are 300 families. These 300 families comprise 2,000 people. On an average, each family has 1 to 2 acres of land. In some cases, people do not have even 1 acre of land. Some Woddars do not have permanent huts. The average monthly income on all sources may be between ₹ 1,000 to ₹ 2,500. Criminal gangs were very active in Siddhapuram in the olden days and these people have relations with other settlements.[203] The reasons for their criminal propensity among a few Woddar families are: (1) Lack of alternative avenues of livelihood, (2) Lack of proper upbringing of children, (3) Poor economic conditions, (4) Easy-going mentality, (5) Harassment of the police and forest departments even after they have given up their criminal activities.[204]

The police conduct raids on the houses of the settlers and loot the same, molest their womenfolk and register false cases against them. To escape from this torture, the settlers unnecessarily own the responsibility of crime. The secretary of ex-criminals welfare association in Siddhapuram K.R. Somanna explained about the inhuman behaviour and harassment of the police department. Many of the members were undergoing trials in various courts and are imprisoned.[205] In addition to the police harassment, the forest department officials apprehend the settlers whenever they go to the forest which adds to the their misery.[206]

The hospital, school, roads and the entire surroundings of Siddhapuram is in a deplorable condition. There has been an overall change in the settlement at present. K.R. Somanna said that they are happy and occasionally the individual officials evince interest in them. For example, Mr Bhaskar Rao, the police sub-inspector, has been very helpful and the entire settlement heaved a sigh of relief under his benevolent administration.[207] However, the present condition of the settlement is very pathetic.

Lingala Settlement

In Telangana, the only settlement, established in the princely state was Lingala settlement (Nizam's dominions). It is about 104 miles from the capital of the state. It looks like a modern village with permanently built structures, including a hospital, police station, jails, schools for boys and girls, work looms, bungalows for the officials and a temple.[208] The Nizam's administration created an opportunity for them to learn spinning and weaving, carpentry, brick-making, laundering and other such useful works. Some of them became proficient in starting business enterprises for themselves and were successful in carrying out these trades. Some of the families chose to take up animal or cattle farming. They also cultivated agricultural lands. The Nizam's Government supplied them with oxen, implements, seeds and provisions. The settlers felt contented and showed no signs of running away.

Lingala settlement is located in the Nallamalai forest in Mahaboob Nagar district of Telangana State. The name 'Lingala' connotes a peculiar meaning because nine 'Saiva temples' surrounded the settlement (including Umamaheswaram and Srisailam temples). The main reasons for establishing the CT settlement at Lingala by the then Nizam Er-Us-Man Nawab Khan (1911–40) were, first, the absconders from other settlements used to take shelter in the Nizam's dominions. They were creating problems in the Nizam's dominions. Secondly, the Chencus who lived in Nallamalai forests depended on the forest produce. The scarcity of food sometimes made them to waylay passengers and rob them. Thirdly, the Sugails, a nomadic tribe of Hyderabad, were creating trouble in the surrounding villages. It was the responsibility of the Nizam to settle all these three tribes in order to maintain peace and tranquillity in his dominions. Fourthly, the CT settlements in the Madras Presidency were exemplary because they were maintained by the Missionaries. All these factors made the Nizam to bestow his attention to wean the wandering and nomadic tribes away from the criminal propensity and make them lead a normal life. The Lingala settlement has a hospital, police station, schools for boys and girls, post office and a temple. The children are well clothed, fed and taught at the expense of the state. They are sent to the workshops to learn the work for which they are best fitted. They are experts in weaving, carpentry, tile, brick-making and laundering. Many families have farming plots given to them by the Nizam's government.

A group of Nizam Woddars, originally belonging to Hyderabad state, migrated to Lingala and Nizam Sagar settlements. They distinguished themselves as Nizam Woddars. They lived by daily labour. They were not regular in their work. Some of them were convicted for burglaries and thefts. They were declared as a CT during the years 1913, 1915 and 1921. Several Christian Missionaries and philanthropic societies who worked for the moral upliftment of the CTs managed the CT settlements. The following Missionaries may be cited: (1) The Canadian Mission, (2) Chief Khalsa Diwan, (3) Deo Samaj, (4) Anjuman-Islamia, (5) Ahmedia Society, (6) Ahmedia Anjuman Isad-i-Islam, (7) Sanatana Dharma Sabha, (8) Arya Samaj, (9) The Punjab Hindu Sabha, (10) The Servants of Indian Society, (11) The Ramakrishna Mission, (12) The Salvation Army, (13) The American Baptist Telugu Mission, (14) The Brahmosamaj and (15) The Social Service League. The government and non-government bodies dealing with these classes were as follows: (1) The Director of Public Instruction, (2) The Board of Revenue, (3) The Depressed Class Mission, Madras and Saidpet, (4) Mr Kesava Pillai, Gooty, (5) The Indian Christian Association, Madras (6) The Theosophical Society, Adyar (7) S.D. Bawaden and (8) A.H. Curtis. In addition to these, the British Government and the Nizam Government managed CT settlements in Andhra Pradesh.[209]

Lingala settlement comprised three tribes, namely, Yerukulas, Chencus and Lambadas. Among the South Indian Tribes, the Yerukulas occupy an important place. They are one of the largest tribes of Andhra Pradesh. These people are found throughout the Madras Presidency.[209] Yerukulas in Lingala originated from Karnataka region. Others came from Lingsoor, Raichur, Adilabad, Nizamabad and Gulbarga. A few of them came from Stuartpuram Settlement. The police department guided these settlers initially.[210] The second tribe that settled in Lingala Settlement was Chenchus, a non-Aryan tribe dwelling in the hilly tracks. The Chenchus are of semi-nomadic nature and considered as one of the earliest of the South Indian tribes. The Chenchus are divided into five endogamous groups: (1) Telugu Chenchus, (2) Adavi Chenchus, (3) Krishna Chenchus, (4) Bonta Chenchus, and (5) Deva Chenchus. The Telugu Chenchus and Krishna Chenchus are beggars. They collect alms by dancing and singing songs in the plains. The Adavi Chenchus are to be found in large numbers in the neighbourhood of Srisailam on the banks of river Krishna. Deva Chenchus and Bonta Chenchus worship Lingamma, Peddamma, Balamma, Yellamma, Pochamma and Lord Venkateshwara of Tirupati. They name their children as Yellamma and Pochamma. They are confined to the secluded parts of the forest and earn their livelihood by hunting. These people, to some extent, were notorious in waylaying passengers.[211] Hence, they were brought to the Lingala Settlement by the Nizam Government.

The Chenchus originated from Komati Kunta, Rayavaram, Chanpet, Peddur and Kotteru of Telangana region. The Nizam Government brought the Yerukulas and Chenchus and provided for each family five acres of land with Lavani Patta and supplied them with necessary agricultural tools.[212] The Banjaras, (Lambadas or Sugalis) are the original inhabitants in Andhra Pradesh.[213] They mostly live in the districts in Telangana, Kurnool, Warangal and Adilabad districts of Andhra Pradesh and Telangana. The Lambadas are an intelligent, good looking, well built, sturdy people. They have weathered many a storm during their journey from their original home in Rajasthan to several districts of Andhra Pradesh.[214] They speak a peculiar dialect, an admixture of Punjabi and Gujarati. Originally nomads, they are mostly agriculturists. Their songs are closely associated with harvest. During their nomadic life, they used to indulge in petty thieving. All these three tribes, viz. Yerukulas, Chenchus and Banjaras are living at present in Lingala settlement. These three tribes are intertwined with each other to the extent that they have marital relations. Some examples of these marriages are cited by them.[215]

Andhra Rashtra Adimajati Sevak Sangh (under the presidentship of Vennalacunti Raghavaiah and under the vice presidentship of Palaparti veeraiah) stopped malpractices like slave trade and ordeal tests in Lingala settlement. The sale of tribal women to buyers from Punjab (for amounts ranging from ₹ 2,000 to ₹ 5,000) right under the nose of the police department was prevalent. The Sangh took active measures to stop such practices. The Sangh suggested tightening the penal code sections relating to slavery. It was approved by the central law department. It was considered by the Home Ministry. With the active support and efforts of the Sangh, they became experts in weaving, carpentry, tile and brick-making and laundering. Many families were given farming plots by the Nizam Government. They also discouraged tribal ordeals like dipping the hand in the boiling oil and lifting the hot iron bars in their hands.[216]

Today, the settlers are engaged either in cultivation, business or manual labour. They have mainly depended on forest produce. Yerukulas bring bamboo from the forest and they are experts in basket-making. Chenchus depend primarily for their livelihood upon forest produce and to some extent agricultural work. The Sugalis are engaged in manual labour because they are more hard working. The officers who deal with these people have neither time nor interest to bestow necessary attention on them with the result that they are discontented with their life. Even for those who have taken to cultivation, there are no sufficient irrigational facilities. Borewells are not constructed. Moreover, the land is a dry land. The rainfall is scanty in this region. On the whole, they are not much satisfied with the income they get. There is plenty of waste land in the vicinity which can be provided to them along with ground water facilities as an alternative measure. Another important issue is their main source of income is derived through the preparation and sale of country liquor. Due to the recent ban on liquor by Andhra Pradesh Government, they have lost their main livelihood. They are looking for alternative means like making of gum, match, bamboo work and preparing paper, preparation of match boxes as small scale industries mainly based on the raw materials available in the forest and a small section of them are committing petty crimes (rafu).[217]

With regard to educational facilities in Lingala settlement, there is a government school and a residential hostel both for boys and girls. Almost all the parents expressed their dissatisfaction with their school. Their economic conditions are not conducive for their proper growth. Some of the parents still feel that education for their children is a sheer waste of time and energy. They are worried about the employment of their children with 7th or 10th class qualifications. There are very few who have studied up to engineering, medicine and other professional courses. The medical facilities are by and large poor. There is a hospital which was established by the then Nizam Government, which is dysfunctional. Generally, the Chenchus are knowledgeable in using herbal medicines. Unfortunately, this practice has been declining in the recent years. They expressed that the Chenchus from Kurnool, Khammam and Dornala have the knowledge of these medicinal plants. They pleaded for a hospital. There is a general awareness among these people about their problems. They want to struggle with the government to get their demands conceded. Although Girijan co-operative society is established to supply the consumer goods, its benefits are cornered by the well-to-do sections in the village.[218]

The members of the settlement are facing problems from the forest department. The main problem is that rich people from surrounding areas like Achammapeta and other places are given preference by the forest officers and they are the real beneficiaries of the government schemes. Moreover, the facilities provided by the government are also meagre. What should be done in this context is that the economic rehabilitation should be combined with social education. Inculcating social values should be preceded by necessary economic measures to provide them with basic necessities. To raise them to a higher level of social values, one will have to inspire confidence in them about the right path they should take in their effort. They should be made aware of the vast potentialities that lie dormant in them. In spite of the development activities undertaken by the government, an atmosphere of general discontent prevails in the settlement. They are not fully convinced that the government is showing as much care and attention on them as they should. When compared to other settlements, the settlement in Lingala is lagging behind, the exception being Siddhapuram settlement, in Kurnool district. The social workers are also not evincing proper interest in this settlement.

To sum up, a large share of allotment of these tribals should be spent on their economic rehabilitation. As it was stated by the Planning Commission about the DNTs, two-thirds of the allotment should be spent on welfare schemes such as hawking business, selling gum and other forest products. They should be provided with alternative means of livelihood. It is a stunning paradox that till today no sociologist or anthropologist has done a complete survey of these people. Officials and non-officials who guide and control the destinies of crores of Indians are unable to solve the problems and suggest measures for the cure of their long standing ills. If this is the position, concerted action on all fronts is a pressing need. The feeling of a 'psychological barrier' will have to be removed among the DNTs. A more responsible and human approach will go a long way in stimulating a change among the DNTs.

Notes

1. The total population of these tribes in India was estimated in different states totalling approximately more than thirteen million population.
2. Y. C. Simhadri, 'Changing Criminal Behaviour of an Ex-criminal Tribe in an Indian Village, in the Journal of Criminology, Vol. 4, No. 1, January 1976, p. 4.
3. Darrow, Clarence, Crime: Its Causes and Treatment, London, 1934, pp. 7–8.

4. Biswas, P.C., The Ex-criminal Tribes of Delhi State, Unpublished Ph.D. thesis, University of Delhi, 1960, p. 188.
5. Government of Bombay, Report of the Criminal Tribes Act Enquiry Committee, Government Central Press, Bombay, 1939, p. 20. Also see, Report of the Criminal Tribes Enquiry Committee, United Provinces of India, 1947, Allahabad, 1948, p. 4 TNA.
6. Government of Madras, Home Department, G.O. No. 1675, dated 2 December 1919, p. 9
7. Booth Tucker, F., Criminocurology or the Indian Criminal and What to do with Him: A Report of the Work of the Salvation Army among the Criminal Tribes, Habitual and Released Prisoners in India, London, (n.d.) p. 14.
8. Government of Madras, Note Showing the Progress Made in the Settlement of Criminal Tribes in the Madras Presidency upto September 1916, Madras, 1917, p. 6
9. Simhadri, Y.C., The Ex-Criminal Tribes of India, National Publishing House, New Delhi, 1979, p. 35
10. See Government of Madras, Home Department, G.O. No. 1675, dated 2 December 1919, p. 14.
11. See Government of Madras, Home Department, G.O. No. 1675, dated 2 December 1919, p. 6
12. Pickett, Waskom, J., Christian Mass Movements in India, Chicago, 1933, p. 297.
13. Ibid, p. 298.
14. Government of Madras, Note Showing the Progress Made in the Settlement of Criminal Tribes in the Madras Presidency upto January 1926, Madras, 1927, p. 3.
15. Mukhopadhyay, Anandita, 'Criminal Tribes and British Policy, 1871–1928', Unpublished M. Phil thesis submitted to Jawaharlal Nehru University, New Delhi, 1988, pp. 30–35.
16. Government of Madras, Madras Criminal Tribes Manual, brought upto 31 March 1927, Government Superintendent Press, Madras 1927, p. 3.
17. Government of Madras, Note Showing the Progress Made in the Settlement of Criminal Tribes in the Madras Presidency upto January 1926, Madras, 1927, p. 6
18. Booth Tucker, F., Criminology or the Indian Criminal and what to do with Him, A Report on the Work of Salvation Army among the Criminal Tribes, Habituals and Released Prisoners of India, London, (n.d.) p. 18
19. Lalitha, V., The Making of Criminal Tribes: Patterns and Transition, New Era Publications, Madras, 1995, p. 14.
20. Radhakrishana, Meena, 'Colonialism, Evolutionism and Anthropology: A Critique of the History of Ideas 1850–1930', Research-in-progress papers, History and Society, NMML, New Delhi, June 1997. Also see Radhakrishna Meena, 'Surveillance and Settlements under the Criminal Tribes Act in

Madras', Indian Economic and Social History Review, 29, 2, 1992. Also see, Radhakrishna Meena, 'Colonial Construction of a Criminal Tribe: The Itinerant Trading Communities of Madras Presidency' in Neera Chandhoke (ed.) Historical Trajectory: Essays in Honour of Ravinder Kumar, Tulika, New Delhi, 2000.

21. See Government of Madras, Public Works (Labour) Department, G.O. No.1551, dated 20 July 1927, pp. 5–6, APSA.

22. Government of Madras, Madras Criminal Tribes Manual, brought upto 31 March 1927, Government Superintendent Press, Madras, 1927, p. 6.

23. Government of Madras, Note Showing the Progress Made in the Settlement of Criminal Tribes in the Madras Presidency upto September 1916, Madras, 1917, p. 9. The settlements had a uniform structure with the following facilities and equipments.

The Structure and Staff of DNT Settlements

Quarters

A and A-1 : Manager's quarters
B : Office building
C and C-1 : A Hall for mid-day meals and a kitchen
D : Clerks' quarters
E : Compounder and midwife's quarters
F : School building
G and G-1 : Roll call shed and settlers' huts
H : Dispensary and store room
I : Teachers and maistries' quarters, etc.

The settlements were also equipped with settlers' huts and a lock-up. The following staff members were appointed in the settlements by the Government:

Settlement Staff

a Inspector (Managers)
b Clerks
c Peons
d Compounders
e Teachers
f Watchers
g Scavengers
h Midwife
i Wardboy
j Agricultural Instructors/Maistries
k Sweepers, etc.

24. Booth Tucker, F., Criminocurology or the Indian Criminal and What to do with Him, A Report on the Work of Salvation Army among the Criminal Tribes, Habituals and Released Prisoners of India, London, (n.d.) p. 20.

25. Government of Madras, Law (General) Department, G.O. No. 1803, dated 24 July 1920.
26. Government of Madras, Judicial Department, G.O. No. 924, dated 10 May 1913. The members were removed to the Kavali Settlement, Nellore District. Also see Boswell, Nellore District Manual, Madras, 1973.
27. Government of Madras, Home (Judicial) Department, G.O. No. 681, dated 26 March 1917. Some of the Dasaris were transferred to Hubli settlement.
28. Government of Madras, Home (Judicial) Department, G.O. No. 681, dated 26 March 1917. Also see Home (Judicial) Department, G.O. No. 2293, dated 7 October 1919. Lalitha V., 'Socio-Economic and Administrative Aspects of an Ex-Criminal Tribe, A Case Study of Kapparalla Tippa', unpublished M.Phil Dissertation Submitted to Sri Venkateswara University, Tirupati 1975.
29. Government of Madras, Judicial Department, G.O. No. 616, dated 13 May 1922.
30. Government of Madras, Judicial (Police) Department, G.O. No. 658, dated 15 December 1924.
31. Government of Madras, Note Showing the Progress Made in the Settlement of Criminal Tribes in the Madras Presidency upto January 1926, Madras, 1927, p. 10
32. Ibid.
33. Government of Madras, Home Department, G.O. No. 2797, dated 2 July 1940.
34. Government of Madras, Home Department, G.O. No. 5303, dated 2 July 1940.
35. Government of Madras, Home Department, G.O. No. 4714, dated 22 November 1940.
36. Government of Madras, Home Department, G.O. No. 2048, dated 4 May 1940.
37. Government of Madras, Judicial Department, G.O. No. 918, dated 10 May 1913. Also see, Judicial Department, G.O. No. 1796, dated 5 September 1913 and Home (Judicial) Department, G.O. No. 414, dated 20 February 1918 and Judicial Department, G.O. No. 52, dated 31 January 1923. In October 1915, the then district magistrate reported that two headmen of the Koracha tribe by name Puli Bangaru Bojjigadu and Koneti Venkatigadu were the heads of two forts. The entire settlement was split up into two groups. They obstructed the whole development of the settlement. They prevented the people from working on the tank project. The manager removed Bojjigadu to Sitanagaram settlement in Guntur District. For other details see Government of Madras, Judicial Department, G.O. No. 520, dated 2 March 1914. (Report on the settlement of Criminal Gangs in Chittoor district)
38. Government of Madras, Judicial Department, G.O. No. 381, dated 10 July 1925 and Judicial Department, G.O. No. 592, date 20 October 1925. The strength of the settlement at the end of the year 1915 was 161 males, 152 females and 135 children with a total population of 448 people.

39. Government of Madras, Note Showing the Progress Made in the Settlement of Criminal Tribes in the Madras Presidency upto September 1916, Madras 1917, p. 12.
40. Ibid.
41. Government of Madras, Judicial Department, G.O. No 1869, dated 30 July 1927.
42. Government of Madras, Judicial Department, G.O. No 562, dated 23 October 1929.
43. Government of Madras, Judicial Department, G.O. No. 506, dated 22 October 1934.
44. Government of Madras, Judicial Department G.O. No. 643, dated 28 November 1935.
45. Government of Madras, Note Showing the Progress Made in the Settlement of Criminal Tribes in the Madras Presidency upto January 1925, Madras 1927, p. 17.
46. Ibid.
47. Government of Madras, Home (Judicial) Department, G.O. No. 1937, dated 13 September 1917.
48. Government of Madras, Home (Judicial) Department, G.O. No. 2874, dated 6 December 1916. Government of Madras, Judicial Department, G.O. No. 784, dated 25 April 1913.
49. Government of Madras, Judicial Department, G.O. No. 917, dated 10 May 1913 and Judicial Department, G.O. No. 1714 dated 4 July 1916.
50. Government of Madras, Home (Judicial) Department, G.O. No. 212, dated 1 February 1917.
51. Government of Madras, Home (Judicial) Department, G.O. No. 373L., dated 14 February 1934, p. 6. Government of Madras, Home Judicial Department, G.O. No. 24, dated 5 January 1918, p. 2.
52. Government of Madras, Public Works and Labour Department, G.O. No. 1794 L., dated 15 July 1931, p. 8.
53. Government of Madras, Judicial (Police) Department, G.O. No. 377, dated 26 July 1923, p. 3.
54. Government of Madras, Home (Judicial) Department, G.O. No. 1017, dated 30 April 1918, p. 4. Also see Government of Madras, Home Department, G.O. No. 1004, dated 27 April 1918, p. 4.
55. Government of Madras, Home (Judicial) Department, G.O. No. 1004, dated 27 April 1940, p. 1. Also see, Government of Madras, Home Department, G.O. No. 242, dated 1 February 1917.
56. Government of Madras, Home Department, G.O. No. 1059, dated 15 January 1940, p. 1.
57. Government of Madras, Home Department, G.O. No. 1269-G, dated 15 January 1940, p. 3.
58. Government of Madras, Home Department, G.O. No. 1004, dated 13 August 1940, p. 1.

59. Government of Madras, Public Works Labour Department, G.O. No. 5248, dated 5 August 1940.

60. Government of Madras, Law (General) Department, G.O. No. 1714, dated 22 October 1921, p. 4. The sub-settlements at Allur and Bitragunta were started in 1917. The services of the manager was given freely by the ABM missionaries. The population of the settlement at the end of the year 1917 was 1, 393. The nature of employment of the inmates were contracts, agriculture, carpentry, weaving, lime kiln, coolie work, stone quarrying and fire wood cutting. See Government of Madras, Home (Judicial) Department, G.O. No. 2294, dated 7 October 1919, p. 6.

61. Government of Madras, Public Works and Labour Department, G.O. No. 1551 L. dated, 20 July 1927, p. 3.

62. Government of Madras, Public Works and Labour Department, G.O. No. 1654 L., dated 6 July 1928, p. 1.

63. Government of Madras, Public Works and Labour Department, G.O. No. 2394 L., dated 23 August 1929, p. 1.

64. Government of Madras, Public Works and Labour Department, G.O. No. 2338 L., dated 19 August 1930, p. 1. Also see, Law (General) Department, G.O. No. 666, dated 26 February 1923, p. 4.

65. Government of Madras, Public Works and Labour Department, G.O. No. 1926 L., dated 30 July 1931, p. 1. Also see, Law (General) Department, G.O. No. 993, dated 8 April 1922.

66. Government of Madras, Public Works and Labour Department, G.O. No. 34 10 L., dated 3 December 1930, p. 2. Also see, Public Works (Labour) Department, G.O. No. 296 L., dated 8 November 1923, p. 4.

67. Government of Madras, Public Works and Labour Department, G.O. No. 1426 L., dated 27 January 1931, p. 3.

68. Government of Madras, Public Works and Labour Department, G.O. No. 1350 L., dated 18 May 1931, p. 1.

69. Government of Madras, Public Works and Labour Department, G.O. No. 1364 L., dated 20 May 1931, p. 1.

70. Government of Madras, Public Works and Labour Department, G.O. No. 413 L., dated 16 February 1931, p. 1., Also see, Judicial Department, G.O. No. 2874, dated 6 December 1916, and Judicial Department, G.O. No. 212, dated 1 February 1917.

71. Government of Madras, Public Works and Labour Department, G.O. No. 194 L., dated 24 January 1933, p. 2.

72. Government of Madras, Public Works and Labour Department, G.O. No. 427 L., dated 20 February 1933 p. 4.

73. Government of Madras, Public Works and Labour Department, G.O. No. 5554, dated 17 November 1938, p. 2.

74. Government of Madras, Public works and Labour Department, G.O. No. 5860, dated 7 December 1938, p. 1.

75. Government of Madras, Administration Report of the Labour Department for the year ending 31 March 1933, Madras 1934, pp. 25–26.

76. Government of Madras, Public Works and Labour Department, G.O. No. 373 L., 14 February 1934, p. 3.

77. Lalitha, V., Making of Criminal Tribes Patterns and Transition, New Era Publication, Madras, 1995, p. 18.

78. Until 1933, Kavali Reformatory Settlement and Bitragunta Settlements were under the management and control of the American Baptist Mission. The total population of the settlement on 31 March 1933 was 1111 people out of which 378 were men, 287 were women and 446 were children. The Employment for the Yerukulas in Kavali was inadequate and a number of Yerukulas continued to be employed on unremunerative labour. See Government of Madras, Administration Report of the Labour Department for the year ending 31 March 1933, Madras, 1934, pp. 24–25, TNA.

79. Government of Madras, Home Department, G.O. No. 1059, dated 1 January 1940, p. 1.

80. Ibid.

81. Lalitha V., Socio-Economic and Administrative Aspects of an Ex-criminal Tribe, Unpublished M.Phil Thesis, Tirupathi University, 1977, p. 32.

82. In making the grants the government recommended first persuasive methods should be adopted to settle the families of Yerukala tribe. If the persuasion failed, then to apply the Provisions of the CT Act.

83. Sitanagaram settlement was the first of its kind in Madras Presidency. It was actually opened in the month of January 1913 with a few men who were released from the jail before their arrival to Sitanagaram. The government adopted some persuasive methods to settle the Yerukulas. Since the persuasive methods adopted by the government failed the Government submitted the proposals to declare the Yerukulas as the CTs under the CTA and restricted their movements under section 12 of the 1911 Act. The recommendation of the government was carried out immediately. The Yerukulas of Godavari and Guntur districts were restricted in their movements to the areas comprised within the settlement area. See Government of Madras, Note Showing the Progress Made in the Settlement of Criminal Tribes in the Madras Presidency upto Septembers 1916, Madras 1917, p. 5.

84. Note, 1925: 1.8

85. Lalitha, V., The Making of Criminal Tribes Patterns and Transition, New Era Publications, Madras, 1995, p. 143.

86. Robert Eric Frykenberg, Manual of Guntur District 1960: 17.

87. Home (Judicial), Department G.O. No. 1420, dated 9 July 1917, p. 1.

88. Home (Judicial) Department G.O. No. 1225, dated 20 May 1918, p. 1.

89. Home (Judicial) Department G.O. No. 1234, dated 22 May 1918, p. 1.

90. Home (Judicial) Department G.O. No. 927, dated 20 April 1918, p. 3

91. Home (Judicial) Department G.O. No. 2715, dated 6 December 1918, p. 1.
92. Home (Judicial) Department G.O. No. 2615, dated 13 December 1917, p. 1.
93. Judicial Department, G.O. No. 573, dated 29 February 1916, p. 1.
94. Home (Judicial) Department G.O. No. 2373, dated 4 October 1916, p. 3.
95. Home (Judicial) Department G.O. No. 625 dated 18 March 1918.
96. The then District magistrate, Guntur, inspected Sitangaram in November 1916, and reported that the place was in a very insanitary condition owing to floods. The government appointed a committee consisting of the Deputy Inspector General of Police (CID and Railways), the Executive engineer, the manager of the settlement and the district magistrate. The Committee recommended: 1) Improvement of Sainyapuram by thinning out the village, 2) Building of new huts at Kondapet, 3) Construction of a road and improvement of drainage, and 4) Construction of a well. Home Judicial Department, G.O. No. 22, dated 5 January 1920, p. 1.
97. The children attended the school regularly. The strength of the school at the end of the year 1915 was 92. See, Home (Judicial), G.O. No. 795, dated 4 April 1918, p. 1.
98. A.G. Cardew the then government officer on the settlements visited Sitanagaram during the year 1917. There was a thorough discontentment among the Yerukulas in Sitanagarm. The government carefully examined the question whether Sitanagaram should be completely closed and to transfer the Yerukulas to Stuartpuram in Guntur. The then SA Manager adopted new ventures to settle the Yerukulas in Sitanagaram. But all his ventures were terminated by the Government and the Yerukulas. In the month of February 1915 a number of Yerukulas formed into gangs walked out of Sitanagaram defied the management. The then district Magistrate remarked 'I regret that I cannot regard the working of the settlement as satisfactory'. See Home (Judicial) Department G.O. No. 946, dated 27 April 1918, p. 1.
99. Home (Judicial) Department, G.O. No. 216 dated 23 September 1918.
100. The Annual Report on CTs during the year 1918–1919 showed that the condition of Sitanagaram under the administration of the new management progressed satisfactory. The total strength of Yerukulas in Sitanagaram on 31 March 1919 was 720 people of whom 122 Yerukulas had absconded. The school contained only 94 children due to severe influenza epidemic. Home (Judicial) Department, G.O. No. 2233 dated 29 September 1919, p. 1.
101. Law (General) Department, G.O. No. 2454, dated 7 October 1922, p. 1. The future of the Sitanagaram came up for consideration during the year 1920–21. The new manager enforced better discipline among the Yerukulas. The debts incurred were wiped off gradually. The then Inspector General of police said: "the settlement should be continued. The early difficulties were mainly due to mismanagement of the missionaries". After careful considerations of all the circumstances, the government ordered the management authorities to retain Sitanagaram permanently.

102. Employment was freely available for the Yerukulas throughout the year. The wages earned by them amounted to ₹ 22,600. The strength of the Yerukulas during the year 1922 was 728 people out of which 58 people had absconded. There were 70 boys, 57 girls of school-going age children. All of them attended the school regularly. A night school was also maintained at Sitanagaram. A total number of 83 acres was cultivated by the Yerukulas. Agricultural operations were successful. A new masonry drain was built. The level of the road was raised. Housing conditions were improved. The Yerukulas showed improvement in all directions. The government congratulated Adjutant and Mrs Mabe for their continuous and good hard work for improving the conditions of the Yerukulas. See, Law (General) Department, G.O. No. 2314, dated 19 September 1922, p. 4. Also See Home Department, G.O. No. 2451, dated 3 June 1940, p. 1
103. Home Department, G.O. No. 2150 (c), dated 20 August 1936 p. 1.
104. Public works (Labour) Department, G.O. No. 2172 B, dated 25 August 1933.
105. Public Works (Labour) Department, G.O. No. 5649, dated 5 March 1936, p. 1.
106. Ibid, p. 4.
107. Home Department, G.O. No. 372, date 28 January 1937.
108. Government of Madras, Administration Report of the Labour Department for the year ending 31 March 1938.
109. Government of Madras, Administration Report on Habitual Offenders Settlements for 1951–52, Madras 1953, p. 5
110. Home Department, G.O. No. 2900, dated 8 August 1952, p. 4. The District Medical Board Guntur Contributed an amount of ₹ 25 per month for the maintenance of the hospital. The government have also sanctioned an amount of ₹ 500 to the SA manager for the purchase of equipment for the hospital. See, Note showing the Progress Made in the Settlement of Criminal Tribes in Madras Presidency upto September 1916, Madras, 1917, p. 6.
111. Home Department, G.O. No. 2900, dated 8 August 1952, p. 4.
112. Home Department, G.O. No. 1837, dated 13 June 1944, p. 1.
113. Home Department, G.O. No. 2214, dated 26 July 1946, p. 3.
114. Home Department. G.O. No. 3953, dated 20 July 1939, p. 1.
115. The Manager of Sitanagaram settlement during the year 1938 was S.V.V. Gopala Rao Nayudu. The population of the Yerukulas in Sitanagaram on 31 December 1938 was 298 people (195 men and 103 children). In addition to the above people there were 763 people (110 men, 167 women and 484 children) who were exempted and unregistered. They were freed from the restriction of the CT Act. A total number of 163 acres of land was brought under cultivation by the Yerukulas. The crop raised in Sitanagaram did not thrive well. The Yield was very poor. See Government of Madras, Home Department, G.O. No. 3953, dated 20 July 1939 pp. 31–32 Government of Madras.

116. Government of Madras, Administration Report on Kallar Reclamation, Korava Reclamation, Yenadi Reclamation (Criminal Tribes) and settlements for 1947–1948, Superintendent Government Press, Madras, 1949, pp. 36–39.
117. Ibid, p. 37
118. Ibid, p. 38
119. Home Department, G.O. No. 2960, dated 2 August 1948, p. 22.
120. Home Department, G.O. No. 3587, dated 16 November 1946, p. 38
121. Ibid, p. 34
122. Ibid, p. 35
123. Administration Report on Kallar Reclamation, Korava Reclamation, Yanadi Reclamation and Settlements for 1950–51, Government Press, Madras, 1952.
124. Government of Madras, Administration Report on Habitual Offenders Settlements for 1951–52, Madras 1953, p. 1.
125. Home Department, G.O. No. 2900, dated 8 August 1952, pp 4–5
126. Lalitha, V., 'A Profile of Sitanagaram settlement', Proceedings of Andhra Pradesh History Congress, 17th Session held at Guntur, 1986, pp. 171–177
127. Government of Madras, Administration Report on Kallar Reclamation, Korava Reclamation, Yanadi Reclamation (Criminal Tribes) and Settlements for 1949–1950, Superintendent Government Press, Madras, 1951, pp 11–12.
128. Lalitha, 1995: p. 144
129. Hemalatha Lavanam, Jeevana Prabhatam (Telugu), Vijayawada, 1984, p. 3. Also by the same author Nerastula Samskarana (Reform of the Criminals) (Telugu), Vijayawada, 1985, p. 4 and Problems of Denotified Tribes: An Experiment on Stuartpuram, Vijayawada, 1975.
130. Lalitha 1995: p. 147
131. Captain Robilliard of the Salvation Army, Manager of the Stuartpuram Criminal Tribes Settlement, Bapatla, Madras, Written Statement on the Work of Sturtpuram Settlement, p. 6. Stuartpuram settlement was opened on 1 June 1914. Few families lived at No. 8 division, known then as Ratnapuram in a few dilapidated huts. Since the settlement was opened by Mr Stuart the then acting chief secretary to Government of Madras, it was called as Stuartpuram settlement.
132. Government of Madras, Note Showing the Progress Made in the Settlement of Criminal Tribes in the Madras Presidency upto September 1916, Madras, 1917, p. 7.
133. Home (Judicial) Department, G.O. No. 1093, dated 16 May 1918, p. 1.
134. Note, 1916, p. 7.
135. Home (Judicial) Department, G.O. No. 305, dated 7 February 1918, p. 1.,
136. Home (Judicial) Department, G.O. No. 3003, dated 3 December 1920, p. 1.

137. Home (Judicial) Department, G.O. No. 1298, dated 6 September 1921, p. 1.
138. Home (Judicial) Deportment, G.O. No. 357, dated 13 May 1921, p. 2.
139. Home (Judicial) Department, G.O. No. 2233, dated 29 September 1919, p. 4.
140. Home (Judicial) Department, G.O. No. 2150, dated 20 August 1936, p. 1.
141. Home (Judicial) Department, G.O. No. 716, dated 30 March 1917, p. 1.
142. Note, 1925, p. 8.
143. Home (Judicial) Department, G.O. No. 212, dated 1 February 1917, p. 3. Also see Home Judicial Department G.O. No. 1579, dated 1 August 1917, p. 1.
144. Judicial Department, G.O. No. 2491, dated 12 October 1915, p. 1.
145. Home (Judicial) Department, G.O. No. 1579, dated 1 August 1917, p. 1.
146. Home (Judicial) Department, G.O. No. 305, dated 7 February 1918, p. 1.
147. Home (Judicial) Department, Memorandum No. 2123/A-4, dated 25 September 1917, TNA.
148. Home (Judicial) Department, G.O. No. 625, dated 18 March 1918, p. 1.
149. Home (Judicial) Department, G.O. No. 818, dated 5 April 1918, p. 2.
150. Home (Judicial) Department, G.O. No. 1234, dated 22 March 1918, p. 3. See Home (Judicial) Department, G.O. No. 1402, dated 13 June 1918, p. 1.
151. Home (Judicial) Department, G.O. No. 1224, dated 20 May 1918, p. 3.
152. Home (Judicial) Department, G.O. No. 1402, dated 13 June 1918, p. 4.
153. Home (Judicial) Department, G.O. No. 795, dated 4 April 1918, p. 3.
154. Home (Judicial) Department, G.O. No. 2163, dated 23 September 1918, p. 1. Also see Judicial Department, G.O. No.553, dated 28 April 1922, p. 1.
155. Government of Madras, Public Works and Labour Department, G.O. No. 1654 L., dated 6 July 1928, p. 3. Also see Home (Judicial) Department, G.O. No. 475, dated 19 February 1920, p. 2.
156. Home (Judicial) Department, G.O. No. 2074, dated 18 August 1916, p. 1.
157. Home (Judicial) Department, G.O. No. 475, dated 19 February 1920.
158. Meena Radha Krishna, 'From Tribal Community to Working class consciousness case of Yerukula women', Economic and Political weekly, Vol. XXIV, No. 17, 29 April 29 1989 pp. 3–4.
159. Law (General) Department, G.O. No. 3187, dated, 14 November 1924, p. 1. APSA.
160. Public Works (Labour) Department, G.O. No 1551, dated, 20 July 1927, p. 4.
161. Public Works (Labour) Department, G.O. No. 170, dated 21 January 1931, p. 3. APSA. Also see Public Works and Labour Department, G.O. No. 1623 L., dated, 1 August 1932, p. 1.
162. Public Works (Labour) Department, G.O. No. 1926, dated 30 July 1931, p. 3. APSA. Also see, Public Works and Labour Department, G.O. No. 1662 L., dated 1 August 1932, p. 1.

163. Public Works (Labour) Department, G.O. No. 170, dated 21 January 1931, p. 4. APSA. Also see Public Works and Labour Department, G.O. No. 1452 L., dated 24 June 1935, p. 1.

164. Government of Madras, Administration Report of the Inspector General of Police, during the year 1936, Government Superintendent Press, Madras, 1937, p. 1. Also see Home (Judicial) Department, G.O. No. 716, dated 30 March 1917, p. 2 APSA

165. Public Works (Labour) Department, G.O. No. 2671, dated 6 December 1934, p. 4. Also see Public Works and Labour Department, G.O. No. 1551L., dated 20 July 1927, p. 3.

166. Law (General) Department, G.O. No. 1714, dated 22 October 1921, p. 4, APSA. The manager of the settlement during the year 1937–38 was Major H. Stevens.

167. Home Department (Judicial) G.O. No. 2615, dated 13 December 1917, p. 1. Also see Home Department Judicial, G.O. No. 1592, dated 13 August 1917, p. 1.

168. Public Works (Labour) Department, G.O. No. 973L, dated 3 April 1928, p. 1. The Manager of Stuartpuram settlement during the year 1950–51 was Brigadier F. Ratna Singh.

169. Government of Madras, Administration Report on Habitual Offenders Settlements for 1951–1952, Superintendent Government Press, Madras, 1953, p. 1

170. Government of Madras, Administrative Report on Habitual Offenders Settlements for the Year 1952–53, Government Superintendent Press, Madras 1954, p. 10.

171. Government of Madras, Administration Report on Kallar Reclamation, Korava Reclamation, Yenadi Reclamation (Criminal Tribes) and Settlements for 1947–48, Superintendent Government Press, Madras, 1949, p. 14.

172. Lavanam and Hemalatha Lavanam, 'The Criminal Background of Stuartpurm, Althiest Centre Vijayawada, pp 10–14. Also see by the same authors, Mrutyma Amrutargamaya, Autobiography of Smt Hemaltha Lavanam, Visalandra Publications, Vijayawada 2004, pp 1–10 (Telugu).

173. Public Works (Labour) Department, G.O. No. 137, dated 19 January 1927, p. 1, APSA.

174. Siddhapuram settlement was started during the year 1913 for the benefit of Woddars. The Woddars were employed by the Public Works Department on the Siddhapuram Tank Project in Kurnool district. The government settled the Woddars as agricultural labourers. A block of 650 acres of forest land was allotted for the opening of the settlement by the government in 1918.

175. Home (Judicial) Department, G.O. No. 1860, dated 25 October 1920, The Siddhapuram tank project work was completed during the year 1919. The government did not provide any work for the Woddars. The strength of the Woddars in Siddhapuram during the year 1920 was 65 males, 65 females and 74 children. 150 acres of forest land was distributed to the Woddars.

However, only 15acres were brought under cultivation by them. Cumbly-weaving was started as a subsidiary industry for the Woddars. See Home Department, G.O. No. 2661, dated 25 October 1920, p. 1.

176. The wool industry was developed in Siddhapuram during the year 1920. There were 12 looms working during the year 1921. The Woddars manufactured 182 comblies (blankets). The cumblies were sold locally. A wool shed was constructed and a total number of 18 males and 15 females were engaged in the wool shed. The males were given 5 annas and the females were paid 3 annas per day. See Public Works (Labour) Department, G.O. No. 137, dated 19 January 1927, p. 1.

177. Owing to unfavourable seasons the cultivation activities of the Woddars was a great failure. Some Woddars were employed in weaving industry. There was no market for the cumblies prepared by the Woddars. The police department refused to purchase the cumblies prepared by the Woddars.

178. Public Works (Labour) Department, G.O. No. 1843, dated 25 August 1927, p. 1. Also see Public Works and Labour Department, G.O. No. 1764, dated 19 August 1932, p. 3

179. Public Works (Labour) Department, G.O. No. 2190, dated 28 July 1930, p. 7, Also see, Public Works (Labour) Department, G.O. No. 2671, dated 6 December 1934, p. 4.

180. Public Works (Labour) Department, G.O. No. 2671, dated 6 December 1934, p. 5. Also see Home Department, G.O. No. 1123, Miscellaneous series, dated 26 June 1936, p. 1.

181. Home Department, G.O. No. 1217, dated 6 March 1939, p. 4. Also see, Home Department, G.O. No. 3889, dated 23 September 1940, p. 1.

182. Home Department G.O. No. 568, dated 23 February 1944, p. 1.

183. Home Department, G.O. No. 2113, dated 12 May 1927, p. 1.

184. Public Works (Labour) Department, G.O. No. 2671, dated 6 December 1934, p. 5. APSA.

185. Home Department, G.O. No. 568, dated 23 February 1944, p. 1. TNA.

186. Home Department, G.O. No. 2113, dated 13 July 1944, p. 1.

187. Home Department, G.O. No. 3889, dated 23 September 1940, p. 2.

188. Home Department, G.O. No. 2482, dated 9 July 1940, p. 1.

189. The following were the managers of the settlement during the year 1951–52: N.R. Vasudeva Nayudu was the manager of the settlement during the year 1938. Janab Syed Abdul Gaffar was appointed upto 3 August 1951, Later, V. Ramanathaiah upto 2 May 1951. G. Audiseshiah (Accountant in Charge) from 3 May 1951 to 11 May 1951, T. Gopala Rao from 12 May 1951 to 1 October 1951, G. Sreenivasulu Naidu from 2 October 1951, T. Govindarajulu from 4 to 18 August 1951, K. Sreemantham (Accountant in charge) from 19 August to 7 November 1951, K.V.R. Patnaik from 8 November to 2 December 1951 and T. Govinda Rajulu from 3 December 1951 to 9 March 1952. These managers were constantly absent for many days and the responsibility of the administration of the Woddars were

given charge to the Accountants in the office. The Inspector of police Atmakur used to supervise the settlement. The total population of Woddars on 31 March 1952 in Siddhapuram was 613 people consisting of 172 males 173 females and 268 children. See Government of Madras, Administration Report on Habitual Offenders Settlements for 1951–52, Government Superintendent Press, Madras 1953, p. 4. Also see, Government of Madras, Report on Habitual Offenders Settlement for 1953–54, Government Superintendent Press, Madras, 1955, p. 6.

190. Home Department, Memorandum No. 29831-G/47-7 dated 4 December 1947, p. 1.
191. Home Department, Memorandum No. 5539-G/48-2, dated 11 February 1948.
192. Home Department, G.O. No. 2960, dated 2 August 1948, p. 3.
193. Home Department, G.O. No. 2877, dated 10 July 1940, p. 1.
194. Home Department, G.O. No. 2482, dated 1 January 1940 p. 1.
195. Home Department, G.O. No. 2877, dated 10 July 1940 p. 3.
196. Development Department, G.O. No. 238, dated 31 January 1940, p. 1.
197. Education and Public Health Department, G.O. No. 204, dated 29 January 1937, p. 4.
198. Government of Madras, Administration Report on Habitual Offenders Settlements for 1951–52, Madras 1953, p. 6
199. Law (General) Department, G.O. No. 3187, dated 14 November 1924, p. 1. APSA
200. Public Works (Labour) Department, G.O. No. 1551, dated 20 July 1927, p. 4.
201. Public Works (Labour) Department, G.O. 170, dated 21 January 1931, p. 3. APSA
202. Public Works (Labour) Department, G.O. No. 1926, dated 30 July 1931, p. 4. APSA
203. Public Works (Labour) Department, G.O. No. 170, dated 21 January 1931, p. 4. APSA.
204. Administration Report of the Inspector General of Police, 1936, Madras, 1937, p. 26.
205. Interview with K.R. Samanna an ex-settler of Siddhapuram settlement dated 22 November 2006.
206. Ibid.
207. Ibid.
208. Haikerwal, B.S., Economic and Social Aspects of Crime in India, Lucknow, 1934, p. 166. Also see, Government Andhra Pradesh, Report on the Administration of the District Police of H.E.H. The Nizams Government, 1918: pp. 27–28.
209. Home Judicial Department, G.O. No. 1678, dated 13 March 1916.

210. The remnants of a fort, jail, post office and temple are still there in Lingala. One bungalow is used as the present post office. It shows how much attention the Nizam's government paid on Lingala settlement. Yerukulas were brought from the surrounding areas and were kept in the jail which was called as Juramfis. They used to get the written permission of the police officers to leave the settlement for going to some other place. For this, the well-known social worker Sangam Laxmi Bayamma pleaded for their freedom. Then the 'Juramfis' was removed.

211. Haikerwal, B.S., op.cit., p. 166.

212. Lalitha, V., The Making of Criminal Tribes Patterns and Transition, Madras, 1995, p. 49. Also see, Government of Andhra Pradesh, Report on the Administration of the District Police of H.E.H. The Nizams Government, 1918: 24.

213. Edgar Thurston, Castes and Tribes of Southern India, Vol. 3, Madras, 1909.

214. Sayyad Siraz-ul Hassan, The Castes and Tribes of the H.E.H. The Nizam's Domination, New Delhi, 1989.

215. Government of Madras, The Chenchus and the Madras Police, Madras, Part I and Part II Madras, 1921.

216. Giridawar, an Officer in-Charge was responsible in supplying them agricultural implements. Interview with Peram Hussain, ex-sarpanch in the settlement, Lingala, 20 October 2006. Palaparti Veeraiah, What we did, an article on 'Andhra Rastra Adimjati Sevak Sangh' published in the report of the 7th Conference from scheduled tribes and tribal (scheduled) areas Guntur, Andhra Pradesh, 9 and 10 November 1964, New Delhi.

217. Interview with M. David, Lingala Settlement, 20 October 2006.

218. Kapila Vatsayan, Traditions of Indian Folk Dance, 1976, Samata, R.K. and L. Shayam Sundar, 'The Lambadas their Socio-Psychological and Agro-Economic Characteristics', Man in India, Vol. 65, No. 3, September 1985.

2

Reformatory Education for the Children of 'Criminal' Tribes in Madras

The present chapter reflects on the issues related to education among India's CT children, particularly the way it was imparted to them during the colonial rule in South India. The aims and objectives of the chapter is to deal with the reformatory schools, training imparted to CT children, character building, treatment meted out to the children in the schools, facilities provided, vocational training and how the government intended to develop the children of CTs through reformatory schools and its implication for the empowerment and development of the CTs in the Madras Province.

From the beginning, education had remained a dream for the overwhelming majority of Indian population due to their lower status in the stratified society. Due to lack of education their fate remained much lower with dejection, lack of identity, status and illiteracy. They lead an unfulfilled life for centuries with some of them continuing in the same position even now. Modern education system leading to development was completely denied to the children of CTs for generations. During the colonial rule, reformatory education was imparted to CT children in the Madras province for their development. The implicit development strategy of the children of the CTs adopted by the colonial government was reformatory education. Reformatory schools developed the self-perception of the children as juvenile delinquents, and a way of life which made them as sub-humans, low wage employees, stigma of criminality in the society. Often this was not the type of education for the majority of children in the country. Children of poorer sections were far away from the development rhetoric. The wandering communities did not have the required power to fight with the society. They led a contended life to improve their existing circumstances living in the internal places or in the secluded hilly forest regions. They did not have any opportunity for any type of education. A few questions arise here: Why the colonial government planned reformatory education, industrial training, night schools and Missionary education for the children of CTs in the Madras province? Why these children were completely detached from general education that was imparted to the children in state run schools? How the colonial government imparted education to the children of the CTs?

Research studies on these communities show that the status of the CTs remained at the bottom in the socio-economic and educational development. First of all, this needs to be understood. They remained invisible in the dominant society. Owing to the increased pressure on the industrial labour, cheap labour contract work and the forces of colonisation they remained backward in the colonial society. The colonial government totally neglected their education and aspirations. These communities lead their life as grazers, petty traders, mendicants, acrobats, etc. They occupied a unique position in the rural society. They were closely linked with their ethnic roots of life. Though the higher sections of the people utilised their services enormously, their representation in the dominant society was very much limited. Official accounts, ethnographic accounts and the colonial administrators made many complaints about them with regard to their culture, immoral ways of living, and poverty stricken conditions in the society.

There was a vast difference between the culture of education in the settlement schools and the general population. Imparting reformatory education was an agenda of the colonial government to certain communities declared as CTs and strictly imposed the regulations of the CTA on them. The colonial government undermined their social life. The result was that a large number of communities were suspected and kept under the control of the police department and the Missionaries to watch them and control and restrict their movements. They were placed in different settlements such as penal, reformatory, voluntary and agricultural settlements. Night schools were opened for the CTs in the settlements. This had not helped their education and development. Education was provided to the children based on the provisions of the CTA. Missionaries such as the Salvation Army, American Baptist Telugu Mission, Canadian Mission imparted education to the children of the CTs. Majority of their children were converted to Christianity. Often, the teachers were recruited by the Missionaries from the community itself. They did not evince much interest in the education of the children of CTs. Thus, the children were deprived of their basic education.

The colonial government placed many communities in the settlements in Madras Province. These settlements were placed near the industrial places. The industries in the nearby places and the contract works were linked with the education of the children. Education and schooling was meant to serve the needs of the industrial recruits or the private owners. The general atmosphere of the schools was pathetic. However, residence of the children in these schools meant that understanding the provisions of the CTA and training under the Missionary bodies. Children were isolated from the traditional knowledge. Children were isolated from their parents, community and the village at tender age. Parents were never allowed to meet their children. Children were trained to cope with arduous work. There were conflicts between the police and the Missionaries on the one hand and the parents, Missionaries and the police on the other. Children were often meted out ill-treatment, low wage payment and exploitation. These schools did not bridge the gap between the general schools and the Missionary schools for the CTs. The Missionary schools often alienated CT children from proper education. As the community and the parents were always under strict supervision of the CTA provisions, they could not seriously resist reformatory schooling system in the Madras province. Parents who resisted the kind of treatment received in these schools were strictly penalised. Wealthy merchants, landlords, zamindars, high caste Hindus used to send their children to the state-owned schools to secure government jobs. Children of poorer sections remained as workers in their houses. In the settlements, the Missionaries imparted Bible education to the children. Education was imparted in a language other than their mother tongue. Often teachers were recruited from the community or from the headquarters of the Missionaries. Most of the time, the Missionaries did not understand the langue of the native people. The Missionaries could not bridge this gap.

In the settlement schools, children were often denied the opportunities for the development of their imaginative world. Their parents and the community were always surrounded by the laws of the CTA and police control. Often, the police would ill-treat the parents of the children and Missionaries used to protect them with different measures. Children were severely affected due to the harsh treatment given to their parents. They could not actively participate in their adult world. They completely lost their freedom in schools and at home. Their development or evolvement creation was disturbed. The problems of children were never understood by the colonial administrators. Virtually, no value was attached to these children in the society. Sophisticated skills, knowledge systems and complex institutional structures were all missing for the children of the CTs in schools. In effect, they continuously failed at every level. The virtual absence of education, either formal or technical kept the children out of the gear of development. However, it is important to note that the communities and their children possessed in-depth knowledge about the geographical terrains, flora and fauna. Their knowledge to adjust to the new environment was unmatched. The colonial state could not explore their in-depth knowledge in various fields. These communities trained their children in the traditional knowledge of medicinal plants, herbs, roots, petty trade, acrobatics, etc. Colonial education did not empower these communities rather it virtually hampered their development.

Beginning of Reformatory Schools

The colonial government established reformatory schools for the children of CTs in India during the year 1880. The colonial government justified the existence of the reformatory schools for the CTs due to the increased rate of crime. The reformatory schools were intended for the benefit of CTs in order to improve the mental and physical conditions of their children. The children had received special treatment in these schools. The government intended the welfare of the children of the CTs and, therefore, entrusted the educational activities to the reformatory schools.[1] The reformatory schools were first started in North India for the education of Dom children. At the same time, the government also started reformatory schools in Chingleput (now Chengalpattu) district in Tamil Nadu, in South India for the children of various 'criminal gangs'.[2] The reformatory school in Chingleput functioned as an auxiliary institution of North Indian Reformatory schools. The school was started as a model school. The colonial government affiliated reformatory schools to the jails. These reformatory schools were established very near to the premises of the prisons.[3] Thus, the reformatory schools worked as sub-jails in India. H.B. Grigg, the then jail department superintendent, advised the government to establish reformatory schools for the 'criminal' classes in order to reduce the number of convicts in jails. The government gained experience with regard to the supervision of the reformatory schools under the supervision of the jail department superintendents. The CTs were treated badly by the superintendents of the jail department.[4]

Reformatory schools grew up as open jails as a result of the supervision of the police and jail department officials. They supervised the reformatory schools mechanically and indiscriminately.[5] Therefore, the Madras Government handed over the reformatory schools under the supervision of education department. The government expected better results from these schools under the guidance of education department authorities.[6] The Madras Government wanted to make the reformatory schools as exemplary institutions of reform and rehabilitate the CTs in Madras province. The government doubted the credibility of the jail department in running these institutions. The reformation work carried out by the education department was better than the jail department. The main task, aims and objectives of the reformatory schools were to bring a change in the attitude, behaviour, and mindset of the CTs children who were in the prison whose mind was totally occupied with the idea of the jail.[7] Thus, the Madras Government started schools for the children of CTs in South India.[8]

The reformatory schools in Madras presidency were opened exclusively for the children of CTs who were going to be released from the jails very shortly. The reformatory schools were simple in nature and character.[9] There were many advantages for the colonial government in establishing the reformatory schools under the supervision of the education department. The advantages were: (1) The government did not want to waste a lot of time and money on the reformation of CTs. (2) It was easy for the government to find suitable educational officers to train the minds of CTs. (3) Well educated and trained people were very useful in the reformation activities of CTs (4) The government can easily change the behaviour of the children in the reformatory schools (5) To encourage orderly behaviour of the children through physical training, etc.[10] Mr Cardew, the then Inspector General of Police, once remarked: 'when I drew a comparison between the Chingleput reformatory school and the reformatory school at Ailapore which were under the control of the jail department the orderly appearance of the children struck me forcibly at the first visit. Another pleasing result is that the old boys visited the school to recall their old memories, and gave expression to feelings of pleasure. It was a great sight to find the ex-pupil in the full uniform of a bandsman of a native regiment, spend the day in the reformatory, join in the boys sports and before leaving, taken the photograph to the amusement and delight of the whole school'.[11]

The superintendents of the medical department also assisted the government to administer the reformatory schools. The medical superintendent was a commissioned medical officer. He was the chief superintendent and executive officer of the reformatory school. A deputy medical officer used to assist him. He was responsible for all the matters affecting the health conditions of the children in the school. They administered the reformatory schools effectively.[12]

Aims and Objectives of Reformatory Schools

The main purposes of the reformatory schools were: (1) providing industrial training and imparting basic skills for the children of CTs, (2) providing general elementary education, (3) development of physical and moral training, (4) equip children with life skills, (5) orient the children to earn their livelihood by providing physical and moral training, etc.[13] The reformatory schools were also intended to develop good physique among the children. They were trained to cope with any amount of physical exertion. Physical training formed an important part of the reformatory schools. As soon as the child was admitted in the school, the government asked the school authorities to train them in garden classes for the first six months. Gardening is considered as an open-air course and training for the young children. They were taught elementary agriculture, use of agricultural tools such as spade, shovel and basket. Children were taught how to draw water for irrigation with the help of a rope and leather water bag. The schools provided an opportunity for the development of physique of the elderly children. The schools developed keen aptitude towards their life. Children were provided with staple food. Thus, children very soon got accustomed to the new food habits. Further, children were trained in gymnastics, physical drill, football and other local games and sport. Physical training was also imparted in the reformatory schools for the children.[14]

Moral Training in Reformatory Schools

Moral training was based on the broad principles of morality of all religions. These schools were infused with moral values and ideas. The children in the schools were expected to obtain a good name and opinion from the higher sections of the society about them. Religious instruction was given to children based on religion. Muhammadan children were allowed to go to the mosque on every Friday.[15] Children were encouraged to recite their prayers in the evening. The Hindu priests were asked to instruct various duties to be performed by the children. Children from Christian families were encouraged to go to the Church. School reading textbooks were provided to the children with frequent references of rich moral values.[16] The school textbooks impressed children very much. During Sundays, teachers used to instruct children with selected moral stories and moral principles. The students were questioned on the following day to see how much of the subject they had learnt or carried away every day. The lessons provided on Sundays to the children had a powerful impact on the character of the children. The boys were asked to sing the lyrics, high-toned songs in order to relieve them from the pains of monotonous work habits. They were asked to narrate interesting tales to train them. Thus, children showed additional interest to learn the lessons in the school.[17]

Development of Sense of Loyalty to the British Raj

The main objective of the reformatory schools was to provide a sense of loyalty to the British Raj. The sense of loyalty to the colonial government had to be maintained with the aid of the Union Jack. The government asked the school authorities to hoist the flags on the anniversary days of the Royal Families of the British Empire and on the occasion of the visits of higher officials to the schools. The school authorities explained to the children about the importance of the British Flag. The colonial administrators emphasised that the British Flag stands for the symbols of justice, good government and liberty.[18] The boys were asked to wear 'Miniature Union Jacks' on the day of British Empire. At the conclusion of the party, children were asked to sing the British National Anthem with utmost devotion.[19]

Supervising Officers

The personal influences of the chief supervising officers were enormous on the children in the reformatory schools. The children came into contact with them every day with their instruction in the school. The supervisors imposed heavy rules and restrictions on children. The deputy superintendent was a permanent chief executive officer for the reformatory schools. Children looked upon him as a guide, philosopher and friend. The deputy superintendent was treated as the head of the institution.[20] Domestic relationship was encouraged among other superintending officers, training staff and children. One deputy superintending officer remarked: 'the reformatory schools worked on the simple principle of reformation. Too much was exercised in the selection of the superintendents, their character and personality. Advice and warning both were laid upon the students. Even in the selection of the lower subordinate staff, necessary care and caution was exercised. They possessed plenty of human sympathy, happy temperament, tact, firmness and patience. They were provided training on life work and a life study. The government provided them with free quarters. They were never allowed to lead an isolated life'.[21]

Character Building

Another important objective of the reformatory schools was to develop character among the children of CTs. They were encouraged to play on the ground. Physical instructors were appointed. The European Sergeant judiciously handled the boys and controlled their habits during their stay in the school. Boys were encouraged to develop healthy competition in the day-to-day activities in the school. They were encouraged to develop healthy temperament. Good qualities of human nature formed an important part of moral instruction. Children were carefully supervised by the teachers. The use of obscene words or language by the native children was strictly condemned. The teachers summarily checked this behaviour among the children and those habituated were trained to speak moral proverbs.[22]

Development of Habits of Obedience

The reformatory schools developed habits of obedience, speaking truth, regularity in work habits, industrious nature, orderly behaviour, cleanliness, judicious system of rewards and punishment. Children with good conduct were awarded with a good conduct badge. The good conduct badge had a monetary value attached to it. Sometimes, children were given cash prizes. They were endowed with a good character badge.[23]

Physical Development of Children

Physical drill was another effective tool for the school instructors to mould the character of children. The reformatory school moulded the character of children, inculcated the mechanical habits of smartness, orderly behaviour, physical development and orderly obedience through physical education. Children after attaining 18 years were placed in the reformatory, voluntary, penal and agricultural settlements. The reformatories looked after them until they were grown up and were able to depend upon their hard work. They were hedged by rules and regulations for several years in the reformatory schools. However, soon after attaining 18–19 years of age all of a sudden, they were thrown into the world of settlements with no guiding hand or discipline of any kind. Thus, it became difficult for CT children with good habits. They suddenly developed certain negative values. Thus, they were placed under the supervision of Missionary organisations like the Salvation Army, the American Baptist Telugu Mission, Lutheran Mission and Canadian Mission.[24] These Missionary societies started exercising their missionary approach over them for many years after they were placed into the settlements. The Missionaries started boarding schools, night schools for the children of CTs. The Missionaries started imparting knowledge according to their methods and belief.

Development of Skills in Theatre Arts

Reformatory schools were also intended to develop theatrical performances among children. Magic lanterns were used to illustrate and impress moral truths among children. Concerts, gramophone recitals were used. The dangers of the stains of criminality in their blood were intended to be removed through value and aesthetic education. Children were able to stage dramas with credibility. Children were trained with coloured papers and stencils. Elderly children were trained to prepare costumes. The ultimate aim of the reformatory school was to make the children happy and contended. These schools intended to develop the discipline of British Empire. Games were introduced with a view to improve the physical fitness and moral intellect of the children. Football was very much favoured in the reformatory schools. Children evinced great enthusiasm on the final match and keen interest in their play. Children were provided with a match dress. They possessed great feelings and charm for their match dress. On Sunday evenings, childron were taken for a walk into the town along the side of the fields. They were allowed to swim in the ponds. They were taken to see the circus. Picnics were also arranged by the teachers on experimental lines.[25]

Treatment of Children in the Reformatory Schools

Children were admitted in the reformatory schools by obtaining the details of residence, caste, parentage, previous occupations of the parents, offences committed by their parents, sentences given by the courts, and the period of detention of the parents in the jails, etc. All the particulars of the parents of the CTs were recorded on the note sheets. Parents were not allowed to correspond with their children. Often the children were separated from the parents with a view to bring them up in a wholesome atmosphere. However, children were allowed to correspond with their parents for a brief period when their parents visited the schools. The occupation of the children's parents, their interest was taken into consideration. Children were taught according to their interests and avocations of life. Initially, the children were admitted for four years. On satisfactory behaviour and progress of the children, their stay in the school was extended until they attained 18 years of age. They were made to earn their living during the course of the training.[26]

Penalties and Rewards in the Reformatory Schools

The rewards and punishments in the schools were explained to the children along with their parents at the time of admission. If the children do not commit any offence for the whole year they were rewarded with a good conduct badge. The badge was made out of copper. These badges possessed money value. Money was sanctioned to the children as an incentive for their good conduct. Children whose conduct was found bad were strictly punished even for their smallest mistakes. Punishment was fixed for misconduct. The fear of punishment and expulsion remained permanently fixed in the minds of children. No offence was excused without a punishment. In exceptional cases, warnings were given. The discipline maintained in the reformatory schools was of military nature. The government felt that such a discipline was very much needed to deal with children of CTs. The government followed the principle of one offence, one punishment on these children. Punishment was administered immediately on the children. Children were made to feel for their mistakes.[27]

Treatment of Children by the Supervising Officers

The chief supervising officers used to act like local parents to children in the reformatory schools. They used to have private talks and conversation with the children. They tried to mould the character of children. They used to give occasional treats. They showed their specific acts of kindness. They were sympathetic towards the miserable conditions of their parents. The personal talks of the supervisors were emotional. These talks used to bring tears of contrition from the eyes of children and parents. The parents and the children were softened by and would give in to such talks and advices of the experienced supervisors. Friendly supervision was exercised over them. Every day, individual attention was paid on children. Proper treatment of the children was meted out to suit their temperament and character. Sometimes, personal interviews were conducted with their parents by personally visiting them at their homes. Their visits helped the supervisors to inform the parents about the conduct of their children. Teachers encouraged parents to counsel their children.[28]

Meetings with Parents

The meetings of the poor parents with their children were often heart rendering scenes. Parents frequently used to tell about their miseries and hardships. They used to leave their children with a good advice and take a promise to behave properly in the school. The visits of the parents used to ignite in the hearts of their children the will to work hard. Regular correspondence was encouraged between parents and children. Children who misbehaved were punished in various ways for their offences. Some supervising officers never allowed their parents to see their children also. There was a friction between parents, children and the supervising officers. Many children used to leave the school and commit petty offences. Children used to abscond from the reformatory schools. The government asked the supervisors to prevent such escapes by maintaining strict supervision and control on the children in the reformatory schools.[29]

Children's Stay in the Reformatories

The stay of children in the reformatory schools was made happy and comfortable as far as possible. Their discipline was strictly supervised. They were not allowed to do anything that degraded their position. Detentions from the schools were made even for small mistakes. They were made to remember their stay in the schools. Children were called by their names rather than attaching a number. Children generally were treated as good human beings. Children were encouraged to work with the elders and supervisors. They were made to correct their mistakes while doing their work. During recreation hours no supervision was allowed on any child. The newcomers were under the influence of their seniors.[30]

General Education

The general education imparted to the children in the reformatory schools was elementary in its nature. They were taught to do sums, accounts, reading, writing in vernacular language, etc. Some children were taught colloquial English also.[31]

Industrial Training

Industrial training was intended to train children to develop physical abilities, use of tools and techniques in order to earn a livelihood. Best abilities of the children were encouraged. They were trained how to use their abilities by making good efforts. Due to India's poor economic conditions they were oriented towards basic education. There was no proper technical education in the reformatory schools. Factory system was not developed in the rural side.[32] The demand for the skilled artisans in the rural areas was very less. Some children of reformed families of CTs were living in towns. They were working in railway workshops.

Majority of them left the settlements due to their occupations and avocations. However, majority of the new tribal communities were turned into the settlements. They were attracted towards labour work. It had formed an excellent preparatory training for them to handle the machines. The youth were able to make things on their own. They were trained to run the machinery. Children were trained to prepare finished goods and articles for sale. Carpentry work was encouraged among children. These children were kept under the strict supervision during the training period. They used to get into hard work very easily. They used to compete with others and worked hard to complete the assigned portion of the work allotted to them.[33] In reformatory schools, children were made to work under three conditions: (1) scope to succeed in life, (2) always children were under the control of a *maistry* (instructor), (3) to become a free agent of his/her own work. The government proposed more hours of work in the industrial and reformatory schools and few hours of general education to children.[34] Children with less age were given more general education and children who were elderly were provided with more industrial training. Every child was given four hours of industrial training and three hours of general education. Majority of the children were provided industrial work rather than literary work. In reading, writing, and arithmetic, children showed better skills rather than the children of ordinary primary schools. Children were regular in their attendance and showed good discipline. The visitors of the reformatory schools admired the brightness of school children. The children were more interested in their routine work. Nobody believed that the schools were meant for the children of the 'criminal' classes as the appearance and the discipline of the children showed in the schools was of high order. Children showed keen interest in gymnastics, intricate movements in drill, drawing and handwriting.[35] Reformatory schools in the Madras province had good reputation with a high position and tried to shape children as honest citizens. It is worthy to note that an inspector of schools commented once: 'With little stumps between their fingers, they held the pencils at anything but the proper angle made them write good letters. The children possessed vanity to show their skills at the best of their abilities'.[36]

Library and Museum in Reformatory Schools

Reformatory schools were also equipped with a library. The library had a good collection of vernacular books. The schools were attached with laboratory. The schools were equipped with a museum. The children used to have access to all of them. Most of the children were encouraged to read during their holidays. The curriculum was elastic and flexible. Reformatory schools provided a series of object lessons. The reformatory schools were considered as special type of institutions in their intent and objective. Practical training was very much insisted upon. In general education, the courses were made to assist the practical work done in the fields attached to the school.[37]

Vocational Education: Training in Weaving

Of all the vocational training imparted to the children, weaving occupied an important position. The government equipped weaving sheds with all facilities in the industrial schools. The turnout of the children was very good. The government asked the education department to train the school children in weaving industry on modern lines in order to develop the economic conditions of the country. The education department asked the teachers of reformatory schools to give first preference to the boys in the schools. It was hoped that technical and industrial schools protect the handloom industry. The reformatory schools helped the government by providing well-trained employees. Soon after completing their training in reformatory schools, children were recruited as weaving industry *maistries* in the state weaving schools and handloom factories in Madras Presidency.[38] The instructors trained the children in the technique of plain-weaving. The weaving skill of the children was much appreciated. They were paid good amount of money for the better turnout of the work in the schools. Reformatory schools tried to improve the skills of children in weaving. The aim of introducing weaving in the reformatory schools was to provide children certain amount of dexterity or expertise in weaving and to produce better cloth by the industrial and reformatory schools. The government very much appreciated the efforts of the reformatory school authorities in producing a good amount of towels and gauze-cloth. Children were trained to print good designs on the cloth. They were trained to bring certain changes necessary in the tuning and treading motion. Children were well aware of the different patterns of weaving or honeycomb weaving. They knew the defects in the manufacturing of cloth. They were able to provide suitable suggestions to the weaving industrial supervisors. In short, the children were fully trained to control the overall management of a small weaving shed in the Reformatory settlements. Children were provided simple cloth. In turn they were able to produce the cloth on the looms. Thus, the reformatory schools in the Madras province provided training to the children of CTs.[39] The handlooms provided to the children in the reformatory schools required further improvement. There was a great demand for the power looms in the urban centres. Children showed keen interest to develop their skills for producing cloth from the power looms. The schools showed keen interest to train the children in warping and sizing the cloth. These schools intended to train children not for commercial purpose or for business activity. The schools spread the idea among the children that if the size of the cloth was better, automatically the quality of the cloth will be better. The school authorities intended that better weaving techniques should be learnt by children. The reformatory schools did not show keen interest to extract more work and manufacturing of clothes by the machines. The reformatory schools asked the government to handover the making clothes on the machines to well established private agencies in Madras Province to meet the demands of the government from time to time.[40]

Training in Carpentry Work

The other type of vocational education imparted by the government in the reformatory schools was training in the carpentry work for the children of CTs. Children showed keen interest in this work. Their annual turnout of the carpentry work was satisfactory. In the carpentry training, there was no manual instruction, syllabus or guidelines. These children were placed under some instructor. The instructors provided some broad principles. Children used to keenly observe the work of the instructors and follow their oral instructions. Gradually, the children developed the required techniques in chiselling, planing and sawing the wooden materials. After some weeks, under guidance of the *maistries*, children were provided with tools to do the assigned work. They were also provided training in sharpening the tools. They were trained to join the wooden materials. Very soon the children were able to make small items like cabinets. Senor children were taught in drawing and scaling the wooden materials. The materials prepared by the children were auctioned for sale. Children were very much appreciated for their skill and talent. Strict supervision and discipline was exercised by the instructors. Children were trained under the supervision of the guidance of drawing teachers and carpentry supervisors. Fine arts exhibitions organised annually in the schools. Children got medals for their skillful work.[41]

Training in Reformatory Bands

One of the special features of the reformatory schools was the introduction of brass band music. Children were trained in physical drill and marching. The reformatory bands played a refined taste of music. Bandmasters were recruited to instruct music to the children. The children showed keen interest in Indian music. They did not understand the importance of European music. The instructors explained to the children the principles of European and Indian music. European music has an elevating art. Each piece of the European music depicts a story. The stories of the great English people were conveyed in the form of melody. The songs were filled with joy and sorrow of the English masters. Children were instructed that the music should be associated with a prayer to god to protect them from evil doings. Parents of children showed their keen interest to sing and dance with the children. It was felt that teaching European music to the children of CTs was a difficult task. They were Hindus. They were familiar with the music and performance of their predecessors only. They were never habituated or had heard about English music. The high caste Hindus protested against teaching of English music in the schools. They criticised English music as intruding the Hindu values and morals. Therefore, the Europeans preferred low caste panchamas, low caste Hindus, Pariahs, native Christians, Muhammadans and CTs in the Madras province. However, some reformed high caste Hindus used to volunteer to offer their services to the bands in the reformatory schools. They soon developed some taste in the European music. It was stated: "the Muhammadans were musically inclined. They are not as intelligent as the Hindus. The panchamas were very slow. The native Christians learn quickly and make first rate musicians, but they are as a rule lazy".[42] Children who were able to sing well in Telugu, Tamil or Hindustani languages only were selected. Thus, the children showed keen interest and exhibited their talents.

Monitoring of Reformatory Schools

The success of the reformatory schools was partly due to the effective monitoring system in Madras province. The education department appointed a full time and one part-time assistant monitoring officers. The best behaved children were appointed as monitors. Separate uniform code was assigned to them by the education department. The monitors used to wear a blue cap with a red band. The assistant monitors used to wear a white cap with red band and a star. The monitors and assistant monitors were very much appreciated for their work. There was a great competition among children for these positions. The monitors hold immense power. They have to maintain proper discipline in the school. They should take part in the teacher-student activities, school parade, etc.[43]

Licence System

The Madras Government had introduced licence system in order to control the CTs during the year 1910. According to the licence system, children in the reformatory schools soon after completing their training were provided with a certificate. With the certificate those children could enter into the social environment they liked. With their full experience in the reformatory schools they could find a job on their own and start a new life. However, in certain cases, some of the children who were released from the reformatory schools reverted to their old habits such as pocket picking and snatching materials from shops. The conduct of the children while in the reformatory schools proved to be good. Soon after they left the reformatories, they again started their old profession. Many complaints from the public were lodged about the children who were released from the reformatory schools with licences. Therefore, the employment opportunities of such children were entrusted to the philanthropic bodies like the Salvation Army and the American Baptist Telugu Mission. The licensing system to the children of CTs was borrowed from Bursham Reformatory system in New Zealand. For the government, the licensing system worked very well. But, the licence system developed the cheap labour colonies in India. Often, healthy children were taken from the settlements and employed in the industrial establishments. The children were escorted by the police with a pass to properly guard them and prevent them from running away from their work. The police used to take the children early in the morning and bring them back in the evening from the work place. They had to produce the licences in order to get employment outside. They had to show proper respect and discipline in their work places.[44]

Provisions for Children in the Reformatory Schools: Food, Clothing and Bedding

Children were provided food, clothes and accommodation in the reformatory schools. Provision for teacher's stay was also provided. Children were provided with vegetarian and non-vegetarian food. Children were also provided two types of dresses, one type of suit for working in the fields, and another dress for Sunday prayers and excursion trips. Children were asked to look smart and clean. Children used to wear caps on their heads. In the beginning, sleeping accommodation was provided in the form of cubical system. Due to their escaping nature some children were locked in separate rooms. However, the system gave birth to prudent ideas. Children used to complain to the higher-ups about their miserable conditions in the lock-ups. Hence, the system was condemned by the higher authorities on moral and humane grounds. In lieu of it, the government had introduced hammock system. This system failed due to the elderly boys who used to change the minds of younger children. Later, the pial (boarding hostel) system was introduced. The government considered the system better due to less expense and more comfort for the children. Majority of the children were Hindus. Therefore, they were accustomed to sleeping on the floor on a mattress. The government had spent lot of money for the running and maintenance of reformatory schools. Best teachers were paid better salaries. The maintenance cost of the tools, bugle troops, weaving maistries, were unremunerative. The cost of the maintenance of the materials, equivalent in the reformatory schools were very high. The workshop materials and tools were purchased from European countries. The cost of the industrial training was very expensive. On an average, the cost of the industrial training during the year 1930 was ₹ 10. The cost of general education was ₹ 6 and the cost of diet was ₹ 5 in the reformatory schools. The cost of bedding, suits and clothing were extra expenditure for the government.[45]

Atmosphere in Reformatory Schools

Generally, the atmosphere in the reformatory schools was very quiet. Strict discipline was imposed on children.

They used to wake up at 5 am in the morning. Elderly children were asked to keep their surroundings clean and tidy. Children were given a small breakfast. They would march to their respective industrial workshop at 6 am and continue with their work till 1.30 pm. Children were provided with two bowls of ragi pudding with vegetable and dal curry in the afternoon. Children were asked to attend the general education classes at around 10.30 am. One hour was allotted for the residential activities after the completion of general classes. Children were taken to industrial training from 2.30 pm to 4.30 pm. Physical drill and gymnastics were conducted from 4.30 pm onwards. Children were strictly ordered to complete their dinner at 6 pm. Children were locked in the hostel rooms at 7 pm. Night schools and classes were conducted from 7 pm to 8 pm.

They were not allowed to talk with one another during the night school hours. During Sundays, moral lessons were given to children in English. English lessons were translated to Telugu and Tamil students. Children were trained in dusting, washing and cleaning their dormitories. The whole school appeared clean and neat. March-Past was organised every day for three times with sound drums and bugle bands. Children were instructed to pay attention to their physical appearance. Children were to apply oil and comb their hair neatly. The children were given a long vacation during Christmas. They were not allowed to go out of their hostels. Cleaning and gardening work was actively conducted during this period. Football matches were organised. Shields, trophies were awarded. Children were encouraged to write letters to their parents and friends. They were also encouraged to read books borrowed from the library. Children were encouraged to stage dramas, draw sketches from nature, play culture-specific games such as marbles, tops, kites, tip cat, *gusti, pallangudi* and *gudgud-chaplam*.[46]

Children of CTs and other Castes in the Schools

Children with criminal background were admitted in the reformatory schools. Along with these children, other caste group children were also admitted. Various communities like Hindu, Christian and Muhammadan were represented in the reformatory schools. These children were from the Telugu, Tamil and Kanarese regions. Children from Korava, Dasari, Wodar communities, children of native Christians, children of Chapparbands from Bijapur district, Muhammadan children who escaped from the Nizam dominions, children of Kapu community, children from Balija community, Jogis, and Dommaras community children were also there. Children of Tamil 'Criminal Tribes and Castes' such as Pariyan, Panisavan, Shanars, Kaikolans, Vaniyans or Pallis, Padayachi Goundans, Kandar, Idians, Vellalas enrolled in the reformatory schools. There were also some tribal children of the Telugu 'Criminal Tribes and Castes' such as: Madigas, Malas, Odderas, Gollas or Kapus, Yanadis, Yerukulas, Sale, Gamandalas, Idigas, Kamsalis, Ganigas, Kapus or Reddies, Kammas, Velamas and Balijas who were also admitted in the reformatory schools due to their poor social status.[47] It was noted that 'the Criminal Tribes of South India were not of Jackal Sheppard type. They were wandering groups of people. They carried their trade with their bullocks to the interior places. With the advent of the railways, they lost their trade and took to stealing. In order to support their livelihood they used to commit petty offences. In order to provide education to their children the government opened reformatory schools in the Madras Presidency'.[48]

The chief occupation of the Koravas was basket-making and selling curry leaves. They were of Tamil origin. They were found in the North Arcot and Kurnool districts. They spoke their own language without a dialect. They used to go from one place to another in order to sell their articles such as beads and combs. Their children used to accompany their parents. Therefore, the government admitted the Korava children in the reformatory schools.[49] The Woddars are Telugu-speaking people. Woddars were known as Pachipas in some places of Tamil Nadu. Some Woddars were living in Gollapalem, Tirutani, in North Arcot district. Some other Woddars were living in Guntur district, in the Telugu-speaking regions of Madras province. Their original occupation was earth-digging and cattle-grazing. Their children were admitted in the reformatory schools.[50] The Dasaris were called as Kattera Dasaris and Golla Dasaris. Some of them were found in Nellore district. Some Dasaris lived in Muttapalli village in Kurnool district. They were employed as labourers. Their children were placed in reformatory schools.[51] Batturajus were a Telugu-speaking race. They used to earn their livelihood by selling articles in the busy centres, markets and towns. Their children were admitted in reformatory schools.[52] Jogis were called as Tottiyans. Most of them were snake charmers. In South Arcot and Tanjore districts, they were called as Koravas. Their children were admitted in the reformatory schools.[53] The Yanadis were primitive sort of people. Their number was more in Nellore district. They were engaged in all kinds of work. The government recommended to admit their children in the reformatory schools.[54] The Yerukulas were widespread community. They possessed different names in different localities. In the Telugu districts, they were called as 'Yerukulavandlu'. In Tamil districts they were called as Koravas or Korwas. They used a peculiar dialect of their own with an admixture of Tamil and Telugu as their mother tongue. They called their language as Kurru Basha or Kurru Vata. Their women go about for fortune telling. The government recommended to keep their children in reformatory schools.[55] Dommaras were found in different places in Madras province. There were two sections of the Dommaras: Telugu Dommaras, who speak Telugu language and Are Dommaras who were well versed in Marathi. Their traditional occupation was performing acrobatic feats, rope dancing and gymnastics. The government recommended that their children should be admitted in the reformatory schools.[56] The children of the Roman Catholic Native Christians were very much deprived. Therefore, their children were also admitted into the reformatory schools.[57] Chappar Bands originated from Bijapur district. They left their homes in the Bombay province due to heavy rains. Their children were sent to reformatory schools.[58] Some Muhammadans lived on the border lands of Nizam dominion and Bombay province. They were familiar with Canaries language. Children used to take part in all dramatic performances. They were also admitted in the reformatory schools.[59]

The colonial administrators showed keen interest in the field of criminocurology, criminal anthropology and anthropometry. They considered this as great field of research. They studied in greater detail about the formation of the cranium and the shapes of ears and heads of Indian population. The study of human parts to consider their character was an essential feature of their interest in their studies. They pointed out that the heads, flat-roofed skulls, and receding foreheads of Indian aboriginal people was abnormal. They noted that the ears of Indian children were very sensitive to nervous disturbances and malformations. Their studies confirmed that the features of the CTs and their children was very abnormal. Their children looked very different from the ordinary settled people in the country. In short, the colonisers strongly believed that the CTs possessed different features and trained their children differently. They were compared and closely related to the savage races. They possessed corresponding traces of character and appearance of the savages in the world. From the close examination of several subjects, they came to the final conclusion that the children of the CTs were offenders by birth and possessed the same physical features, and obtained the behaviour of their parents very quickly. It was, therefore, suggested by the British that the children of the CTs in general required a more regimented and controlled education provided in the reformatory schools.

Notes

1. Coombers, J.W., The Juvenile Criminal in Southern India, Higginbotham, Lawrence Asylum Press, Mount Road, Madras, 1908.

2. Government of Madras, Home Department, Government Order No. 48, dated 7 January 1920.
3. Government of Madras, Home Department, Government Order No. 22, dated 26 January 1920.
4. Government of Madras, Home Department, Government Order No. 451, dated 17 February 1920.
5. Government of Madras, Home Department, Government Order No. 475, dated 19 February 1920.
6. Government of Madras, Home Department, Government Order No. 503, dated 23 February 1920.
7. Government of Madras, Home Department, Government Order No. 596, dated 3 March 1920.
8. Government of Madras, Home Department, Government Order No. 1855, dated 4 October 1921.
9. Government of Madras, Home Department, Government Order No. 1912, dated 12 October 1921.
10. Government of Madras, Home Department, Government Order No. 2332, dated 20 December 1921.
11. Government of Madras, Home Department, Government Order No. 277, dated 2 February 1925.
12. Government of Madras, Home Department, Government Order No. 227, dated 12 February 1925.
13. Government of Madras, Home Department, Government Order No. 243, dated 13 February 1925.
14. Government of Madras, Home Department, Government Order No. 244, dated 13 February 1925.
15. Government of Madras, Home Department, Government Order No. 292, dated 25 February 1925.
16. Government of Madras, Home Department, Government Order No. 267, dated 25 March 1925.
17. Government of Madras, Home Department, Government Order No. 497, dated 2 April 1925.
18. Government of Madras, Home Department, Government Order No. 716, dated 14 May 1925.
19. Government of Madras, Home Department, Government Order No. 71, dated 18 January 1927.
20. Government of Madras, Home Department, Government Order No.12, dated 4 January 1927.
21. Government of Madras, Home Department, Government Order No. 194, dated 10 February 1927.
22. Government of Madras, Home Department, Government Order No. 314, dated 4 March 1927.

23. Government of Madras, Home Department, Government Order No. 852, dated 12 March 1927.
24. Government of Madras, Home Department, Government Order No. 587, dated 26 April 1927.
25. Government of Madras, Home Department, Government Order No. 1790, dated 2 June 1927.
26. Government of Madras, Home Department, Government Order No. 423, dated 8 March 1928.
27. Government of Madras, Home Department, Government Order No. 821, dated 4 May 1928.
28. Government of Madras, Home Department, Government Order No. 1813, dated 25 October 1928.
29. Government of Madras, Home Department, Government Order No. 1816, dated 25 October 1928.
30. Government of Madras, Home Department, Government Order No. 1820, dated 25 October 1928.
31. Government of Madras, Home Department, Government Order No. 1828, dated 27 October 1928.
32. Government of Madras, Home Department, Government Order No. 1704, dated 8 October 1928.
33. Government of Madras, Home Department, Government Order No. 27, dated 5 January 1929.
34. Government of Madras, Home Department, Government Order No. 172, dated 28 January 1929.
35. Government of Madras, Home Department, Government Order No. 231, dated 6 February 1929.
36. Government of Madras, Home Department, Government Order No. 234, dated 7 February 1929.
37. Government of Madras, Home Department, Government Order No. 268, dated 13 February 1929.
38. Government of Madras, Home Department, Government Order No. 385, dated 5 March 1929.
39. Government of Madras, Home Department, Government Order No. 525, dated 8 April 1931.
40. Government of Madras, Home Department, Government Order No. 560, dated 15 April 1931.
41. Government of Madras, Home Department, Government Order No. 905, dated 17 June 1931.
42. Government of Madras, Home Department, Government Order No. 984, dated 4 July 1931.
43. Government of Madras, Home Department, Government Order No. 1283, dated 28 August 1931.

44. Government of Madras, Home Department, Government Order No. 1426, dated 29 September 1931.
45. Government of Madras, Home Department, Government Order No. 1614, dated 7 November 1931.
46. Government of Madras, Home Department, Government Order No. 505, dated 12 April 1932.
47. Government of Madras, Home Department, Government Order No. 1849, dated 15 October 1932.
48. Government of Madras, Home Department, Government Order No. 892, dated 19 May 1933.
49. Government of Madras, Home Department, Government Order No. 154, dated 24 November 1933.
50. Government of Madras, Home Department, Government Order No. 195–196, dated, December 1933.
51. Government of Madras, Home Department, Government Order No. 291, dated 28 February 1934.
52. Government of Madras, Home Department, Government Order No. 472, dated 9 April 1934.
53. Government of Madras, Home Department, Government Order No. 622, dated 8 May 1934.
54. Government of Madras, Home Department, Government Order No. 713, dated 31 May 1934.
55. Government of Madras, Home Department, Government Order No. 855, dated 28 June 1934.
56. Government of Madras, Home Department, Government Order No. 1358, dated 25 September 1934.
57. Government of Madras, Home Department, Government Order No. 1472, dated 11 October 1934.
58. Government of Madras, Home Department, Government Order No. 1652, dated 5 December 1934.
59. Government of Madras, Home Department, Government Order No. 1652, dated 5 December 1934.

3

Vocational Education for the Children of 'Criminal' Tribes

The aims and objectives of the chapter are to gather information and to examine to what extent the vocational education provided to the children of the CTs was helpful in the settlements, and to study the education dimension of the CTs in the Madras province during the colonial period.

The Salvation Army's work in the former settlements of the Denotified Tribes with regard to the education of the depressed classes and former Criminal Tribes began during the year 1910. The Salvation Army had opened several Industrial, Agricultural and Reformatory settlements and schools in the Madras province for the education of the children of the former Criminal Tribes in Madras Presidency under the provisions of CTA 1911. The Salvation Army started an industrial settlement at Madras. The industrial school at Madras was the biggest school in India. G. Watkins, the then Salvation Army officer in Madras Telugu province opened several such industrial settlements in 1914. Many CT members were sent to the industrial settlements from different parts of the country. All these people were richly benefited in every way in the industrial settlements. They were successful in their life. The staff in the industrial settlements was quite capable in handling three or four industries at a time in these centres. The number of children and industrial schools in the Madras province had gradually increased with the efforts of the Salvation Army. The schools in the settlements were developed on industrial lines because training of the children of the CTs was imparted. The training imparted to the children included industrial skills. The Salvation Army used to admit the children of native-speaking vernacular languages with Tamil, Telugu and Canaries languages. Additional teachers were also appointed by the Salvation Army to instruct the children in these schools. The Salvation Army officials requested the settlement managers to send the children of 8 to 18 years to admit in the industrial schools in the Madras province.[1]

The Inspector General of Police, Madras, was in favour of such education for the children. Therefore, the Inspector General of Police, Madras, recommended the government to open more industrial schools in the Madras Presidency. The government asked the Managers to admit more number of children from the settlements. Sometimes, there were very few children in some of the industrial schools. Under these circumstances, the government asked the managers whether there were any children that could be sent to the Madras industrial schools from other settlements. The government used to issue special orders to the managers to transfer the children of the settlements into the industrial training as a special case.[2]

For the wandering communities in India, the colonial administrators organised industrial schools. The Government of Madras had converted the regular schools into training centres for these children. The government had opined that the reformation of the children of the CTs was mainly directed towards the proper upbringing of their children. In each of the CT settlements the government had established a local school for their education. The children used to receive education up to the age of 14 years in the industrial schools. After that age, the children were allowed to associate with their elders. The government felt that it was desirable to take them away from the settlements and place them into boarding schools. The boarding schools were established at a distance from the settlements. Moreover, the land assigned for the settlements was not sufficient to maintain due to growing population. Therefore, the government felt that it was necessary and important to open the industrial schools. The government was able to get many industrial workers from the settlements. It was also important for the government to train the boys and girls on certain occupations other than agriculture with a view to enabling them to earn a good living. Thus, some of the settlers were sent to distant places. They were away from the original settlements. The government also wanted to attract the tribes living outside due to the fact that there was a lot of demand for the settlements and industrial education in the country. Industrial education was considered very popular among the settlers of the CTs in the Madras province.[3]

The Madras Government completely favoured the industrial training for the wandering, nomadic tribal children. Some of the schools were converted as industrial boarding schools for boys and girls belonging to the CTs. They were debarred from the technical, scientific and other general courses of education. The government also opined that the school could not provide accommodation to more than 100 boys and 100 girls at a time. The personal influence of the superintendent was the most important factor for the success of the schools. The schools were fully equipped and up-to-date. The schools acted as models for industrial education. The industrial educational institutions were also filled with strong and committed staff. There was a lot of expenditure involved in running of these schools. The government sanctioned the non-recurring grants in addition to the recurring grants towards the cost of the training of the staff and boarding charges for the boys and girls.[4]

The government proposed separate schools for grown-up girls. The Salvation Army opened an industrial school at St. Thomas Mount, Madras, separately for the girls of the CTs. The institution for the girls was furnished fully. The district magistrates used to ask the government to provide yearly statements showing the number of boys and girls having been admitted separately between the ages of 6 to 16 years from the settlements of the CTs managed by the Salvation Army in the Madras Presidency. The government also decided to open separate schools for boys and girls with the help of the Missionaries. The government considered the idea of establishing separate schools as a wise decision so as to get the immediate cooperation and arrangements to get skillful workers from the settlement boys and girls. The Salvation Army gave some of its buildings for the education of the girl children. The government saved considerable part of the expenditure with the efforts made by the Salvation Army.[5]

In Bhumannagadda settlement, in Chittoor district, there were a large number of boys and girls identified by the then government between the ages of 10 and 16 years. The government transferred all of them to the industrial school at Madras. The boys and girls were under the strict supervision, control, management and influence of the Salvation Army. Many of them were converted to Christianity. They were brought under the great influence of Christianity. The government approved the draft schemes made by the Salvation Army for opening the industrial schools in the settlements without bothering about such conversions. The industrial schools had the capacity to have the intake of 100 boys and 100 girls with a total of 200 children every year. The average intake in the industrial schools managed by the Salvation Army was 200 per year. The admissible age of the boys and girls was 6 to 12 years. The boys and girls were kept in the industrial schools until they had reached the age of 18 years. After completing their education in the industrial training schools they were employed in various forms of employment.[6] Thus, the Salvation Army had managed the industrial schools very effectively under the Christian guidance in Madras province. The government constructed separate bungalows for the purpose of organising classes, study and for the school staff members in the settlements. In an industrial school there were two wings. One wing was exclusively meant for the dormitory and classroom purpose and the other rooms were meant for

Figure 1

The Model Sketch of Industrial School for the Children of 'Criminal' Tribes in Madras

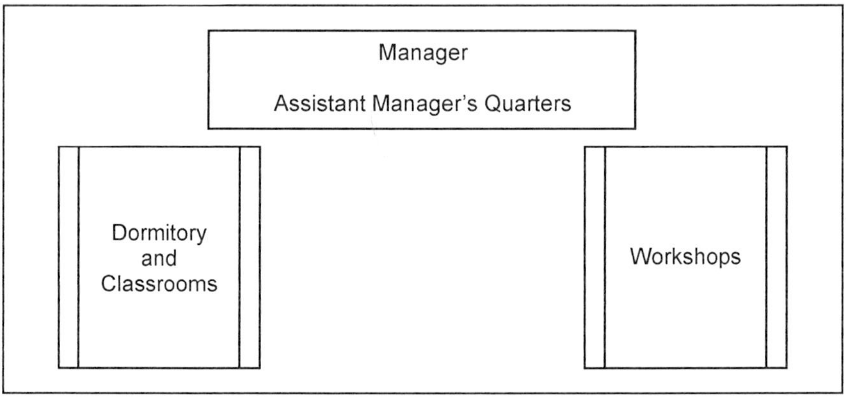

the workshops. Figure 1 is the draft sketch of the model industrial school run by the Missionaries in the Madras province.

The two wings in the industrial schools – dormitories and classrooms – had sufficient provisions to expand in case of increase in the number of intake of the students. The classrooms in the industrial schools were organised on parallel rows. The school authorities felt that it was not desirable to accustom the children to live in the bungalows. The construction of such schools was very cost-effective for the government. The construction cost of an industrial school was not more than ₹ 10,000 during the year 1915. The public works department used to undertake the construction activities. Academic instruction in the industrial schools was restricted to 3Rs (reading, writing and arithmetic). It was not carried beyond the fourth standard. The colloquial knowledge of English was encouraged. The schools were organised only for two hours in a day. Smart boys and girls were trained to become leaders and carried up to seventh standard. The boys and girls who showed their skills and talent were only admitted in the boarding schools. The industries that were more remunerative outside were taught in the schools. After completing their studies in the industrial schools, the boys and girls were encouraged to take up the remunerative industrial occupations. The government felt that it was the best practice not to distract children by teaching too many trades at once. The boys and girls should not become the 'jack of all and masters of none'.[7]

There were two kinds of schools in the Madras Presidency. One type of school was for the Telugu-speaking children and the other type of school was for the Tamil-Canaries speaking children. Different industrial training programmes were designed in these schools. Two languages were taught to the children in the school. For the boys in the industrial schools at Madras and the girls in the Nellore industrial school, the British Government had introduced Tamil and Telugu languages. The choice of introducing industries in the schools completely depended on the government. The government also decided that in future course of time when the children leave the school what type of industrial training should be taken by the children of the CTs. The government made the following options to the CT children: (1) The children may be trained in railway workshops, blacksmithing, carpentry and fitting industries. (2) The government established the mills and other industrial establishments by the private agencies in the province were very close to the settlements. Some children of the CTs were appointed in the mills. They were made experts in weaving industry. (3) The settlements were located in the neighbouring places of the urban centres, cities and towns. The cities and towns opened up a great opportunity for marketing and gardening works. The government, therefore, became keen to establish schools adjacent to the towns and urban centres. (4) There was a lot of demand for the silk industry in the surrounding areas of the settlements. The government encouraged mulberry gardens and silkworm rearing, etc. This had produced considerable income in a short span of time. The industrial schools became a ground for the development of industries in the Madras province. (5) Tea gardens were clamouring for labour contract works. The government and the private contractors had spent lot of money to open the tea gardens in the province. The industrial schools reaped the benefit from opening of tea and coffee gardens in the province. The schools got good profit by sending the tribal people as wage labourers. (6) Many children of the settlements emigrated to Assam, Ceylon, the Straits, West Indies and Andamans as highly paid resources. This relieved the congestion in the settlements. The Missionaries ensured the government to turn the children of the CTs as profitable and remunerative wageworkers.[8]

The British authorities constructed the bungalows in the settlements. Out-houses were used as schools and the staff quarters. The poor tribals in cases of emergency situations like cyclones and other epidemics used the schools and the staff quarters to take shelter. The schools were used as quarantine rooms during the draught period. The dormitories, classrooms, workshop centres were always filled with these people debarring children and teachers to run the schools. The public works department never used to repair the leaky roofs. In the schools, looms and reeling machines were installed. Silkworm rearing, silk reeling and weaving were the principal subjects and industries started in the boarding schools. The government used to purchase silk and cotton yarn, cocoons and silkworm eggs and used to supply to the school for training work. The government also started carpentry and blacksmithing. These skills were imparted to the talented boys and girls. The then Director General of Industries used to supply suitable tools and the requirements needed for the schools. The weaving industry was very popular in the local areas. Therefore, the management of the schools was asked to supply the required local needs regularly. Vegetable gardens were also formed in the settlements. These gardens provided excellent additional income support to the schools. The director of agricultural department was asked to advise the teachers and children to show interest in the agricultural activities. The schools were provided with regular water supply. The director of the agricultural department used to advise the children for proper utilisation of water from ponds, which were readily available there. A school was sanctioned with two acres of mulberry for silkworm rearing. The schools were supervised by the European superintendent with a salary of ₹ 75 per month. The schools were also supported by one assistant (with a salary of ₹ 30), one silk master (with a salary of ₹ 25), one weaving master (with a salary of ₹ 20), one assistant schoolmaster (salary ₹ 10), and two school servants (₹ 10 each). An amount of ₹ 30 was spent by the government on each student in the school every year.[9]

The government provided quality schools for the children of the CTs. Clerks and peons were appointed in the schools. They were entrusted with the responsibility of the school children. Their duty was to collect the children from the settlements and admit them into the schools. The posts of clerks and peons were specially created, as they were not ordinary workers in the schools. They possessed the total responsibility of supervising the schools. In the beginning, the Kallar parents were reluctant to send their children to the school. The authorities chose to rely on the methods of propaganda and persuasion. The parents were warned strictly to send their children to school without fail. The government used to take the assistance of local people and their opinion to develop the school atmosphere.[10]

The efforts of colonial government clearly exhibited in educating the children of the Kallars and Koravars in the Madras province. Reclamation activities of the government were largely confined to the maintenance of the schools, new boarding homes for the boys and girls and the award of the boarding grants to the children. There was an increase in the number of children in these schools. Boarding grants were regularly sanctioned to the children. The boarding homes worked very satisfactorily for the children of the Kallars. The Kallars and Koravars were known as depressed classes in the Madras Presidency. They were the inhabitants of Madura and Ramnad districts of Tamil Nadu. The Madras Government appointed N. Gopala Swami, the then secretary to the government and Rao Sahib T. Devaraja Mudaliyar Avargal as the officers incharge for the reclamation of the Kallar children through education in Madras. They strove very hard for the development of the industrial centre in Madras province.[11]

The Madras Government opened new schools for the development of children of the Kallars. There were a large number of schools functioning in the province by 31 December 1928. The government also opened boarding schools for the boys and girls in the settlements. For instance, in Tanjavore, the government established a number of schools for the Kallar children. Almost all the Kallar villages with a school-going population of 20 had a school. Most of the Kallar schools were located in the districts of Tanjore, Pudukotai Taluk, Papanasanam and Mannargudi Taluks. The government also provided grants for the 120 schools during the year 1929. There was a gradual increase in the percentages of the monthly attendance in the schools. There were 259 schools functioning for the ex-criminal tribes during the year 1940. The Kallar children were admitted in the boarding schools run by the missionaries and other agencies. Very few Kallar children were given the benefit of the faculty. The boarding schools were located in different places in Madras (Usilampatti, Uttampalyam, CSM Madura, CSM Virudhunagar, CSM Usilam Patti, CSM Paramakudi, CSM Dindigal, AMCC Tirumangalam, AMCC Pasumalai, AMCC Palani and Dindigal, AMCC Batlagundu, AMCC Manamadura, Capron Hall Madura and RCM Madura).[12]

There was an increase on the rolls of the children, particularly the girls' side. The then government appreciated the rise of the strength of the schools. It was an indication that the Kallars realised the advantages of elementary education. They showed much interest to avail the opportunity given to them. The attendance of the Kallar children in all the schools was very much satisfactory. In some of the schools the buildings were not adequately sufficient to accommodate all the children and in some villages extra teachers were sent. In some of the villages, the villagers constructed the government buildings and schools by themselves. The teachers were advised to go around the village and congregate the parents and students in the village with the help of the panchayats. Many teachers were employed against the sanctioned strength. The school assistants used to strive hard to develop literacy among the Kallar children. The teachers appointed in the Kallar schools were trained hands. They possessed the training certificates. The Kallar schools were located in the interior places. They did not have the bare necessaries of life. The teachers were paid a poor salary. A greater number of the trained teachers did not show real interest to go and work in the settlement schools.[13]

Trained teachers were necessarily entertained to keep the community in the schools. The labour commissioners were instructed to sanction better scales and pay to the teachers. This attracted the trained teachers in the schools. The government insisted the district education officers to replace the untrained teachers. The government authorities showed greater faith in the reclamation work of the CTs through education. It was hoped that education eventually raises the standard of character and give them a broader outlook of future life to the younger generation. Additional supervisors were sanctioned for the supervision of the schools. There were three ranges of supervisors in the Kallar schools. Some supervisors were kept under the control of the teachers. Other supervisor used to look after the children living within a radius of five miles from the schools. The supervisors acted as scout-masters. The scoutmasters possessed secondary grade teachers training certificate. They used to attend for the preliminaries within the range of the school. The schools were regularly supervised. Special inspectors were also conducted annually. The special sub-inspectors were asked to visit them regularly in the course of their duties. The district education officers were of the opinion that the Kallar schools were much better conducted and functioned than other schools. The Kallar schools were far superior in tone in spite of various deficiencies. Untrained teachers mostly managed the schools. Owing to the close supervision and personal interest taken by the staff, beneficial results were achieved.[14]

With the increase of the children in the hostels, the strength of the hostels increased every year. Some of the students were not promoted to the higher classes. They were weeded out from the schools. Such children were detained in the same class for more than two to three years. The hostels were opened soon after the mid-summer recess. To make up the increased strength of the children the government sanctioned the vacancy positions and filled them up. The poor and promising children only were selected to the schools and hostels. The admissions were restricted as far as possible to the Kallar villages. The selection of the students was based on examinations and their attainment. To look after the general health of the school children the commissioner of labour used to appoint a medical attendant in the hostels. The government also appointed a sub-assistant surgeon from the headquarters and local government hospitals. The doctors were paid an amount of ₹ 20 for their services. To provide food for the children cooks were appointed. Food was provided regularly for the school-going children.[15]

The children were formed into scout troops. Each teacher was given the responsibility of 40 students. The wardens used to manage 24 children. The scout children used to show better results. They used to perform their best skills. They were well qualified in scout crafts. They were taken to scout camps twice in a year for a very short period. The then governor of Madras was the chief of the provincial scouts. The governor used to offer his best advices for the benefit of the children and the teachers.[16]

The settlement boarding schools consisted of five classes. The elderly boys and girls were trained in weaving, tailoring in various batches without causing any detriment to their daily school routine. The headmaster was given a higher scale of pay of ₹ 35/(35–11/2–50–1–60). They were also paid a monthly allowance of ₹ 4. The deputy inspector of schools regularly inspected the schools. The schools were provided with a small library, a small laboratory with scientific instruments and a spacious playground. The schools were the central attraction for the Kallar children. The schools were staffed fully. In the interschool competitions, the Kallar children were rewarded better than other caste groups children in all the subjects. The students were not provided outdoor games for various reasons. The children were divided into batches and were placed under the supervision of the scout teachers. They were trained in various games. On every Sunday, children were taken on a march to the outside places for a distance of 2 to 3 kilometres and they were brought back very safely by the scout teachers.[17]

The Government of Madras retrenched and closed some of the Kallar industrial centres in Madras. The government also closed some of the posts working for the upliftment of Kallars such as clerks, storekeepers, scoutmasters, special inspectors and peons. Some of the teachers like music teachers working in the Kallar boarding home were also abolished. The teachers working in the Kallar schools were trained teachers. The government paid special attention to replace untrained teachers. The teachers working in the Kallar schools attended the meetings of the teachers associations at several centres in the state. Such attendance was insisted on the pain of the disciplinary action in default. The government insisted that the teachers working in the Kallar reformatory schools reside in the villages where the Kallars schools were located. The government for the persistent disobedience of the government orders also dispensed with the services of the teachers. In some cases, the teachers posted in the Kallar schools could not secure accommodation. Therefore, the government made special arrangements with the active cooperation of the Kallar panchayats to house the teachers in appropriate places. There were many conductresses employed throughout the year. The government provided thatched buildings. No new work was undertaken due to retrenchment, repairs to school buildings. The government did not sanction new posts. The government charged heavily for the boarding homes. The grants for the maintenance of the boarding homes were under the direct control of the government; nor which was not sent on time for the running of the schools to the Missionary organisations. The accounts were maintained under separate heads by the government. The boarding grants were sanctioned at fixed rates for the children.[18]

It is necessary to recount the benefits of the boarding homes to the Kallar children. The main objective of the schools was to mould the character of the Kallar children and to inculcate among the children a spirit of self-reliance, to promote self-discipline, etc. The boarding schools became very popular among the depressed classes in the

Madras Presidency. The boarding homes and schools for the Kallar children worked on satisfactory lines. The health of the children was maintained very well. The boarding schools were kept in the charge of selected headmasters. There was strict enforcement of rules regarding the conditions of admissions and conduct of the children in these schools. There was an increase in the strength of the school children every year. Scout troops, cub-packs were attached to the boarding schools. The Kallar boys who attained a fair degree of proficiency were given training in the schools. The headmasters of the board high schools were appointed as wardens of the board homes. They were also asked to take keen interest in the working of the board homes. They were paid an amount of ₹ 25 as honorarium for the supervision of the schools. The headmasters were incharge members of the boarding homes in addition to their responsibilities of regular staff work in the schools.[19]

The work progress of the boarding homes was satisfactory to a great extent. The institutions maintained its prestige for its efficiency and discipline. The district education officers used to visit the institutions regularly. They were impressed with the scouts rally. The number of scouts was increased in the educational institutions. The scouts were attached to the boarding homes. The scouts had been divided into six troops. Some scouts contained 24 troops and two cub-packs. There was tremendous progress in all directions. The scouts had attained a high degree of proficiency. Regular scout rallies were conducted at Periyakulam. They had earned a very good name for their social service activities. Separate boarding homes were constructed for the Kallar girls. Matrons were appointed as incharge members. The district boards paid them better. The matrons were used to engage classes for the Kallar girls. Sewing, needlework, etc. was taught. Particular attention was paid in cultivating the habits of cleanliness and domestic duties. The district education board used to organise games such as football, badminton, hockey, and the district boards appointed ring tennis, etc. by the physical directors. They took keen interest in guiding the Kallar boys in the physical exercises and games. The boys systematised their games. The board high schools were provided with good playgrounds. The playgrounds were furnished with the requisite sports materials. The Kallar children evinced lot of interest in their sports and games.[20]

Agricultural schools were established. They were of much benefit to the children. The agricultural schools imparted practical training. The children were given practical agricultural training on improved methods of cultivation to the boys and girls. Their parents were basically agriculturists. Special facilities were given to the Kallar boys considering their hardwork. The boys and girls were asked to do hardwork during daytime. The labour department sanctioned scholarships for Kallar children. Some of the Kallar children were trained in the government technical institute, Madura. The then commissioners of labour department provided children with the industrial training and scholarships. Some of the Kallar children underwent collegiate education in American college at Madura. Some Kallar boys sacrificed their studies for the sake of employment in the co-operative departments and in Hood Co-operative Institute, Tanjore.[21]

Besides vocational training, Kallar children were trained in farming, gardening, poultry, mat-weaving, string, thread work, etc. They were trained in girl's boarding home at Usilampatti. They were also given special training in domestic economy, nursing, drawing, needlework and embroidery. Boys and girls got merits in their training and in recognising the British Mother Superior. The British authorities congratulated all the boys and girls who showed their proficiency in their work. The district education officers opened night schools, which worked very effectively. There were seven night schools working for the children of Kallar in the state. The Kallars also contributed towards the education of their children. They used to pay ₹ 2 for each Kallar child. The government collected ₹ 6,946.18 and the same was remitted in the government treasury. The Kallar schools were in the charges of six supervisors. The supervisors used to inspect the schools and send their notes to the deputy inspector of schools. Suggestions were taken up for the better working of the schools. The deputy inspectors, sub-assistant inspectors of schools and the district educational officers used to visit the schools regularly. They used to offer their remarks and suggestions to the schools. The school authorities used to attend to the remarks and suggestions made promptly. The officers of the education department used to provide valuable assistance for the improvement of the Kallar schools. Several Missionaries and managements rendered hearty cooperation and assistance for the upliftment of the children of Kallars in the Madras Province.[22]

There were scout troops and cub-packs for the Kallar boys and girls in the schools. The girls were provided with girl guides and blackbirds in the district. They had their aptitude for the movement. They had the true scout spirit with them. The scout troops at Uttamapalyam and Usalam Patti had got the highest appreciation by the district education officers every year. The Kallar boys scouts were always displayed their zeal in putting out accidental fires and doing service during the festivals. The scouts used to attend the district scout rallies. The boys and girls were asked to take part in the excursions regularly. The South India Boy Scout Magazine and the Girl Guide News sheet were published and supplied in the state government schools. Ry. Rao Sahib and R. Krishna Aiyyar Avargal were the then district scout commissioners for the boy scouts and girl guides. The Kallar boy scouts and girl guides showed their active work under their active guidance. Thus, the

British Government imparted education to the children of the denotified communities very effectively in the Madras province with the help of the missionaries like Salvation Army, American Baptist Telugu Mission, Canadian Mission and other philanthropic agencies, of course, with a Christian bias.[23]

Present Concerns

After Independence, the research studies and field experiences shows that the children of the nomadic, semi-nomadic and denotified tribes were systematically kept out of the schools. They were subjected to various types of harassment in the schools. The children of these communities were not welcome into the Municipal schools, Panchayat local and government schools. The parents of the children often complain that their children were regularly beaten and ridiculed by the children of the upper communities and teachers working in the schools. The children of the Yerukala, Yanadi, Nakkala, Dommara, Sikari children were subjected to ill-treatment and bullying. In one case, the headmaster of the DNT School even ridiculed the parents of the DNT children in the school assembly. Therefore, children do not attend the schools. As a result, there is a widespread disinclination among the DNT communities to send their wards to school. They prefer to keep the children out of school, to train the children in traditional skills to ensure some secured life for their living. In some settlements like Lingala in Mahaboobnagar District in Telangana, the children of the DNT communities were sold to the rich people of Bombay and Gujarat for bonded labour. In Siddhapuram settlement in Kurnool district of Andhra Pradesh, there is not even a single person (men and women) who has studied up to graduation. The schools do not care for the children of these communities. In fact, there is a considerable hostility among the youth of these communities. They are engaged in the traditional activities such as rope-making, basket-making, working with the iron implements, etc. From childhood they are engaged in the traditional occupations along with the parents. The parents expose the children to hard work for lesser wages. Thus, there is total unemployment, bonded labour, child labour in the DNT colonies. The reservation system has not given any benefit whatsoever for the children of the DNT communities. They are absorbed in the mainstream of the society.[24]

Providing education to the Denotified Tribes (DNTs) is one of the challenging and urgent issues in front of our government after Independence. The education policy makers, practitioners and other actors have to take serious note to solve the varied problems of the education of the DNTs. They constitute 8 per cent of Indian tribal population. They are found in all states and districts. The national education statistics indicated that the literacy level among these groups is very less. The educational provisions aimed for them are not reaching them in time. If the goals of education like Education For All (EFA) and the Millennium Development Goals (MDGs) have to be achieved then more interventions needs to be designed to increase the educational opportunities for these DNT tribes/communities in India.

The serious issues to be addressed with the education of the DNTs in the country are: (1) How to make education more accessible to the DNTs? (2) What are the different ways and means to include the children of the DNT communities in the education process? (3) What kind of training is required for these children? (4) What kind of educational strategies are effective for them? (5) What innovative interventions are required in their education needs to be taken into consideration. In order to strengthen their education, there is a need to involve the DNTs in the process of planning and implementation of education, health initiatives in their villages, taking the potentialities of the open school system, initiating appropriate curriculum and content, introducing basic adult education and making schools more flexible for their children which are very much essential for their development. The government has to ensure basic education for all. The women and the young girls in the DNT colonies have to be empowered through employment opportunities. The women and the young girls are facing acute problems in the vicinities of the DNTs. They face social, economic and other problems. Gender discrimination persists in the DNT colonies. Therefore, gender discrimination of all types has to be uprooted. Gender parity is the essential goal of Education For All and the Millennium Development Goals. In the colonies of the DNTs, gender disparity needs to be seriously targeted. Gender inequality in the DNTs is a serious concern. Respect for their cultural attitudes, gender sensitive schools, conducive environment for their education in schools, culture specific curriculum and content eradication of poverty, skill development are the essential requirements for their improvement in the society.[25]

The problems faced by the NT/DNT/SNT tribal children in receiving education can be clarified under five areas, viz. economic factors, social factors, cultural factors, school factors and administrative factors. Poverty of parents, lack of parental demand, child labour, lack of Early Childhood Eductaion (ECE) facilities are some of the economic factors. Illiteracy of the parents, early marriages, community loyalties and lack of awareness, tribal festivals, tribal traditions, value system and problem of language are some of the cultural factors, lack of access, incomplete schools, teacher absenteeism, poor quality of teaching, unserviceable curriculum, unsuitable working hours, etc. are some of the school factors, while lack of coordination among different managements, delays in supply of incentives, weak inspectorate, lack of enrolment campaigns, lack of community control, lack of incentives for better performance are some of the administrative factors which are standing in the way of the education of tribal child. Some of the NT/DNT/SNT communities in Andhra Pradesh are involved in occupations like hunting, honey collection, cattle rearing, manufacture of agriculture implements, basket-making, selling bangles and beads, making garlands, forest labour, etc. Some of the traditional occupations of DNT communities of Andhra Pradesh are:

- Acrobatics
- Puppetry
- Singing, dancing and acting
- Snake charming, monkey playing and bear playing
- Hunting
- Handicrafts and artisans
- Fortune telling
- Traditional medico and herbal medicine selling
- Mendicant
- Herdsmanship
- Construction and earth work
- Fishing
- Brewing liquor

The special features of the DNT tribal communities can be listed as follows:

- Geographic isolation/isolated societies
- Simple way of life
- Treat Nature with respect
- Subject to customary laws/without law and order department, they control themselves
- They have their own code of conduct
- Truthfulness and honesty are found in them
- Closed system
- Subsistence economy
- Festivals throughout the year
- Early marriages (13–15 years boys, 10–14 years girls)
- Own dialect (Yerukula, Lambadi, Yanadi, etc.)
- Polygamy
- Divorce
- Limited exposure to outside world
- Beliefs and superstitions

- Limited needs and aspirations
- Parents are interested in immediate gains
- Economic characteristics include food gathering/hunting/fishing
- Low skills/very little specialisation/low productivity/no work training
- Lacks abstract thinking
- Child is looked as potential earner but not a learner
- Women looked as economic assets
- Learning through imitation but not instruction

Present Occupations of DNTs

- Begging
- Rag picking and waste collection
- Prostitution
- Child labour
- Street vendor (Restricted by Corporation Act)
- Unorganised labour
- All traditional occupations being carried not illegally

Socio-Economic Conditions of DNTs

- Extreme poverty
- Landlessness
- Illiteracy
- Homelessness
- Live in slums both in urban and rural areas
- No civic amenities like drinking water, electricity and toilets
- Sub-human conditions of living
- No Ration Card, BPL Card, Job Card, Voter Identity Card, Caste Certificate
- Untouchability/discrimination
- Malnourished (ill-fed, semi-starved)
- Unemployment/non-regular employment)
- No education
- No healthcare facilities
- Non-participation in government welfare schemes

Repercussion of the Social Stigma of Criminality and Beggary

- Police generally treat the DNTs as criminals
- They are falsely implicated in criminal cases
- Restriction in their movement from one place to another in pursuit of their occupations

- Victims of social discrimination by other castes
- Generally not permitted to stay permanently in villages
- Generally not permitted to allot a piece of land for their settlement in villages

Constitutional Safeguards

- Humiliated by sedentarised and established section.
- The DNTs irrespective of their backward categories (SCs, STs and OBCs) are humiliated by the people from sedentarised and established section of the society.
- Sometimes they are humiliated by the people other than DNTs from the backward categories, as they are carriers of social stigma.
- In this situation, effective and efficient implementation of the development policies and programmes is very important.
- Hence, DNTs need to be given separate constitutional status, support and security (Right to Life) to bring them into main stream society speedily.

What Needs to be Done Urgently in the Field of Education

- While efforts are made to bring the DNTs into mainstream education, the traditional knowledge and skills of the communities should be promoted to enable the youth to enhance their traditional skills in the modern context.
- Special play school for DNT children in their localities
- Residential schools be opened for DNTs.
- Free hostels at district and taluka level for the DNT students.
- Special vocational training and pre-recruitment training for DNT youth to enable them to take up jobs and appear in competitive examinations
- Educational facilities like scholarships and other benefits be provided to DNT students on the line of SC/ST students.
- Special academic institutions be instituted by the government for research and studies especially done on these communities to improve their culture, socio-economic condition and leadership.

There is high investment levels and rapidly raising national enrolment ratios with regard to the education of other categories of the people like Scheduled Castes and Other Backward Classes. But with regard to the education of the DNTs, the educational facilities provided to them is inadequate. There are disparities in their education in the country. The gross enrolment ratio of the higher sections of the society is very high when compared to the enrolment ratio of the DNTs. The enrolment of the boys and girls in the school is very less in the schools.[26]

Achieving the goals of Universal Primary Education, eliminating gender disparities in the DNT schools depended on the mass enrolment drives, targeting, reaching the smaller percentage marginalised groups. They are currently unable to access the education system. Therefore, it is time for educational planners and government to explore flexible and innovative approaches in the educational provisions that address to the specific barriers in providing basic education for the children of the DNTs. The DNTs belong to the group that needs to be targeted for educational interventions. It is stated that: 'Education system has to be inclusive, actively seeking out children who are not enrolled, and respond flexibility to the circumstances and needs of all learners'. Inclusive education carries the deliberate and positive action to ensure realisation of access for all kinds and conditions of the learners. What is needed for the children of the DNTs is flexible education at all levels. Great strides are being made by the central and the state governments to increase access, retention and the completion of education of all primary stage school-going children. There is a need to analyse the issues and share the best practices on the flexible education for the DNTs. The government and the stakeholders have to be informed about the policy options and best practices to provide relevant and qualitative education. Qualitative education has to be designed to improve their lives. The main goals of education of the DNTs include: (1) to understand the status of education of the DNTs in India in terms of access, retention and inclusion, (2) to achieve the millennium goals of education for all and quality education for the DNTs, (3) to identify innovative success stories and flexible initiatives for possible replication, (4) to identify the new challenges and formulate appropriate strategies to overcome them, (5) to establish linkages and networks for sharing expertise and resources for the future collaboration, and (6) to create a platform for raising the educational standards of the DNTs and an agenda for the future national, state meetings, etc. The DNTs have to be assured with basic and primary education. They do not have access to education in their localities. There is no training, skill-based orientation to the women and young girls among the DNTs. There is no adequate training for the teachers working in the DNT schools. The children of the DNTs do not get life skills in their schools. In the light of these circumstances, the government should come out with a specific policy and agenda to improve the educational facilities for these communities.[27]

There is a need to enhance their ideas and expertise for the development of the DNTs. The state and central government organisations have to increase the access for education to the DNTs. Free and compulsory education must be provided for them up to the collegiate level. The percentages of the enrolment ratio among the DNTs are very poor. Innovative practices encourage the DNTs to attain literacy in numeracy and the life skills. Globalisation had increased the urgency of the ability to read, communicate, to take the advantage of the technology and information. Education will definitely equip the DNTs. Today their habitats and their simple ways of living are under severe threat. This is due to environmental change, lack of education, harassment by the upper castes, moneyed folk, bureaucracy, etc. Their livelihood options have to be increased. Access to education means access to better future. Knowledge is the key for cultural, social and economic development. There are many advantages of open, distance and technology mediated education or learning. These strategies will provide increased and inevitable access to education and training for the DNTs. The DNTs require support and capacity building. Teacher education, technical education, vocational education and training, agricultural and industrial work, open schooling, establishing mini-universities are essential. What is urgently required is programme-based and result-based management approach for the DNT colonies. Careful planning and evaluation are two supportive pillars for the over-all development of the DNTs.[28]

Denotified tribes are the ethnographic people. They have no fixed home as such. Their movements are necessitated by their culture and economic demands such as cattle rearing, hunting and gathering, shifting cultivation and craftwork. They live in harsh climatic conditions. They lead their life without basic necessities of life. Therefore, under these circumstances there is a need to redesign the concept of education for the communities of Denotified Tribes. In the provisions of basic education, the denotified tribes are receiving the unfair treatment. The education, programmes initiated by the government had failed them. The society considers them as other people. They are depicted as subhumans with inferior caste stigma in the society. They lead semisedentary life. The current status of the delivery of education to the denotified communities had not taken cognizance of the needs of the DNTs in the country. Their interests and aspirations are totally neglected. The basic education for the denotified tribes is feasible and doable. The current research works support the view that the Denotified communities are very much interested in the education of their children. Indeed, they are demanding for English medium and quality education for their children. Research has shown that the percentage of enrolment among the Denotified tribal children in their colonies is very encouraging. In some settlement schools there are cent per cent enrolment. Thus, there is no problem from the side of the Denotified tribes for their education but the real problem is the type of education provided to them, the content and the delivery of the education in the respective schools of the Denotified communities. In order to improve education among children, some of the strategies that are appropriate are: mobile schools in the remotest areas, improvement of the mid-day meal programme, mobilising community participation, adopting non-conventional approaches, innovative interventions and programmes in the denotified tribal schools, etc.[29]

Teachers can travel with the nomadic communities as and when the situation arises. They can take the classes in the temporary structures in the tents or under the trees. In the countries like Nigeria and Kenya, many mobile schools were opened for their nomadic people. These efforts were very much successful in these countries. Nigeria had been one of the first Commonwealth countries in Africa to be able to recruit a large number of teachers for the effective functioning of the mobile schools from the nomadic, Denotified communities themselves. Sufficient training must be provided to the teachers working in the tribal schools. Teachers working in the normal tribal schools were deployed with little more incentives in the mobile schools. Many talented people from the Denotified communities are available in their colonies. Such committed and talented people can be appointed as teachers in such mobile schools. They were properly trained in the transaction of the content, pedagogical, and evaluation practices. Teachers were trained periodically in Nigeria. The teachers were recruited from the nomadic communities itself. Thus, in India also the same practice can be adopted taking into consideration of the success stories of Nigeria.[30]

The schools in the denotified tribe colonies should not be fixed schools. The schools should focus on imparting life skills to children attending the schools. Animal husbandry, industrial training, gardening work, farming and other activities, which are suitable to their life, may be introduced. The schools working in the Denotified Tribe colonies must be child friendly. The life with which the children are familiar must be included in their curriculum. In order to increase the enrolment rate and decrease the dropout rate levels the school feeding programmes have to be properly implemented. Children must be provided with regular incentives. The personnel who are providing mid-day meals to these schools must be paid without any delay. The monitoring committees should take strict action to curb the corrupt practices in implementing the school nutrition programme.[31]

There is an urgent need for the involvement of the Denotified community members in the planning and implementation process of educational schemes in the denotified tribal schools. This will improve the school education scenario. Community participation will provide positive results both in the enrolment drive, retention, and removal of corrupt practices. Their culture can be preserved through the involvement of the community. They will further act as best administrative staff for the effective functioning of their schools. In case of Nigeria, the National Commission for Nomadic Tribes Education had mobilised the support of the nomadic communities and got active support for the effective functioning of their schools. Education centres may be exclusively opened for the nomadic and denotified communities and these study centres can be linked to state institutions like DIETS/BRCs/CRCs, school Complex Resource Centres and Ashram Schools, Welfare schools, etc. The active community leaders must be encouraged for their involvement in the school affairs.[32]

Notes

1. Government of Madras, Note Showing the Progress Made in the Settlement of Criminal Tribes in Madras Presidency up to September 1916, Madras 1917, TNA, p. 19.
2. Government of Madras, Note Showing the Progress Made in the Settlement of Criminal Tribes in Madras Presidency up to January 1926, Madras 1927, TNA, p. 14.
3. Government of Madras, Home Department, G.O. No. 3953, dated 20 July 1939, TNA, p. 1.
4. Government of Madras, Administration Report on Kallar Reclamation, Korava Reclamation, Yenadi Reclamation (Criminal Tribes) and Settlements for 1947–1948, the Superintendent Government Press, Madras, 1949, pp. 2–3.
5. Government of Madras, Public Works Labour Department, G.O. No. 1623 L., dated 1 August 1932, TNA, p. 4.
6. Government of Madras, Home Department, G.O. No. 3587, dated 16 November 1946, TNA, p. 1.
7. Government of Madras, Public Works Labour Department, G.O. No. Mis 752 L., dated 13 March 1928, p. 1.
8. Government of Madras, Public Works Labour Department, G.O. No. Mis 1111 L., dated 13 March 1928.
9. Government of Madras, Public Works Labour Department, G.O. No. Mis 1794 L., dated 15 July 1931, p. 6.
10. Government of Madras, Public Works Labour Department, G.O. No. Mis 752 L., dated 13 March 1928, p. 1.
11. Government of Madras, Public Works Labour Department, G.O. No. Mis 1111 L., dated 6 April 1929, p. 3.
12. Government of Madras, Public Works Labour Department, G.O. No. Mis 423L., dated 17 February, 1931, p. 4.
13. Government of Madras, Report on Kallar Reclamation, Madura and Ramnad districts, Administration Report for the Year 1931, Superintendent, Government Press, Madras, 1932, p. 2.
14. Government of Madras, Public Works Labour Department, G.O. No. Mis 1528L., dated 22 May 1930, p. 4.
15. Government of Madras, Public Works Labour Department, G.O. No. Mis 2152 L., dated 25 August 1931, p. 5.

16. Government of Madras, Administration Report on Kallar Reclamation, Madura and Ramnad Districts, Administration Report for 1932, Superintendent Government Press, Madras, 1933, p. 13, TNA.
17. Government of Madras, Administration Report on Kallar Reclamation, Madura and Ramnad districts, Administration Report for 1935, Superintendent Government Press, Madras, 1936, p. 8, TNA.
18. Government of Madras, Administration Report on Kallar Reclamation, Korava Reclamation, Yenadi Reclamation (Criminal Tribes) and Settlements for 1948–1949, the Superintendent Government Press, Madras, 1950, pp. 24–25.
19. Government of Madras, Public Works Labour Department, G.O. No. Mis 752 L., dated 13 March 1928, p. 2. APSA.
20. Government of Madras, Home Department, G.O. No. 3953, dated 20 July 1939, p. 2. TNA,
21. Government of Madras, Public Works Labour Department, G.O. No. Mis 2152 L., dated 25 August 1931, p. 4. APSA.
22. Government of Madras, Administration Report on Kallar Reclamation, Korava Reclamation, Yenadi Reclamation (Criminal Tribes) and Settlements for 1948–1949, the Superintendent Government Press, Madras, 1950, p. 19, APSA.
23. Government of Madras, Administration Report on Kallar Reclamation, Korava Reclamation, Yenadi Reclamation (Criminal Tribes) and Settlements for 1947–1948, the Superintendent Government Press, Madras, 1949, p. 4, APSA.
24. Radha Krishna, Meena, Urban Denotified Tribes: Competing Identities, Contested Citizenship, Vol. XLIV, No. 18, dated 2 May 2009 (Special Article).
25. Alba de Souza, Reaching Nomadic Populations in Africa, Garissa, Kenya, Commonwealth of Learning, Canada, June 2006, p. 30 (Unpublished Report).
26. Gandhi. Malli, 'Factors Affecting the Literacy of Denotified Tribe Children in the Settlement Schools of Andhra Pradesh', Unpublished ERIC Report, Submitted to NCERT, New Delhi, March 2005, p. 16.
27. Ibid.
28. Gandhi, Malli. Denotified Tribes, Dimensions of Change, Kanishka Publishers, New Delhi, 2008, p. 257.
29. Gandhi, Malli. and Lalitha, V., Tribes under Stigma: Problem of Identity, Serials Publishers, New Delhi, pp. 59–60.
30. Alba de Souza, Reaching Nomadic Populations in Africa, Garissa, Kenya, Commonwealth of Learning, Canada, June 2006, p. 30 (Unpublished Report).
31. Gandhi, Malli, Development of Denotified Tribes: Policy and Practice, Serials Publishers, New Delhi, 2006, pp. 140–141.
32. NCERT, NCF – 2005, Position Paper on Problems of Education of SC/ST Children, New Delhi 2005, p. 30.

4

Educational Status of Denotified Tribes in Andhra Pradesh

Attainments and Challenges

Education of children of the DNT communities is a very important concern of our government. Although schools were provided in their colonies, attendance was made compulsory for the children of school-going age, the expenses on education were met by the governments, children were fed, yet desirable results have not been achieved in the standard of education. The educational problems concerning these DNT children should be tackled by the apex educational organisations as a part of their extension programmes. It is with this background that it has been decided to study the educational pattern available to these DNT children, with a view to improve the achievement levels of DNT children in the present settlement schools. The main focus of the chapter is to examine to what extent education has spread among the DNT communities in Andhra Pradesh.

Profile of Education in Siddhapuram

For the education of the Woddar children, a school was established during the year 1915. Twenty-six boys and 26 girls were receiving instruction during the year 1916. Education was imparted in three Rs (reading, writing and arithmetic) and no attempt had been made to give them industrial training. The attendance was fairly regular. The school was run by two masters and one mistress who were paid ₹ 15 and ₹ 12 and ₹ 10, respectively.[1] Educational Department was inspecting the school now and then.

The average attendance during the year 1924 was 76.[2] The boys were made to learn agricultural work in the fields during the season. Carpentry, weaving tapes, masonry and brick-making were taught. The girls were taught sewing. They had the proficiency in making their own jackets. Taylor, the then Labour Commissioner, said: 'the children look well cared for and show satisfactory knowledge of their subjects'.[3] The settlement school was excellent in every way. Most of the boys used to read and write Telugu well. They were smart, clean and well drilled. Table 1 shows the class-wise distribution of children during the year 1927.[4]

Table 1

The Strength of Siddhapuram School, 1927

Standard	*Boys*	*Girls*	*Total*
Infant	8	7	15
1st Class	2	2	4
2nd Class	–	3	3
3rd Class	3	2	5
4th Class	5	–	5
5th Class	4	–	4

Strength of the School during the Year 1930

Standard	*Boys*	*Girls*	*Total*
1st	24	26	50
2nd	2	1	3
3rd	2	2	4
4th	3	–	3
5th	5	–	5
Total	36	29	65

The scout troop of boys was started in 1923. The boy's scouts were prepared for the inspection of officers. The officers were pleased with their smart turnout. The educated Woddar settlers were sent to teachers' training at Kurnool and were later appointed as teachers in the school. The school worked for 252 days in a year.[5] The school mistress, the wife of the compounder, took care of the girls in the lower classes. Elementary school boys were given practical lessons in agriculture on the government farm. The school was regularly inspected by the Deputy Inspector of Schools, the District Educational Officer and the Sub-Assistant Inspectors. Elderly boys were taught some agricultural theories in the class and then they were given manual work on the government farm. Some were sent to weaving. Some were trained as scouts. The best boys were presented with eight goats as school prizes to promote interest in education.[6]

The headmaster was a secondary grade trained teacher. He possessed good teaching ability and organising capacity. English was introduced as an additional subject in the IV and V standards during the year 1937, as suggested by the collectors. The headmaster was the only person who was competent to handle that language.[7] We can draw comparisons between Siddhapuram children and the students of advanced localities in the district. The Woddar children were brought under excellent discipline. They were trained to become self-reliant and useful members of society. The old boys of the school were encouraged to form into a drama troupe and they enacted four street dramas. It served them as a diversion and moral instruction. The Animal Week was celebrated and the settlers were taught how to show sympathy towards their animals. Leaflets were read out and explained to them. The supply of mid-day meals to the school children commenced in Siddhapuram from 13 March 1937.[8]

Sometimes the settlement manager used the innocent Woddars in scandals. Since the manager was the incharge of the school, tuition work was given to grown-up girls. It was very sad to know that 'in a school, especially of criminal settlers, a strict standard of discipline was absolutely essential and any chastisement by the headmaster in the exercise and maintenance of such a discipline should not be criticised. Exercise of discipline must be measured with a different standard'.[9]

The school was developed into a first grade elementary school during the year 1938. Pupils who completed fifth standard joined higher elementary school.[10] The government gave sanction to open the sixth standard in the school at Siddhapuram during 1947–48 and to convert one of the higher elementary grade teacher's post into a secondary grade post. The students who passed the sixth standard were sent to Velgode for further studies in the Telugu lower secondary school. The settlers' girls who passed the sixth standard were sent for training in midwifery.[11] The students of elementary school and secondary grade school were too slow to understand lessons due to lack of proper motivation. The children in each class were more in number. This was not an easy task for a teacher to coach up more than a reasonable number. The parents of the children did not appreciate the value of education. They were constantly goaded to send the children to the school. The strength of the school during the year 1948–49 is shown in Table 2.[12]

Table 2

Strength of Siddhapuram School During the Year 1948–49

Standard	*Average attendance strength, 1948–49*	
	Boys	*Girls*
1st Class	18	17
2nd Class	10	6
3rd Class	9	6
4th Class	10	2
5th Class	6	1
6th Class	4	11
Total	57	43

At present, the location and condition of the school at Siddhapuram is in a deplorable condition. A teacher with the secondary teacher training qualification (SGT) is running the school. It is not planned properly, since there is no syllabi or curricula prescribed for the school. The environment is not conducive for the children to study. There are only two graduates in the entire settlement and they too are still unemployed.

Profile of Education in Stuartpuram

The SA thought that education was compulsory for the Yerukulas of this settlement and, therefore, started an elementary school in 1916. Elementary education was made compulsory and those not attending the school were strictly punished. Out of 481 children in the settlement, 250 children were school-going during the year 1916. Seventy-four children attended the school regularly. The children in the school were very bright. The Governor of Madras was delighted with the school and took a photograph of the boys.[13] The school was run in a Palmyra shed of the size 60' x 20' which was leaky. In the elementary school, the children were taught three 'Rs' (reading, writing and arithmetic) and general knowledge including rural science, gardening, nature study, English, physical training and the Bible. In the higher standards of the school, industrial education and moral training were introduced. Instruction in agriculture was made compulsory in school education. The school was a co-education school. Class books, maps, slates and slated pencils, pictures of animals and plants, a globe, Ananda Primer and Ananda Readers for standards one, two and three, and garden implements for children were purchased by the manager. Night classes were conducted for adults. The teachers employed in the day school taught in the night schools also. The wives of the teachers evinced keen interest in girls' education. For this, the teachers were given extra salary of ₹ 8 to headmaster and ₹ 5 for assistant teachers. The subjects taught in the night school were reading, writing and arithmetic.[14] The strength and attendance of students in the elementary school on 29 October 1917 was as shown in Table 3.[15]

The management of the school and the employment of teachers were left entirely to the SA. The government desired that the rules prevailing in the education department should be adopted. An interesting feature of that time was that qualified teachers from the Yerukulas, both men and women, were appointed as teachers in the school.[16] This was done with the intention of creating an atmosphere in the settlement primarily to promote the self-confidence of the whole tribe and, secondly, to prove that those who were committed to do any work they were asked to do so seriously. To strengthen this, periodical inspections were arranged by the educational officers of high mental caliber.[17] The teachers were given better salaries and provided with free quarters in the settlement. *Ganji* (boiled rice water) was supplied at noon to the students who were present both in the morning and in the evening.[18] Table 4 describes the teachers in the school during the year 1918.[19]

Table 3

Strength of Elementary School, Stuartpuram, 1917

Standards	*No. on rolls*		*No. present*		*Total*
	Boys	*Girls*	*Boys*	*Girls*	
Infants A	14	11	14	9	23
Infants B	22	14	13	11	24
Infants C	15	23	10	18	28
Infants D	30	34	25	27	52
1st Standard	8	3	6	2	8
2nd Standard	11	1	8	1	9
3rd Standard	7	3	7	3	10

Table 4

Position of Teachers in Stuartpuram Elementary School

Name of the Teacher	*Qualifications*	*Scale of Pay*
K. Jacob	L.S.P.T.C. of 1915	25
Ch. Joseph	S.S.L.C. of 1915	20
Santhoshammal	L.S.P.T.C. of 1915	15
Soubhagyammal	L.S.P.T.C. of 1915	15
P. Simon	Unpassed	12
Lyssammal	Passed 4th Std.	12
B. Solomon	Unpassed	12

The newly established boarding school helped the settlers in withering away of the crime atmosphere. The boarding school was established for the sake of (1) orphan children, (2) children whose parents were in jail, (3) children of parents who were miserably poor, (4) children of parents just returned from jails, (5) children of parents from whom separation was made because of the bad character of parents or because of the suspected character of children and (6) children of absconding settlers.[20]

The boarding school was very well managed and in a report the manager stated that the school was an asset to the settlement. In order to improve the sleeping conditions of the children of the settlers, the Commissioner of Labour constructed separate dormitories for boys and girls. Two matrons were appointed separately to take care of them.

Another classification was the young children and the older ones. A separate building was arranged for recreation purpose.

The meeting of parents and children either at the school or at home added to the disturbance of the children's minds. It was felt that reformation was impossible in an atmosphere where the crime culture was not forgotten. The SA dissuaded the parents from meeting their children. But the influence of the parents on their separated children was very severe. The new generation was made up of honest people. The SA visualised the hours of work as to make use of timings in such a way that no time was left for them to visit their parents and, hence, no perpetuation of crime among the youth.[21] Thus, they segregated their children from their parents and arranged a boarding school in the settlement and permitted occasional visits of the parents.

The SA appointed peons for the reformation of the children of the ex-settlers. The peons for these schools were selected from the settlers themselves.[22] Their duty was to go round and collect the children for the school. At the age of 5 years, the settlers' children were sent to schools.[23] In the elementary school, instruction was given up to fifth standards. The headmaster was with a certificate of higher grade training.[24]

There was an increase in the number of children attending the school every year. During the year 1924, there were nearly 401 children on the rolls. A total number of 261 children attended the school regularly in the school.[25] Furthermore, the outside influence on DNT children was more. The SA authorities considered that the solution to the problem was in sending girls to Nellore and boys to Perambur, near Madras city.[26] It would help them in reformatory process. Mackenzie, the SA official wanted to change the structure of the building to create a new atmosphere in the settlement. The availability of buildings at Nellore was a positive factor and this was congenial to the growth of children. The SA suddenly closed the boarding school in Stuartpuram and shifted some of the girls to Nellore girls' school. But the closing down of the Stuartpuram Boarding School (1926) gave a severe blow to the settler's children.[27]

A significant feature of the settlement school was that manager L.R. Gale gave a Christian bias to the whole atmosphere of the school. When the first children batches of Yerukulas were brought into this settlement, school boys and girls were dirty looking and they got involved in petty thefts and road robberies. It was not an easy task to teach CTs to be on the path of righteousness. But much had been done towards this good end. The younger generation understood and responded well.[28] The SA constructed a church in the year 1915, ostensibly to reform the Yerukulas by giving Bible education and thereby making them disciplined. All the settlers were gathered and brought into the church.

S.H. Slater, the Labour Commissioner, bestowed attention on the school children. Some students got through the SSLC (Secondary School Leaving Certificate) examination. Those who failed were also given utmost care. They were admitted either in Paddison hostel or in the industrial school, Perambur, Madras.[29] Some of the boys who passed through the five standards in the settlement school were admitted in the fourth and sixth forms of the high school at Bapatla.[30] Dowson, the then Deputy Inspector General of Police, Madras, inspected the settlement school on 8 July 1931 and wrote 'I knew this settlement in its earliest infancy. My visit today was peculiarly interesting. My first visit was in 1914. Today, i.e. 8 July 1931, it is possible to see that the settlement has completely filled the purpose for which it was instituted'.[31] After inspecting the school, he said: 'The kiddies looked fat and happy. Neither the manager nor the police had any controversies. The settlement is in a most flourishing condition'.[32]

The SA opened a new girls' school for the development of women's education. During the year 1921, there were nearly 100 girls in it.[33] During the year 1926, few girls were transferred to Nellore Industrial School. Owing to the closure of the girls' reformatory school at Nellore, a number of girls were sent back to their parents. There were no classes above the fifth standard. The girls who studied at Nellore in the higher classes were again sent to the higher elementary boarding school at Kavali. Nursing and sewing training were given to the girls. The manager of Stuartpuram settlement selected some women who were familiar with three 'Rs and talented with the art of conversation and possessed with the ability to describe, explain them completely to have an idea of such topics. In addition to that, they were also trained in the proper maintenance of the house or the working place by sweeping, dusting and cooking. For extracting talent from them, they were encouraged. For example, on 10 March 1928 a model was done by a girl for essay writing on 'Home Sanitation' during *Health Week Competition*.[34]

The settlers had a brigade of scouts since 1923. Although the members were constantly changing, owing to employment and other circumstances they had a creditable brigade. A small bugle band had been formed and equipment supplied. The Assistant Manager had taken a keen interest in the movement and himself went into camp with the scouts.[35] The scouting activities in the schools were conducted by the school teachers who were trained as scout masters.[36] All the adult-reformed settlers were expected to give importance to morality. Polygamy was prevalent and the traces of polyandry were rare among them. The SA thought that religious and moral instruction were the greatest factors for their improvement. They used to instruct the women-folk of the settlement to take stern steps to control their crimes. But it happened to the contrary that even the wives were also involved in the culture of crime.[37]

The supply of mid-day meals was started at Stuartpuram for the first time only from December 1947. Other settlements' school children were also supplied with mid-day meals at the government cost of ₹ 3. The introduction of mid-day meals to the school children was to encourage the children to attend the school regularly and make them fit to receive instruction.[38] The school children were taken to excursions. The government authorities, the DIG of Police, CID and railways sanctioned the expenditure not exceeding ₹ 50 per year.[39]

It is striking to note that among the Yerukula community of Stuartpuram some already secured good employment both in central and state governments. At present, more than 150 members even received University Education. This is obviously to some extent due to the efforts of the SA and the awareness among the youth. Separate hostels are also being maintained by the SA for these children. Consequently, there are nearly 155 students in these hostels today. In the hostels, there are 101 boys and 54 girls studying in class I to the S.S.C (10th class). It is providing scholarships, food, hostel facilities and clothes to the students. The SA had requested the Secretary, Government of Madras, to sanction a general library for children outside the premises of the school, and it was conceded.

In the year 1958, the SA combined with the Inspector General of Police, opened a new high school for the children of the settlers. The school comprised of mainly Yerukula children and some converted Christians together with the children of upper castes. Later, it was converted into a middle school from the academic year 1958–59. It was run by the Social Welfare Department.[40] The high school followed the syllabi prescribed by the Board of Secondary Education, Andhra Pradesh, Hyderabad. The strength of the high school as per the annual record of the year 2006 is 277. The division of boys and girls from class VI to X is shown in Table 5.[41]

Table 5

Strength of High School in Stuartpuram, 2005

Class	*Boys*	*Girls*	*Total*
VI	34	26	60
VII	29	18	47
VIII	26	17	43
IX	34	28	62
X	41	24	65
Total			277

After the repeal of the CTA in 1952, it was contemplated that all state governments should undertake welfare schemes especially education. In the second five-year plan, funds were sanctioned by the government for the education of these tribal children.[42] During the Third Five-Year Plan, a plan provision of ₹ 375 lakh was made for the purpose. An estimated expenditure of ₹ 55.36 lakh was incurred during 1962–63. In the Fifth Five-Year Plan, no separate provision has been made under centrally sponsored programmes for undertaking educational and other schemes for DNT communities.[43]

Various societies such as Bharatiya Adimjati Sevak Sangh (New Delhi), Andhra Rastra Adimjati Sevak Sangh and Andhra Rashtra Yerukula Maha Sangam came forward to reform these people.[44] The main aims and objectives of Andhra Rashtra Adimjati Sevak Sangh were education, literature, liberation, sadachar work, etc.[45] Yerukulas, Yanadis and Banjaras were included in the list of Scheduled Tribes by the Parliament in 1956 owing to the efforts of the B.N. Datar, the then Minister of Home Affairs.[46] The first school for Scheduled Tribes was started by the Sangh in 1934. The first Harijan hostel was started in 1929. The first tribal hostel was started in 1939. Female education among tribals was taken up by the Sangh.[47] Various types of books, magazines and articles were published in Telugu and English. The best examples are Kallumunta, Rama Rajyam, Yekalavya, which are ballads. *Adivasi, Dalit Marg, Girijana Jyoti, Yekalavya Patrika and Harijanoddharana* were other important newspapers published by Andhra Rashtra Adimjati Sevak Sangh.[48]

In addition to the SA and various social organisations, social workers namely Gora, Lavanam, Hemalatha Lavanam of Atheist centre Vijayawada, M.V. Thomas, the former Superintendent of Police and T. Gopala Rao, the former collector of Guntur district, endeavoured hard to reform these people, through education. During the year 1983, DNT students who secured highest marks in public examinations in eighth and tenth standards in the school at Stuartpuram were awarded prizes by Lavanam and Hemalatha Lavanam.

The welfare measures initiated for Yerukulas, Woddars, Yanadis and Sugalis bear a resemblance to the efforts of squeezing oil from sand. The development of scheduled tribes is a real challenge to the present government. The utterances of the government on the welfare measures are making much noise emanating from empty vessels. Policy formulation and its execution, most often, fall apart. Tribal children are required to pay special fee at the time of admission, though they are exempted from other fees. Poor tribal students are not in a position even to pay this. Added to this, tribal welfare scholarships are generally delayed and released at the end of the year. As a result, students are bound to face many problems. There is a lot of injustice being done to tribal children.

In the sphere of employment too, tribal children are facing serious problems. Though the public advertisements earmark a number of vacancies to these people, they appear so with a clause saying that the posts would be convertible to other castes in the absence of the eligible tribal candidates. In such a situation, the very policy of reservation loses its meaning and validity. It is suggested that the government takes appropriate measures to overcome these problems. The elected representatives from the tribal region should educate the government about these fundamental hardships of tribal children.

It is evident that in the quagmire of poverty, they prefer immediate gains to long-term benefits that accrue to their children after a continuous schooling of 10 to 15 years. They are under the false impression that the schooling eats away their economic fruits. Therefore, need-based or job-oriented education is an effective alternative to the existing monotonous and unproductive education. In the interviews, we found from the settlers that their children could not reach higher echelons of society because of the psychological barriers they suffer from. For this, revamping the present school set-up on ashram or gurukula type would make a considerable difference. Trained teachers and well-equipped schools would be a significant factor in moulding the personalities of children in these colonies. This is what we have observed in Siddhapuram settlement. There is no proper schooling for the children. Hence, no advancement is found in that settlement.

There should be a major drive to eradicate illiteracy among these people. It goes without saying that any positive change in their attitude towards earning their livelihood, necessarily drives them towards a positive realisation of the important aspect like education. The aim of social education can best be achieved only when feelings of deprivation, discrimination and aloofness are erased from their minds. A dynamic group of young volunteers and social workers will have to shoulder the responsibility of disseminating enlightened ideas among these people.

Today, there is a strong objection raised regarding the pathetic conditions of education and educational institutions prevailing in the settlement schools. The status of Andhra Pradesh in respect of these tribes stands in unique contrast to the rest of the country. There are social and behavioural changes taking place among the members of the Denotified Tribal Settlement areas in Andhra Pradesh. The Denotified Tribal Settlements such as Stuartpuram, Sitanagaram (Guntur district), Kapparallatippa and Bitragunta (Nellore district), Siddhapuram (Kurnool district) and Lingala (Mahaboobnagar district) Settlements constitute a major segment of the total scheduled tribe population in Andhra Pradesh. In all these settlement areas Yerukulas, Woddars, Katheras, Chenchus, Sugalis, Yanadis and other nomadic tribes form a major part of population. Some of the settlers are still having some serious problems of crime and illiteracy. On the whole, the scenario in Andhra Pradesh offers contrast on any comparison.

One of the main problems identified by the field experiences and the field survey is about the social treatment meted out to the families of these tribes. For generations together, the families and their members have been labelled as criminals, thus suffering dishonour and social negligence. The reasons are not far to seek given the background of the socially despicable avocation as practised by some of the people belonging to these tribes. The children and women, in particular, have suffered ignominy from mainstream society. The stigma of criminality is still one of the major impediments in the smooth run of educational progress of children and youth. Children often faced a kind of social alienation in most of the walks of social life. Social alienation, particularly in young age, hampers the growth of psycho-social faculties of the children. Social practices of the mainstream society have denied opportunities for the children coming from the so-called criminal families residing in the settlement areas. The approaches of the government often times, remain impersonal and lack human element and eye on social cohesiveness, in its approach. However, there can be education without even the formal modes and methods of schooling. But mere efforts on mainstream socialisation do not open wide social canvas for the children because there is already a hostile attitude in the outside society. The school or the process of schooling in settlement areas or settlement schools may be used as instruments or tools to impart social culture, feelings of common fraternity, community approach, adjustment mentality, atmosphere of working and learning together and finally, moral dynamics of social and cultural behaviour. The schools in settlement areas are to be treated or perceived from a different angle where they are expected to combine the role of an instructor, and change agent.

Profiles of Schools (Pen-Pictures of Primary Schools) in Settlements

The following is the situational analysis of Primary School facilities and educational needs of DNT settlement schools of Andhra Pradesh:

Salvation Army Aided Primary School, Stuartpuram, Guntur District

This school was established by a Missionary group, viz. Salvation Army and later the Government of Andhra Pradesh provided aid and presently it is functioning as an aided primary school. It is a two-teacher school. Both the teachers are not residing in the same school village but are residing in places up to a distance of 4 to 5 kilometres. Table 6 shows the details of roll of the school at present.

The strength in each class is low, ranging from 15 to 24. On the whole, the number of male students is more than the number of female students except in class IV. Multigrade teaching is going on in the school and the head teacher is taking classes I to III and the assistant teacher is taking classes IV and V. Instead of subject teacher system, class teacher system is adopted. Children are provided free textbooks and mid-day meals. No other incentives are enjoyed by the pupils. Except for the teachers, there is no furniture for students. The school and classrooms do not possess the minimum required equipment. Teacher grant and school grant are provided and from the school grant a radio was purchased and the students are exposed to radio lessons. Daily school assembly is organised and news is read. The children need to be exposed to moral education stories, wise sayings, etc. Further, there is need to organise activities which develop honesty among the children. The school is situated in a place having railway line on one side and road on the other side. It is not accessible to children in the sense that parents are afraid of sending their children to school for fear of accidents. The school is being run in a tiled building having five rooms. Only two rooms are under use and the other three are vacant. The roof leaks and needs immediate repairs. Neither the aided management, nor the government which is providing aid is looking after the repairs of the building. Because of craze towards English medium education, many parents are sending their children to nearby towns, wherein conveyance facility by school bus or auto or riksha is available. There is no compound wall to the school and no garden and no demarcated playground. Only open space is used as playground. Socially useful productive work (SUPW) activities are also not given the required attention in the school.

Table 6

Strength of Salvation Army Aided Primary School, Stuartpuram, 2006–07

	Boys	*Girls*	*Total*
I Class	10	10	20
II Class	10	05	15
III Class	11	06	16
IV Class	07	10	17
V Class	16	08	24
Total	54	39	93

Some children belonging to well-to-do families are studying elsewhere and a few children whose parents are very poor, are left out and they need to be enrolled. Limited play material is available with the school, like skipping ropes, rings, etc. Last year (2005–06), about 20 students who completed class V were admitted to class VI in the High School situated in the same village. Some of the problems faced by the teachers are as follows: (i) repairs needed in the school building and lack of compound wall, (ii) lack of equipment, like furniture for students, (iii) lack of medical aid, (iv) lack of learning aids and play materials, (v) lack of sanitation facilities, (vi) absence of students for long periods because of the harassment of their parents by the police. The students are psychologically depressed because of this and are not able to attend the school and concentrate on their studies, (vii) lack of facilities for organisation of SUPW activities, (viii) owing to social stigma attached to the community, the educated children are neither employed nor able to support themselves and so there is a chance of reverting back to the old practice of thefts and robberies, and (ix) early childcare education centre (ECE) is not present in the school campus.

Table 7

Population Details of the Settlement (Colony)

	Males	*Females*	*Total*
Population	661	688	1349
School-age children	139	143	282
Enrolled children	54	39	93
Remaining children	85	104	189

In view of the present conditions of education prevailing in the colony the following are some of the suggestions that can be made to improve condition of the school: (i) to provide for close supervision facilities by the Department of Education/Tribal Welfare to the teachers, (ii) to provide facilities for the organisation of SUPW activities, (iii) to organise such activities which develop honesty among the students, (iv) arrange extension lecture by local educated youth and others who are employed, (v) in the broader interest of the village the solution lies with the voluntary organisations of the specific programmes, (vi) formation of co-operatives for providing self-support to the settlers (villagers) such as milk cows, mushroom growth, autos, piggery, cashew plantation growth, etc. (vii) establishment of industries by inviting the interested industrialists which provide employment opportunities to the settlers in the settlement itself, (viii) some of the NGOs (Samskar) should think of these programmes in the interest of the settlers, (ix) convert these settlement schools as Ashram schools and introduce vocational courses, (x) provide incentive facilities more in number like uniforms, writing materials, etc. and finally, (xi) lack of safety to girl students. Therefore, security measures should be adopted for the welfare of the girl children also.

Government Denotified Tribal Elementary School, Siddhapuram, Kurnool District

This school was established by the British Government during the year 1913 for the benefit of DNT children and Table 8 presents the strength of the school during the year 2006.

Table 8

Strength of the School in Siddhapuram (2006)

Class	*Boys*	*Girls*	*Total*
I	13	18	31
II	18	23	41
III	17	2	29
IV	16	06	22
V	10	10	20
Total	74	69	143

In lower classes, the strength of girls is more than that of the boys. The school-age population (children 5–11 age group) of the village is 168. Yet, 25 pupils are to be enrolled in the school during the year 2006. The population of the village is 571 males and 564 females with the total of 1,135. The literacy rate of the village is 34 per cent. This is a four-teacher school. Class teacher system is followed in the school in place of subject teacher system. Only one teacher is incharge of multiple class teaching; he is handling classes III and IV. None of the teachers are residing in the school village. All are residing outside school village. Some are residing at a distance of 10 kms and some at a distance of 5 kms. The school is being run in three buildings (two RCC (reinforced concrete cement) buildings and one tiled old building.) The tiled old building wherein class I is located needs immediate repairs. The two RCC buildings have a verandah and one room each in which two classes each are located. There is no furniture for the pupils and it is available only to teachers. Playground is available in the school. No equipment is available to the school. Teacher grant and school grant are provided to the school. It is reported that the major occupation of the villagers is illegal preparation of arrack. Even the students are involved in the preparation and transportation of the same. The dire need of the village is to have an upper primary school. The girls are afraid of going to nearby upper primary schools because of eve-teasing and lack of social security. The village needs area-specific programmes. Some of the areas in which some industries can be established are sericulture, match stick industry, weaving gauge clothes, honey collection and preservation, *beedi* leaf collection, bamboo work, etc. Some NGOs can come forward and help the local villagers in their development and self-support. SUPW scheme needs special care and attention in the school to train students to support themselves in life.

Bitragunta Salvation Army Government Upper Primary School, Kapparallathippa, Bogole Mandal, Nellore District

This is an upper primary school with seven classes and strength of the school during the year 2006 is as given in Table 9.

The population of the village is 640 men and 660 women: 1,300 people. There are about 10 children yet to be enrolled in the school. None of the teaching staff are residing in the school village. The headmaster and some teachers are coming from a distance of 20 km and others are residing at a distance of about 2 kms. The headmaster is incharge of classes VI and VII and the others are teaching one class each. Class teacher system is in vogue in the school. The school is being run in three buildings – a tiled one, an asbestos roofed one and an RCC building. All the three buildings need repairs. Up to class V, furniture is available for students. The school needs equipment and aids. Teacher grants and school grants are also received by the school. The following are the problems of the school: lack of equipment and AV aids (audio-visual aids), upgradation to High School and eve-teasing. Social security is also needed for girls in the colony.

Table 9

Strength of the School, 2006

Class	*Boys*	*Girls*	*Total*
I	22	27	49
II	16	16	32
III	08	13	21
IV	03	11	14
V	09	17	26
VI	04	12	16
VII	08	09	17
Total	70	125	175

Government Upper Primary School, Sitanagaram Colony, Tadepalli Mandal, Guntur District

The school was established by the erstwhile British Government during the year 1916. The Government of Andhra Pradesh provided the aid under Social Tribal Welfare Department. Presently, the school is managed by Tribal Welfare Department, Government of Andhra Pradesh. The school has the strength of nine teachers, viz. two B.Ed. qualified teachers, five secondary grade teachers and two pandits. The following is the details of the enrolment of DNT children of the colony during the year 2006.

Subject teacher system, class teacher system is going on. Children from other communities, such as Christians, Muslims and Hindu caste groups are undergoing instruction simultaneously with the DNT group children. The DNT (tribal) children are not provided free textbooks, uniforms, notebooks, scholarships, mid-day meals, etc. Other incentives are also not provided by the government to the school so far. The children have to sit on the floor. Furniture is not available to the students. The school building had collapsed. The school does not possess the minimum equipment and aid. The settlement population are scattered in three areas Tadepalli 1st Ward, Tadepalli 2nd Ward and Annapurna Devi Nagar. The well-to-do family settlers are sending their children to the nearby English medium schools. Some elderly girls who dropped out of the school were provided tailoring work in the school. The headmaster is handling maths and science subjects for all classes. Teaching Learning Material (TLM) grant, though provided, is still not utilised by the headmaster.

Table 10

Strength of DNT Children in Sitanagaram School

Class	*Boys*	*Girls*	*Total*
I	1	2	3
II	1	1	2
III	2	1	3
IV	2	2	4
V	1	3	4
VI	1	1	2
VII	0	0	0

Conclusion

The social conditions, living standards, income and educational level of the tribal people living in these settlements are much below than the conditions of non-tribal people living in Andhra Pradesh. Lack of census data, absence of policy-level discussions on DNTs, treatment of DNT issues seems outside the purview of Planning Commission estimates (always Primitive Tribal Groups (PTGs) other than DNTs are covered), weak community participation in the settlements or colonies and lack of need-based training (contextual) given to teachers teaching in settlement schools, are some of the gaps identified during the visit of the settlements which are seriously affecting the progress of the DNTs in their colonies.

A complete and comprehensive survey conducted in the five settlements hints at the establishment of separate schools with English as the medium of instruction. Many of the reformed parents in the selected settlements wish to send their wards to schools at different places. For, they perceive English medium of instruction as one important tool of mainstream social integration. The NGOs working in the settlements look for a time bound tie-up between Regional Institute of Education (RIE)/National Council of Educational Research and Training (NCERT) and wish to ground a separate school with an eye on social integration. NGOs also expressed their wish to shoulder the responsibility of land procurement, construction, recruitment, school infrastructure and admissions of students from settlements (also from non-settlement areas of the surrounding settlements). The NGOs are also looking at RIE/NCERT or similar apex educational bodies for help in training the teachers. The NGOs should be in a position to shoulder complete responsibility of the education of the DNT children. The future tie-up will be confined to teacher training and teaching aid support from RIE/NCERT or similar institution. A comprehensive census data collection may be undertaken in all the existing settlement areas by the NCERT as a part of educational survey reports, Programme Advisory Committe (PAC)/Educational Research Innovative Committee (ERIC) programmes. To undertake advocacy campaign and networking meets with government departments and NCERT so that issues and problems of these tribes in transition will be put on the agenda of general discussion on tribal welfare. In view of the above analysis, few suggestions can be made to improve the educational scenario of the denotified tribes of Andhra Pradesh:

1. The government has to conduct sample surveys to know about their present position pertaining to the present state of literacy achievement levels of the DNT children in primary schools.
2. They should be provided with jobs which give them immediate remuneration and relief. Some of them who are minimum educated, may be recruited into the departments of police as constables, water boys and sweepers.
3. Educational facilities as they exist today are not adequate. A few more schools may be established and all these schools should be provided with necessary infrastructural facilities.
4. Rigid enforcement of the provisions of the Compulsory Primary Education Act is highly essential. The government should issue strict orders to various school boards to enforce primary education in schools situated in areas where the members of DNT are residing in considerable number.
5. Free coaching centres should be opened in these colonies for educated unemployed youth. Coaching facilities should be provided for the students of both technical and general courses.
6. Best sports persons are available among these denotified tribe children. Physical education should be improved and special training facilities should be provided to make them national and state level players, etc.

Notes

1. The teachers were supplied clothing, rations and all sorts of contingency grants. A special pay, unhealthy locality allowance of ₹ 5 per month was sanctioned to the assistant teachers in Siddhapuram elementary school. The higher elementary grade teachers were placed in the scale of ₹

27-1-1-50 from 1 April 1932. ₹ 10 were paid as unhealthy locality allowance from 1 April 1932. See Public Works (Labour) Department, G.O. No. 1675 dated 9 August 1932, pp. 1–2, APSA.

2. Of the 76 children at the settlement, 23 boys and 17 girls attended the school. The average attendance was 19 for the whole year 1924. See Note Showing the Progress Made in the Settlements of Criminal Tribes in the Madras Presidency upto January 1926, Madras, 1927, p. 30, AP State Gazetteers Office, Hyderabad.
3. Public Works (Labour) Department, G.O. No. 137 dated 19 January 1927, p. 5, APSA. The children are kept away from their parents. The younger children are sent home at night. Others sleep in the school building. Also See Public Works (Labour) Department, G.O. No. 1719, dated 9 August 1927, p. 2, APSA.
4. Home Department, G.O. No. 3557 dated 6 September 1937, pp. 1–3, National Archives of India (NAI).
5. Public Works (Labour) Department, G.O. No. 2190 dated 28 July 1930, p. 7–13, (APSA)
6. Public Works (Labour) Department, G.O. No. 2671 dated 6 December 1934, p. 5, Andhra Pradesh State Archives.
7. Home Department, G.O. No. 6170 dated 22 December 1938, p. 36, NAI.
8. Public Works Labour Department, G.O. No. 2671 dated 6 December 1934, p. 6, Andhra Pradesh state Archives.
9. Home Department, G.O. No. 6170 dated 22 December 1938, p. 3, NAI.
10. Ibid.
11. Home Department, G.O. No. 149, dated 11 January 1947, pp. 1–2, NAI.
12. The strength of the school improved after the internment of Golla Kuppam Dasarees. After passing V Standard, the children were sent to Kurnool for studies. See Administration Report on Kallar Reclamation, Korava Reclamation, Criminal Tribes settlements and Yanadi Reclamation for the year 1947–48, Madras, 1949, p. 13.
13. Home (Judicial) Department, G.O. No. 2074, 18 August 1916, p. 4, Tamil Nadu State Archives.
14. Home (Judicial) Department, G.O. No. 1225, 20 May 1918, p. 6, TNA.
15. Op. cit., p. 6.
16. Mildred Mackenzie, The Mud Bank, Pennsylvania, 1959, p. 12.
17. Law (General) Department (Annual Report), G.O. No. 3187, 14 November 1924, p. 3, APSA.
18. Ibid.
19. The two unpassed teachers were sent up for the sessional school. See, Home (Judicial) Department, G.O. No. 1225 dated 20 May 1918, p. 6.
20. Law (General) Department, G.O. No. 1714, 22 October 1921, p. 4, APSA.
21. Settlers criticised that it was cruel to separate the children from their parents. The SA made the parents to understand that the separation was

done to enable them to get in future an honest employment. The parents put forward no objections. However, we can note that both Mabe and Robilliard were strongly opposed to the separation of children from their parents. They did not object for the boarding schools in the settlement where the parents were allowed to see the children under supervision. See, Home (Judicial) Department, G.O. No. 1759, 5 August 1918, p. 1, TNA.

22. Law (General) Department, G.O. No. 2267, 16 June 1925, p. 2, APSA.
23. PWLD, G.O. No. 2338, dated 19 August 1930, p. 2, APSA.
24. Ibid.
25. Law (General) Department, G.O. No. 3187, 14 November 1924, p. 3, APSA.
26. Law (General) Department, G.O. No. 1907, 15 June 1925, p. 1, APSA.
27. Law (General) Department, G.O. No. 2267, 16 July 1925, p. 2, APSA.
28. PWLD G.O. No. 1551, 20 July 1927, p. 6, APSA.
29. PWLD G.O. No. 2061, dated 21 August 1928, p. 1, APSA.
30. PWLD G.O. No. 1926, dated 30 July 1931, p. 2, APSA
31. PWLD G.O. No. 1313 dated 17 June 1932, p. 7, APSA.
32. Ibid.
33. Booth Tucker said that, 'If a man wished to marry one of the girls in the settlement he had to come into the settlement and live there'. Gillman pointed out that the proposed husband would in the majority of cases, be already a member of the tribe. Home (Judicial) Department, G.O. No. 1759, 5 August 1918, pp. 13–17, APSA.
34. Home (Judicial) Department, G.O. No. 1639, 8 August 1917, p. 2, TNA.
35. The Scouts went to the camp during the year 1931 for 5 days and enjoyed the outing. See, PWLD G.O. No. 1313, 17 June 1932, p. 6, APSA.
36. Home Department, G.O. No. 1571, 21 April 1947, p. 1, NAI.
37. Home Department, G.O. No. 1508, 21 March 1938, p. 1, NAI.
38. Home Department, G.O. No. 1571, 21 April 1947, p. 1, NAI.
39. Home Department, G.O. No. 1571, 21 April 1946, p. 1, NAI.
40. Interview with the Headmistress, Stuartpuram High School dated 6 February 2006.
41. Ibid.
42. Interview with The Manager of Stuartpuram settlement, Stuartpuram dated 2 February 2006.
43. Report of the Commissioner for Scheduled Castes and Scheduled Tribes for the year 1962–1974.
44. L.M. Sreekant Report of the Commissioner for Scheduled Castes and Scheduled Tribes for the year 1953, 3rd Report, New Delhi, 1954, p. 200.
45. L.M. Sreekant, Report of the Commissioner for Scheduled castes and Scheduled Tribes for the year 1954, 4th Report, New Delhi, 26 February 1955, p. 232.

46. Adivasi, Issue No. 9 and 10 dated 15 December 1962 and 15 January 1963, p. 1.

47. Adivasi (Telugu monthly) Published by R. Nagaiah, Vol. 10, Nos. 9 and 10, Guntur dated 15 December 1962 and dated 15 January 1963, p. 1.

48. *Kallumunta* is a ballad. The authors of the work are Ponna Koteswara Rao and Ponna Satyanarayana. It was published in 1950. *Rama Rajyam* is another ballad on Yerukulas by Ponna Koteswara Rao. It was published by Jayanti Publications, Vijayawada during the year 1960. These two sources, though valuable, are out of print today. The two important sources give detailed information of the culture of Yerukulas, how they perform their marriages. They also provide information on the general conditions in the settlements. *Adivasi Patrika* is a Telugu monthly published by Rameswaram Nagaiah from Guntur in 1943. Each issue was priced at 1 anna and the annual subscription rate was ₹ 1. *Yerukula Patrika* was published by Kampa Punnaiah during the year 1943. *Dalit Marg* was another monthly by Ponna Koteswara Rao. Some other papers of the same kind were *Girijana Jyoti* and *Yekalavya*. Due to financial crisis, these publications were stopped from 1980 onwards.

5

Factors Affecting Literacy of Denotified Tribes' Children in Schools

The Context of the Study

In the state of Andhra Pradesh there are 35 tribes living in different parts of the state. The Denotified Tribes constitute a major segment of the total Scheduled Tribes population. Some of the Denotified Tribes are living in the hilly areas, some are living in the forest areas, some are leading nomadic lives wandering from place to place to eke out their livelihood. But the tribal communities coming under the specific nomenclature 'Denotified Tribal Settlements' in Andhra Pradesh at present are only five in number. The social conditions, living standards, income and educational level of the DNTs living in these settlements are much below the conditions of tribal and non-tribal people living in Andhra Pradesh. This fact remains as a grim reminder to the more privileged sections of people in spite of the efforts and huge amount of money allocated and spent by the government over the years and in spite of the efforts put in by the missionary groups such as Salvation Army and other Christian voluntary organisations, NGOs, etc. Whatever be their present condition, the future of the tribal people lies in their children, especially in the education imparted to them. It is in this context that the present study has been undertaken focusing on the school education which they receive in the primary schools, the achievement (success in school subjects) attained by them and various factors and problems which affect their academic achievement and overall development.

One primary school is available (Classes 1 to 5) in each tribal settlement for the children to attend. The schools with higher classes (Upper Primary Schools and High Schools in most of these settlements) are situated several kilometres away and hence only a few are able to pursue and continue their school education. Thus, the education which they receive in these Lower Primary Schools lays the foundation for their entire future life. Therefore, a study like this becomes relevant and necessary to enquire into the factors and problems affecting the learning of these tribal children and to review the current status of education of the DNTs in the present scenario and to suggest possible solutions and remedial measures.

Preparation for the Study (before data collection)[1]

A summary of the planning done for the study, the context of the present study and variables included are given below.

Preliminary Discussions with Tribal Welfare Department Authorities and Education Experts

Correct and reliable information was gathered from the Tribal Welfare Department authorities Tribal Cultural Research & Training Institute (TCR & TI) Hyderabad, State Education Department Authorities: Sarva Shiksha Abhiyan and State Council of Educational Research and Training (SSA and SCERT) faculty and state education experts (from the universities) regarding the tribal communities coming under the label of Denotified Tribal Communities and Settlements (Colonies) in the State of Andhra Pradesh. Though there are presently 33 tribal communities (two more communities are added to the list) living in the hill areas, agency tracts, plain areas and thick forests it was found that 59 sects were classified/noted under 'Denotified Tribes/Communities' living in Denotified Tribal Settlements (DNTS). They are predominantly living in the selected five settlements:

1. Siddhapuram settlement in Kurnool district
2. Bitragunta (Kapparalla Tippa) settlement, Nellore district
3. Stuartpuram settlement, Guntur district
4. Sitanagaram settlement, Guntur district
5. Lingala settlement, Mahaboob Nagar district

The Denotified Tribes presently living in these settlements are Yerukulas, Woddaras, Katheras, Sigalis (Limbadis) and Yanadis. The Yerukulas were called as Koravas in Tamil Nadu, the Woddaras were categorised under BCA category and the Yanadis are still under primitive tribal conditions. The Katheras were also called as Woddars in some places like Nellore, Kurnool districts and the Sugalis are the plain tribes in Andhra Pradesh.

Library Consultancy

From libraries in Mysore and Hyderabad (Anthropological Survey of India, Mysore and State Archives and Research Institute, Taranaka, Hyderabad) relevant literature, information was gathered regarding the DNT communities. Discussions with experienced state education experts at Hyderabad and Regional Institute of Education experts at Mysore were made to identify on the workable activities of the project.

Pilot Study

Based on their valuable suggestions regarding identification of the schools in the settlements, population statistics, socio-economic conditions of the settlers, the present conditions of the schools and education imparted to the children, a pilot study was conducted. After a visit to these tribal settlements, the principal investigator got the following preliminary information. There is one primary school with classes I to V in each of these five tribal settlements. Two of the schools (Government Upper Primary School, Bitragunta and Government Upper Primary DNT School, Sitanagaram settlement, Tadepalli) have classes I to VII. Thus, the total number of five schools (the population itself) was taken for the present study rather than a sample of two or three schools out of five. And the entire population of 452 students in these five schools was included in the study.

List of Schools Identified

1. Government DNT Elementary School Siddhapuram, Atmakur Mandal, Kurnool District.
2. Government Bitragunta Salvation Army Upper Primary School, Bogole Mandal, Kapparallatippa, Nellore District.
3. Salvation Army Aided Primary School, Stuartpuram, Bapatla Mandal, Guntur District.
4. Government Upper Primary, DNT School, Sitanagaram settlement, Tadepalli Mandal, Guntur District.
5. Subhash Chandra Bose Government Primary School and Library, Achammapeta Mandal, Mahaboob Nagar District.

Visit to DNT Settlements, Schools and Gathering Preliminary Data

All the selected five schools' head teachers were contacted and preliminary data regarding students' enrollment, retention and dropouts were gathered. Primary information about the problems relating to the schools, habitation, personality of the children, head teachers, teachers, parents, community participants, school records, school health programmes, achievements of the children in the school and curriculum related information were gathered. The photographs of the schools, some students, teachers, and habitation were taken. Looking at them will provide first-hand information of the conditions prevailing in these DNT schools (Appended at the end of the chapter).

Identification of Education Experts for the Preparation of Tools

Prior to preparation of the tools, discussions were made with the senior faculty of the RIE, Mysore, Principal and Dean of Instruction regarding the preparation of the tools for data collection and to study the prevailing situation of tribal education in DNT settlement schools. A five-day workshop was also organised at SCERT, Hyderabad, from 24–28 June 2006. Discussion was carried out with the retired RIE senior faculty members for the possible preparation of tools. Experts from SSA, Hyderabad, University Faculty, (Central University, Hyderabad),

SCERT Faculty, NGOs (Samskar, Varni, Nizamabad) who are working presently in the settlements, Tribal Welfare Department Authorities (TCR & TI) and the head teachers of the schools were identified and they were involved in the preparation of tools.

Workshop for the Preparation of Tools

A five-day workshop was organised at State Council of Educational Research and Training (SCERT), Hyderabad, from 24–28 June 2006. Elaborate discussions were done by the experts on the present conditions of the DNTs in Andhra Pradesh and after detailed discussions a total number of 11 tools were prepared and finalised with the assistance of head teachers working in schools and state education experts.

Selection of Tools

The following tools were prepared and used in order to gather data required for the study.

Tools to Assess Students' Performance[2]

Achievement Tests in Telugu Classes I to V

A test in Telugu (maximum marks: 15) to assess the achievement of tribal students in class I was prepared. Similarly, achievement tests in Telugu for class II (maximum marks: 15), class III (maximum marks: 20), class IV (maximum marks: 30) and class V (maximum marks: 35) were prepared. Thus, the total number of achievement tests constructed in Telugu was five. They were prepared with the assistance of the head teachers of the five schools and experts by using the State Government textbooks currently used in the schools.

Achievement Tests in EVS Classes I to V

An achievement test in Environmental Science to assess the achievement of tribal students in class I (maximum marks: 25), class II (maximum marks: 30), class III (maximum marks: 50), class IV (maximum marks: 50) and class V (maximum marks: 50) were prepared by the head teachers and experts based on the state prescribed textbooks for the schools.

Achievement Tests in Maths Classes I to V

The achievement tests in Mathematics to assess the achievement of tribal students in class I (maximum marks: 10), class II (maximum marks: 20), class III (maximum marks: 20), class IV (maximum marks: 50) and class V (maximum marks: 35) were prepared by the head teachers and experts by using the state prescribed textbooks.

Attitude Test to Assess the Attitude (or Behavioural Pattern) of the Tribal Children

Attitude Test to assess the behavioural patterns (desirable and undesirable) of the students studying from classes III to V was prepared by head teachers with the help of state education experts.

Tools to Assess Other Variables

School Schedule

The school schedule was prepared to gather data regarding furniture available, compound wall, drinking water facility, toilets for teachers and students (male and female), teaching aids, etc.

School Record Schedule

School record schedule was prepared to gather data regarding school management, student teacher strength, instructional time, number of teachers (male and female), school facilities such as teaching-learning material, audio material, kits, books, newspapers, charts, tables, etc.

Questionnaire for Head Teachers

(a) The questionnaire was prepared to gather data regarding the enrolment of children from classes I to V, number of school-going children and (b) Regarding their perception/opinion about the students.

Teachers' Schedule

This was prepared to gather data regarding qualifications, training, teaching process, teacher opinion on tribal children, medium of instruction, etc.

Classroom Observation Schedule

This tool was prepared to gather data regarding engagement of classes, i.e. single, multiple class, preparation for the class, lessons taught, use of teaching, learning material and use of kits, charts, etc.

Interview Schedule for Parents (Focus Group Discussion)

Parents schedule is prepared to collect data regarding literacy level of parents, occupation, economic position of parents and their opinion on children's education, etc.

Habitation Schedule

The habitation schedule is prepared to gather data regarding the total number of families, school age and school-going children, literacy levels of the DNTs in the habitation, facilities of the habitation such as roads, electricity, drinking water and children attending the school from nearby villages, etc.

The above 11 tools were prepared and printed both in English and Telugu. The same tools were photocopied into the required number for the implementation and to gather the required information from the selected schools. The head teachers were also informed about the field survey in the selected schools and they accepted the use of the tools in the schools.

Selection of Sample and Sampling Techniques Used

The present study is a census survey covering entire population (with respect to the topic related) of all the schools in the DNT settlements – not a sample survey of two or three schools out of five and some students out of the total population of 452 students (see Table 1). Hence, descriptive statistics and tables and graphs have been used in data analysis.

Table 1

Sample Table of Boys and Girls Strength in five DNT Settlement Schools

Sl. No.	*Schools (Boys and Girls)*	*Number of students*											
		Class 1		*Class 2*		*Class 3*		*Class 4*		*Class 5*		*Total*	
		B	*G*	*B*	*G*	*B*	*G*	*B*	*G*	*B*	*G*	*B*	*G*
1	Government DNT Elementary School, Siddhapuram, Kurnool District	13	19	18	24	16	6	18	12	11	10	76	71
2	Government BRS Upper Primary School, Bitragunta, Nellore District	18	28	15	15	6	14	3	11	8	13	50	81
3	Government UP DNT School, Sitanagaram Colony, Tadepalli, Guntur District	1	2	1	1	2	1	2	2	1	3	7	9
4	Salvation Army Aided Elementary School, Stuartpuram (Betapudi), Bapatla, Guntur District	6	6	2	6	9	6	4	7	13	6	34	31
5	Subash Chandra Bose Government DNT Primary School, Lingala, Mahaboobnagar District	10	10	10	5	11	6	7	10	16	8	54	39
	Total	48	65	46	51	44	33	34	42	49	40	452	

With respect to parents, only a sample of 50 parents of children studying in the five schools, taking 10 parents from each settlement, was used for collecting data.

Interventions

The present investigation is a survey study to find out the existing status/condition(s) of the schooling and achievement of Denotified Tribal Children in the primary schools and the factors which affect negatively their learning, etc. Thus, no intervention is envisaged within the ambit of the present study to promote their scholastic achievements (which can be another study).

Data Collection and Scoring

All the 11 tests/tools were administered in the five schools where the DNT settlement children are studying. The tools used for gathering data are of two types:

A: Tests administered to the school children.

B: Questionnaires administered to the headmasters, teachers, parents and community leaders.

A Type: Tests

1. Test to assess the achievement of students in Telugu.
2. Test to assess the achievement of students in Environmental Science.
3. Test to assess the achievement of students in Mathematics.
   These three tests were administered to all the tribal children studying in classes I to V in all the five schools.
4. Test to assess the Attitude (or Behavioural Pattern) of the students – administered to students of classes III, IV and V in all the five schools.

B Type: Questionnaires/Schedules

5. School Schedule.
6. School Record Schedule.
   Both these tools (5 and 6) were filled in by the head teachers and they contained detailed information regarding the school: infrastructure, staff, incentives/support received from the government, etc.
7. Questionnaire for head teachers to gather information about the functioning of the schools: number of classes, students, teachers, facilities, special provision for ST students, etc. in each of these five schools – administered to the head teachers and data was gathered.
8. Teachers' Schedule used to collect information about the teachers, their qualification, experience and to elicit their opinion/ perception regarding various aspects of the teaching-learning process prevailing in the schools.

9. Classroom Observation Schedule: Through direct observation of some classes while teaching was going on, actual data regarding the teaching-learning process, single class teaching, multigrade teaching, etc. were recorded using this tool.
10. Interview Schedule for Parents (Focus Group Discussion): The responses of parents to the items in this schedule were gathered to find out (a) their literacy level, occupation, economic condition, etc. and (b) their opinion about the learning and education process of their children, reasons for dropout children and about the functioning of the schools. This was administered to a total of 50 parents, taking 10 parents of children in each of the five schools.
11. Habitation Schedule: This was administered to gather data regarding the total number of families, school-age children and school-going children, facilities in the habitation such as roads, drinking water, electricity, etc. in order to understand the living conditions of the children and parents in their habitats.

These 11 tools were administered and data gathered to meet the objectives of the present project.

Scoring

The maximum marks scorable in each test is as shown in Table 2:

Table 2

Maximum Marks in Tests

Subject	*Class 1*	*Class 2*	*Class 3*	*Class 4*	*Class 5*
Telugu	15	15	20	30	35
Environmental Science	25	30	50	50	50
Mathematics	10	20	20	50	35
Total	50	65	90	130	120
Attitude Test	–	–	10	10	10

But for the purpose of analysis, the maximum score in each test was converted to 30 and the total in the three subjects came to 90. This was done for the five classes in order to facilitate inter-subject comparisons and between class comparisons.

Grouping of Students

Three subjects: Out of the total of 90 marks scorable in the tests for Telugu, Environmental Science and Mathematics put together, each student has scored a particular mark (obtained score) – may be 10, 25, 32, 45, 56, ... up to 70, 80 or any mark up to the total 90. Accordingly, the performance of students in each class has been classified into five groups based on the range of marks obtained by each student as shown in Table 3.

Table 3

Performance Categories in Total of three Subjects

Sl. No.	*Category*	*Range of marks out of 90*
1	Group–1: Very Poor	0 to 12.9 (14.33%)
2	Group–2: Poor	13 (14.44%) to 31.4 (34.88%)
3	Group–3: Average	31.5 (35%) to 49 (54.44%)
4	Group–4: Good	49.1 (54.55%) to 64 (71.11%)
5	Group–5: Very Good	64.1 (71.22%) to 90 (100%)

In the next section: Data Analysis, the number of students in each class, coming under these five categories, has been presented.

Attitude Test: Scoring and Grouping of Students

There are 10 items in this test to assess the Attitude or Behavioural Pattern of the students. Based on the response of each student, each item is scored 1 or 0 – which means a student can score a maximum of 10 marks. Based on this quantification or score, the students have been grouped into three categories, as shown in Table 4:

Table 4

Grouping of Students on Attitude

Sl.No.	*Category*	*Range of marks out of total 10*
1	Negative attitude	0 to 3 marks
2	Positive attitude	4 to 6 marks
3	More positive attitude	7 to 10 marks

The number of students coming under each category in each class, data analysis, scoring, tabulation, data entry and analysis for all the tests mentioned above for students in classes I to V, was completed and the analysis with results are presented.

Analysis of Data, Statistics Used and Results[3]

The analysis of data was carried out using the computer software SPSS – after doing the appropriate paper tabulation, coding of variables and data entry.

Statistics Used[4]

The present study is a survey of all the schools and all students in every school coming under the nomenclature of Denotified Tribal Settlements (DNTS) in Andhra Pradesh. Thus, the census survey covering the entire population (with respect to the selected topic) of DNTS – not a sample survey, under which only two or three schools out of five and only some students out of the total might have been included. Hence *descriptive statistics* (mean, standard deviation, range, etc.) have been derived and presented (not inferential statistics like t-test, ANOVA, etc.) regarding the performance of students in the three school subjects. *Data summary* in the form of frequency tables, cross-tables and graphs have been used more in the analysis since they are very suitable for extensive survey type data gathered in this project. The analysis and results for each class – classes I to V – are presented in the following pages.

Class I

Class I: Performance of Students in Three Subjects

As already stated in the previous section, the test marks in the three subjects, Telugu, Environmental Science and Mathematics add up to 90 total (30 in each subject). A total of 113 students are studying in the five schools under DNTS. Their overall performance is shown by the values of *descriptive statistics* in Table 5:

Table 5

Class I: Descriptive Statistics – Three Subjects (90 Marks)

	N	*Range*	*Minimum*	*Maximum*	*Sum*	*Mean*	*Standard Deviation*
Total–Telugu, EVS and Maths–90 final	113	77	0	77	4636	41.03	21.320
Valid N (listwise)	113						

Descriptive Statistics: Class I

Discussion of Results: The mean achievement of 113 students in three subjects (Telugu, Environmental Science and Mathematics) out of a total of 90 marks is given as 41.03 (rounded to the second decimal place) which comes to 45.6 per cent. This average for the whole group comes between 40 per cent and 50 per cent and may be termed as average or medium performance. The fact that the marks are ranging from 0 to a maximum of 77 shows that it is a very heterogeneous group with poor students at one extreme and very bright students at the other.

Frequency Table – 5 Groups: Class I

Table 6 presents the frequency of students falling in five groups – group 1 to group 5 (very low marks to very high marks) – the details of grouping already presented in Table 3. The frequency table, Table 6, is discussed next.

Discussion: The values in Table 6 show that 38.1 per cent of students (20.4% + 17.7%) have performed in the group 4 and group 5 categories; 32.8 per cent (14.2% + 18.6%) in the low categories of group

1 and group 2 and 29.2 per cent in the middle/average category (group 3). This shows quite an even distribution of students when the categories are collapsed into three groups and also when five groups are considered.

Table 6

Class I: Three Subjects – Performance (90 marks)

	Frequency	*%*	*Valid %*	*Cumulative %*
Group 1: 0 to 12.9	16	14.2	14.2	14.2
Group 2: 13 to 31.4	21	18.6	18.6	32.7
Group 3: 31.5 to 49	33	29.2	29.2	61.9
Group 4: 49.1 to 64	23	20.4	20.4	82.3
Group 5: 64.1 to 90	20	17.7	17.7	100.0
Total	113	100.0	100.0	

Gender-wise Distribution in five Categories: Class I

Table 7 shows the male/female distribution of students in class I with respect to total performance in three subjects.

Table 7

Students' Gender Class 1–3 Subjects – Performance (90) Cross Tabulation

			Class I: Three Subjects – Performance (90)					*Total*
			Group 1	*Group 2*	*Group 3*	*Group 4*	*Group 5*	
Students' Gender	Boys	Count	10	9	10	11	8	48
		% within Students' Gender	20.8%	18.8%	20.8%	22.9%	16.7%	100.0%
	Girls	Count	6	12	23	12	12	65
		% within Students' Gender	9.2%	18.5%	35.4%	18.5%	18.5%	100.0%
Total		Count	16	21	33	23	20	113
		% within Students' Gender	14.2%	18.6%	29.2%	20.4%	17.7%	100.0%

Discussion: The cross-table shows that 39.6 per cent of boys have performed in the top categories of group 4 and group 5 while 37 per cent of girls are in the same top two categories, which shows that the performance of boys and girls are nearly equal in the higher categories. But in the lower two categories (group 1 and 2) there only 27.7 per cent of girls while the percentage of boys is 39.6 per cent which shows poor performance of boys when compared to girls.

The contingency coefficient (C) is used as a measure of association (or relation) between the two variables in a cross-table – which may also be called as a bivariate distribution. The low value of C, 0.2 in Table 8 shows that there is very little association or relation between the gender of students and their performance in the three subjects.

Table 8

Symmetric Measures

	Value	*Approx. Sig.*
Nominal by Nominal Contingency Coefficient	0.205	0.293
N of Valid Cases	113	

a. Not assuming the null hypothesis.
b. Using the asymptotic standard error assuming the null hypothesis.

Figure 1

Graph of Gender-wise Distribution

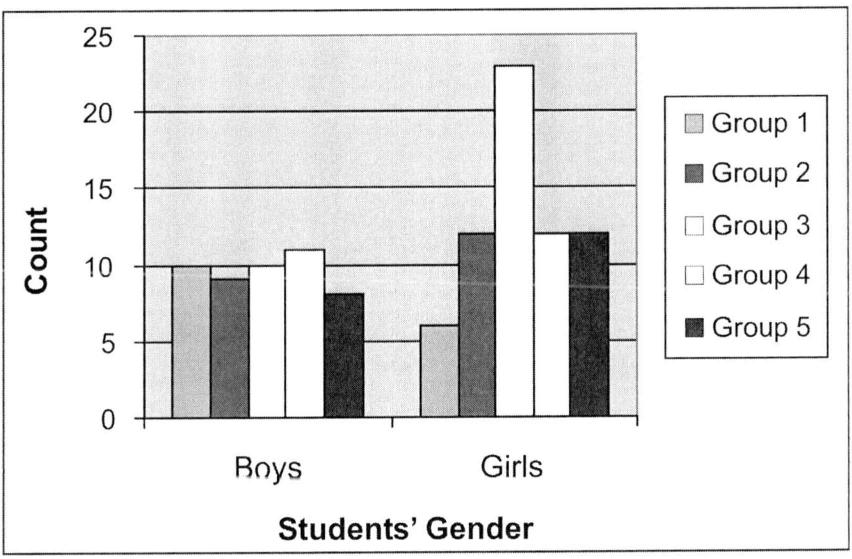

The graph, Figure 1, gives a visual representation of the gender-wise distributor (boys, girls) Table 7. The height of the third bar (girls) stands out showing better performance of girls (23) in group 3 compared to only 10 boys in group 3.

School-wise Distribution of Students in Five Groups: Class I

This is shown in Table 9. Out of five schools, one school, Government Upper Primary DNT School, Sitanagaram, has only three students and two of them are in group 4 and group 5 which shows good performance.

Of the remaining four schools, Subash Chandra Bose DNT School, Lingala tops in the performance of three subjects since 50 per cent of the students (35% and 15%) come in the top two categories (groups 4 and 5). Government Salvation Army UP School, Bitragunta (39.1%) and Government DNT Elementary School, Siddhapuram (34.4%), respectively, occupy the second and third ranks considering the percentage of students in groups 4 and 5. The Salvation Army Aided Elementary School, Stuartpuram, comes last in performance with 16.7 per cent of students in group 4 and none in group 5.

Table 9

Class I: Schools three Subjects–Performance (90) Cross Tabulation

		Class I: Three subjects – Performance (90)					*Total*
School		*Group 1*	*Group 2*	*Group 3*	*Group 4*	*Group 5*	
Government Elementary School, Siddhapuram	Count	3	5	13	6	5	32
	% within School	9.4%	15.6%	40.6%	18.8%	15.6%	100.0%
SA UP School, Bitragunta	Count	6	7	15	7	11	46
	% within School	13.0%	15.2%	32.6%	15.2%	23.9%	100.0%
Government UP School, Sitanagaram	Count	0	1	0	1	1	3
	% within School	0%	33.3%	0%	33.3%	33.3%	100.0%
SA Elementary School, Stuartpuram	Count	4	5	1	2	0	12
	% within School	33.3%	41.7%	8.3%	16.7%	0%	100.0%
S Bose Government Pr School, Lingala	Count	3	3	4	7	3	20
	% within School	15.0%	15.0%	20.0%	35.0%	15.0%	100.0%
Total	Count	16	21	33	23	20	113
	% within School	14.2%	18.6%	29.2%	20.4%	17.7%	100.0%

The contingency coefficient of 0.4 (value rounded to first decimal place) shows moderate association or relation between schools and the performance of students in the five categories, which is also supported by the school-wise discussion in the previous section. We may say that the performance of students or academic achievement in class I depends to some extent on the schools which they attend, assuming other factors equal.

Table 10

Symmetric Measures

	Value	*Approx. Sig.*
Nominal by Nominal Contingency Coefficient	389	0.216
N of Valid Cases	113	

a. Not assuming the null hypothesis.
b. Using the asymptotic standard error assuming the null hypothesis.

Figure 2

Graph of School-wise Distribution

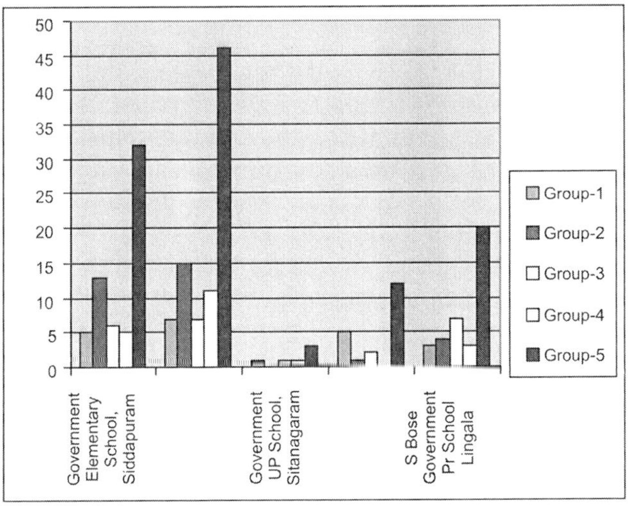

The graph shown in Figure 2 is self-explanatory. The performance of Subash Chandra Bose DNT Primary School, Lingala, is shown less here, because the graph shows the number of students; it does not show the percentage of students in groups which is more relevant while comparing the performance of different schools.

Comparison of Performance in Three Subjects: Class I

The performance of 113 students in five schools in three subjects is shown in Table 11. The maximum marks in each subject (Telugu,

Environmental Science and Mathematics) is 30. The performance in two subjects, Telugu and Mathematics, is nearly equal as shown by the means 14.3 and 14.6, respectively – but the level of performance in both is less than 50 per cent which is 15. The achievement in EVS is still lower: Mean 12.1.

Table 11

Class I: Summary of Performance in Three Subjects – Comparison

	Telugu (Marks 30)	*EVS (Marks 30)*	*Maths (Marks 30)*
Total N	113	113	113
Mean	14.34	12.064	14.63
Sum	1620	1363.2	1653
Minimum	0	0	0
Maximum	28	30	30
Range	28	30	30
Standard Deviation	7.824	8.2780	10.661

Summary regarding Class I: Students' Performance: It is found that the mean achievement in three subjects total 90 is 45.6 per cent marks which may be termed as Average Performance (in the range 35% and 54.4%) according to the five categories shown in Table 3 in the previous section. Similar also is the result in the individual subjects (Telugu, EVS and Mathematics) – mean score below 50 per cent. Much remains to be done if the level of performance is to be raised to the next category – Good performance: 54.5 per cent to 71.1 per cent (group 4). There seems to be no relation between the gender and performance of students but there is moderate relation between schools and performance of students.

Class II

Class II: Performance of Students in Three Subjects

The performance of students (total 90 marks) in class II (N = 97) in the three subjects (Telugu, EVS and Mathematics) is discussed and the relevant tables and graphs are also presented.

Descriptive Statistics: Class II – Discussion of Results

Table 12 shows the important statistics for students' performance.

The Mean marks (out of total 90 for three subjects) is 38.1 which works out to be 42.3 per cent which is even less than the mean for class 1: 45.6 per cent. The range of 74 also shows the wide disparity in performance of some students who have secured very low marks out of 90, and other students who have scored high marks approaching 74 which is 82 per cent.

Table 12

Class II: Class 2 Descriptive Statistics – Three Subjects (90 Marks)

	Statistic								
	N	*Range*	*Minimum*	*Maximum*	*Sum*	*Mean*	*Std Dev*	*Skewness*	*Kurtosis*
Total Telugu, EVS and Maths 90 final	97	74	0	74	3694	38.08	17.787	–0.733	–0.171
Valid N (listwise)	97	—	—	—	—	—	—	—	—

Frequency in Table – Five Groups: Class II

The frequency distribution shown in Table 13 reveals the large concentration of students in class II in group–3 (46.4%) and only 2.1 per cent (just two students out of 97) in group–5. This is a reflection of overall poor performance of class II students in the three subjects (Telugu, EVS and Mathematics).

Table 13

Class II: Three Subjects – Performance (90 marks)

		Frequency	*Per cent*	*Valid per cent*	*Cumulative per cent*
	Group 1	14	14.4	14.4	14.4
	Group 2	12	12.4	12.4	26.8
Valid	Group 3	45	46.4	46.4	73.2
	Group 4	24	24.7	24.7	97.9
	Group 5	2	2.1	2.1	100.0
	Total	97	100.0	100.0	

Gender-wise Distribution in Five Categories – Class II

Table 14 shows that the combined percentage of girls in groups 3 and 4 comes to 76.5 per cent (49% + 27.5%) which is higher than the figure 65.2 per cent (43.5% + 21.7%) for boys. Hence, the overall performance of girls is better than that of boys in Class II.

The graph as in Figure 3 shows the visual presentation of the data shown in Table 14 and it is self-explanatory.

Figure 3

Graph of Boys/Girls Performance

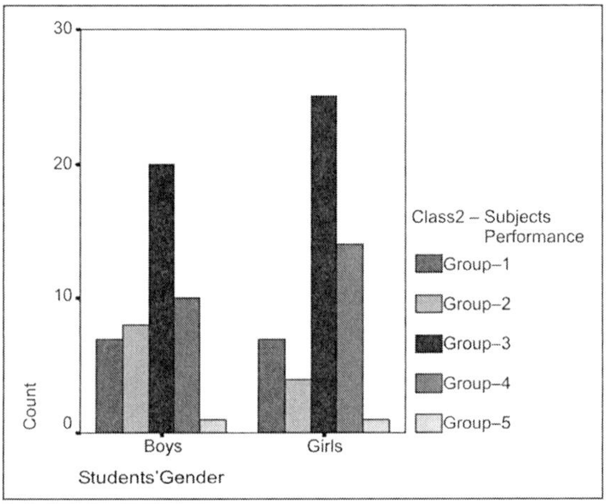

Table 14

Students' Gender Class II – Three Subjects – Performance Cross Tabulation

		Class 2 – 3 subjects – Performance (90)					*Total*
		Group 1	*Group 2*	*Group 3*	*Group 4*	*Group 5*	
Boys	Count	7	8	20	10	1	46
	% within Students' Gender	15.2%	17.4%	43.5%	21.7%	2.2%	100.0%
Girls	Count	7	4	25	14	1	51
	% within Students' Gender	13.7%	7.8%	49.0%	27.5%	2.0%	100.0%
Total	Count	14	12	45	24	2	97
	% within Students' Gender	14.4%	12.4%	46.4%	24.7%	2.1%	100.0%

School-wise Distribution of Students in Five Groups: Class II

Two schools (Government DNT UP School, Sitanagaram and SA Aided Elementary School, Stuartpuram) have only two and eight students, respectively. Observation of the frequencies in the 3rd and 4th rows reveals clearly that the performance of Stuartpuram school students is lower than Sitanagaram school students considering the frequencies in the very low performance category: group 1. But it is compensated by the fact that 25 per cent of students in Stuartpuram are in the very high performance category: group 5 which points to better performance compared to the other school (Table 15).

Table 15

Class II: Schools – Three Subjects – Performance Cross Tabulation

		Class II – Three subjects – Performance					*Total*
School		*Group 1*	*Group 2*	*Group 3*	*Group 4*	*Group 5*	
Government Elementary School, Siddhapuram	Count	0	7	22	13	0	42
	% within School	0%	16.7%	52.4%	31.0%	0%	100.0%
SA UP School, Bitragunta	Count	5	3	16	6	0	30
	% within School	16.7%	10.0%	53.3%	20.0%	0%	100.0%
Government UP School, Sitanagaram	Count	0	0	1	1	0	2
	% within School	0%	0%	50.0%	50.0%	0%	100.0%
SA Elementary School, Stuartpuram	Count	2	0	3	1	2	8
	% within School	25.0%	0%	37.5%	12.5%	25.0%	100.0%
S Bose Government Pr School, Lingala	Count	7	2	3	3	0	15
	% within School	46.7%	13.3%	20.0%	20.0%	0%	100.0%
Total	Count	14	12	45	24	2	97
	% within School	14.4%	12.4%	46.4%	24.7%	2.1%	100.0%

Regarding the other three schools, the ranks in performance are: first is Government, Elementary School, Siddhapuram with 83.4 per cent students in groups 3 and 4 (52.4% + 31%); second is Salvation Army Aided School, Bitragunta with 73.3 per cent students in groups 3 and 4 and third Subash Chandra Bose School, Lingala with 40 per cent in group 3 (Average) and in group 4 (Good Performance). The above statement refers only to the relative performance between the three schools. But in absolute performance there is not much to claim since the number of students in group 5 is zero in all these three schools.

The graph as in Figure 4 shows visually the above conclusions especially the first two schools ranked in performance (Siddhapuram and Bittragunta schools).

Figure 4

Graph of Performance: School-wise Distribution

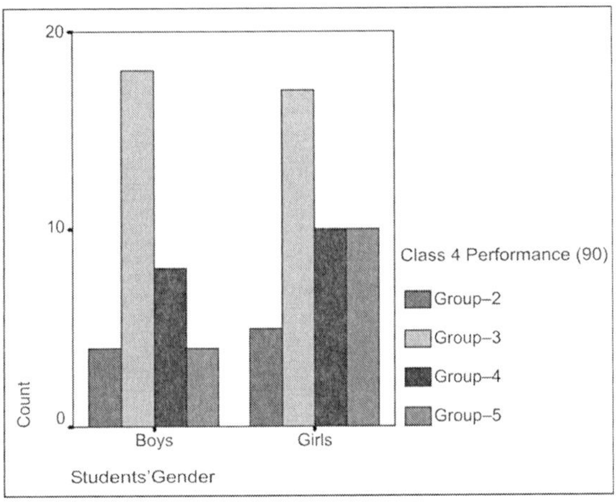

Table 16

Symmetric Measures

	Value	*Approx. Sig.*
Nominal by Nominal Contingency Coefficient	0.572	0.000
N of Valid Cases	97	

a. Not assuming the null hypothesis.
b. Using the asymptotic standard error assuming the null hypothesis.

As shown in Table 16 the contingency coefficient of 0.6 (0.572 rounded to the first decimal place) shows moderately high association or relation between schools and the achievement of students in the three subjects (Telugu, EVS and Mathematics). This shows that other things being equal, the achievement of students depends on the schools which they attend to a fairly good extent.

Comparison of Performance in Three Subjects: Class II

Findings from Table 17 are as follows. The mean values obtained by 97 students in class II shows that the achievement in Mathematics is moderately good: Mean score of 16 out of 30, which is 53.3 per cent, followed by mean 13.4 in Telugu (44.6%). The performance of class II students in Environmental Science is poor with mean 8.6 (28.7%).

Table 17

Class II: Summary of Performance in Three Subjects – Comparison

	Telugu (Marks 30)	*EVS (Marks 30)*	*Maths (Marks 30)*
Total N	97	97	97
Mean	13.44	8.62	16.02
Median	12.00	9.00	16.50
Sum	1304	836	1554
Minimum	0	0	0
Maximum	30	22	30
Range	30	22	30
Standard Deviation	8.370	4.805	8.673
Kurtosis	–0.980	–0.116	–0.800
Skewness	0.171	–0.010	–0.295

Summary of Class II Students' Performance

The mean performance of students in the total of three subjects (90 marks) is 42.3 per cent, lower than that of class II students: 45.6 per cent. The performance in the separate individual subjects (presented in the previous part) shows poor performance in Environmental Science.

Class 3

Class III: Performance of Students in Three Subjects

The achievement of 77 students in class III in the five schools considering the total of three subjects (90) in Telugu, EVS and Mathematics and also considering separate performance in each of the three subjects, are presented here.

Descriptive Statistics: Class II Discussion of Results

According to Table 18, the Mean score of 77 students out of total 90 in three subjects, is 56.4 which is 62.6 per cent which shows good performance. This is much better than the mean for class 1: 45.6 per cent and the mean for class II: 42.3 per cent.

The range of scores from minimum 11 to the maximum 88 shows the widespread dispersion of scores – but a much better picture compared to classes I and II where the minimum is zero in both classes.

Table 18

Class III: Descriptive Statistics – Three Subjects (90 Marks)

	Statistic								
	N	Range	Minimum	Maximum	Sum	Mean	Std Dev	Skewness	Kurtosis
Total — Telugu, EVS and Maths – 90 final	77	77	11	88	4341	56.37	17.184	–0.600	–0.229
Valid N (listwise)	77								

Frequency Table – Five Groups: Class III

The frequencies shown in Table 19 is also evidence for the much better performance of class III students, where it shows increasing percentage of students in all the five groups. Notable is the increase in percentage of students from group 3 to group 5: 19.5 per cent (group 3), 31.2 per cent (group 4) and 37.7 per cent (group 5).

Table 19

Class III: Three Subjects – Performance (90)

	Frequency	Per cent	Valid per cent	Cumulative per cent
Group 1	1	1.3	1.3	1.3
Group 2	8	10.4	10.4	11.7
Group 3	15	19.5	19.5	31.2
Group 4	24	31.2	31.2	62.3
Group 5	29	37.7	37.7	100.0
Total	77	100.0	100.0	

Gender-wise Distribution in Five Categories: Class III

Table 20 shows the better performance of girls: 71 per cent in group 4 (28.9%) and group 5 (42.1%) together, compared to 66.6 per cent of boys in groups 4 and 5.

Table 20

Students' Gender Class III Subjects Performance (90) Cross Tabulation

		Class 3 – Performance (90)					Total %
		Group 1	Group 2	Group 3	Group 4	Group 5	
Boys	Count	1	2	10	13	13	39
	% within Students' Gender	2.6%	5.1%	25.6%	33.3%	33.3%	100.0

Cont'd...

...Cont'd

Girls	Count	0	6	5	11	16	38
	% within Students' Gender	0%	15.8%	13.2%	28.9%	42.1%	100.0
Total	Count	1	8	18	24	29	77
	% within Students' Gender	1.3%	10.4%	19.5%	31.2%	37.7%	100.0

Relation between Gender and Performance

The value of contingency coefficient 0.3 shows only a small relation or association between gender and achievement in the total of three subjects (90 marks). The achievement of class III students is to a great extent independent of whether they are boys or girls.

Table 21

Symmetric Measures

	Value	*Approx. Sig.*
Nominal by Nominal Contingency Coefficient	0.250	
N of Valid Cases	77	0.274

a. Not assuming the null hypothesis.
b. Using the asymptotic standard error assuming the null hypothesis.

Figure 5

Genderwise Performance of Class III

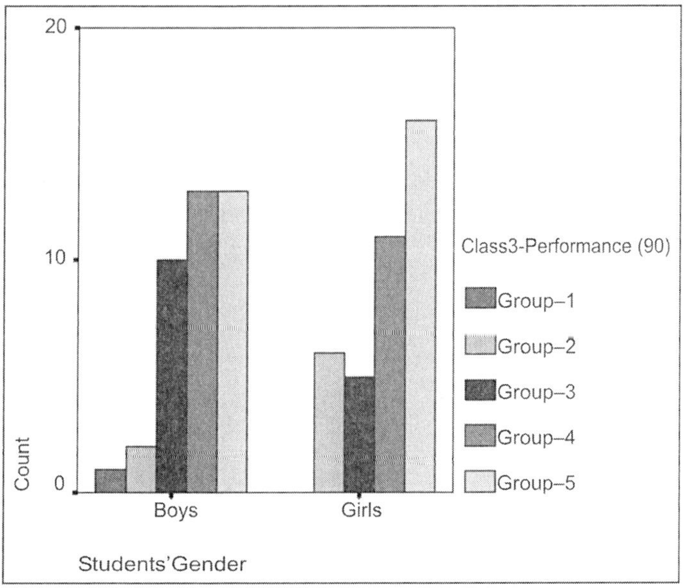

Table 22

Class III – School Performance (90) Cross Tabulation

School		*Class III – Performance (90)*					*Total*
		Group 1	*Group 2*	*Group 3*	*Group 4*	*Group 5*	
Government Elementary School, Siddhapuram	Count	0	0	3	8	11	22
	% within School	0%	0%	13.6%	36.4%	50.0%	100.0%
SA UP School, Bitragunta	Count	0	1	1	10	8	20
	% within School	0%	5.0%	5.0%	50.0%	40.0%	100.0%
Government UP School, Sitanagaram	Count	0	0	0	3	0	3
	% within School	0%	0%	0%	100.0%	0%	100.0%
SA Elementary School, Stuartpuram	Count	0	3	5	0	7	15
	% within School	0%	20.0%	33.3%	0%	46.7%	100.0%
S Bose Government Pr School, Lingala	Count	1	4	6	3	3	17
	% within School	5.9%	23.5%	35.3%	17.6%	17.6%	100.0%
Total	Count	1	8	15	24	29	77
	% within School	1.3%	10.4%	19.5%	31.2%	37.7%	100.0%

School-wise Distribution of Students in Five Groups: Class III

As shown in Table 22, there are only three students in Government DNT School, Sitanagaram, but their performance is good – all three in group 4.

Regarding the other four schools, notable is the performance of Bitragunta Salvation Army UP School, which comes first with 90 per cent of students in groups 4 and 5 put together and Government DNT School, Siddhapuram comes second with 86.4 per cent of students in groups 4 and 5. The performance of the other two schools is poor.

Contingency Coefficient (C)

The value of C, 0.6 in Table 23, shows moderately high relation or association between schools and performance of students. Other things being equal, the achievement of students of class III depends to some extent on the schools they attend.

Table 23

Symmetric Measures

	Value	*Approx. Sig.*
Nominal by Nominal Contingency Coefficient	0.556	0.005
N of Valid Cases	77	

a. Not assuming the null hypothesis.
b. Using the asymptotic standard error assuming the null hypothesis.

Figure 6

Graph of Performance School-wise

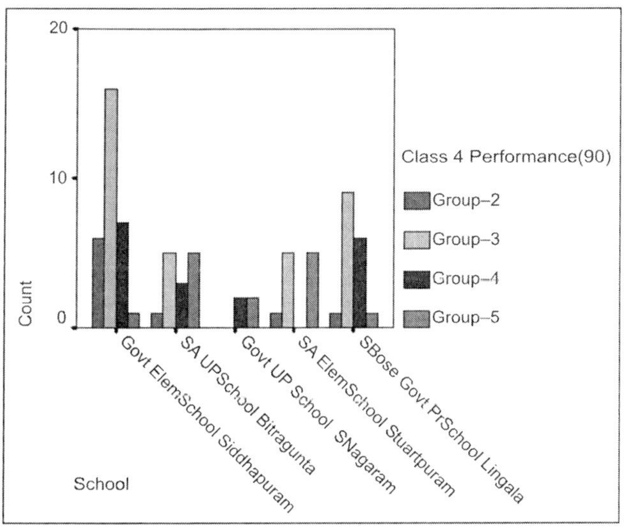

Graph of Five Schools: Class III

The graph in Figure 6 gives a visual picture of the data shown in Table 22.

Comparison of Performance in Three Subjects: Class III

Table 24 shows that the performance of students in Telugu and Mathematics is quite good: a mean of 23.9 out of 30 in Telugu which is 79.6 per cent and a Mean of 20.8 in Mathematics which is 69.3 per cent. The performance in Environmental Science is poor in comparison: Mean of 11.6 which comes to 38.6 per cent only.

Summary of Class III Students' Performance

The mean achievement in the total (90 marks) of three subjects (Telugu, EVS and Mathematics) is good with 62.6 per cent – much better than the mean achievement of class III students (45.6%) and class II students (42.3%). The performance of students depends to some extent on the schools which they attend, shown by the contingency coefficient of 0.6. In individual subjects, the performance in Telugu is very good (79.6%) and the achievement in Mathematics is good; but the achievement in EVS is poor: 38.6 per cent.

Table 24

Class III: Summary of Performance in Three Subjects – Comparison

	Telugu (Marks 30)	*EVS (Marks 30)*	*Maths (Marks 30)*
Total N	77	77	77
Mean	23.94	11.59	20.84
Median	27.00	9.60	21.00
Sum	1844	892	1605
Minimum	6	2	2
Maximum	30	28	30
Range	24	26	29
Standard Deviation	6.919	6.501	7.046
Kurtosis	–0.218	–0.483	–0.565
Skewness	–0.985	0.754	–0.487

Class IV

Class IV: Performance of Students in Three Subjects

The performance of class IV students in Telugu, EVS and Maths is presented in Table 25.

Table 25

Class IV: Three Subjects Total – Descriptive Statistics

	Statistic								
	N	*Range*	*Minimum*	*Maximum*	*Sum*	*Mean*	*Std Dev*	*Skewness*	*Kurtosis*
Total Telugu, EVS and Maths (90) final	76	73	16	89	3690	48.56	14.281	0.175	0.067
Valid N (listwise)	76								

Descriptive Statistics: Class IV Discussion of Results

The Mean score of 76 students in class IV in the three subjects is 48.6 out of 90, which comes to 53.9 per cent – better than the performance of class I and II students but less than class III students. The marks range from 16 to a maximum of 89 which is a record 98.9 per cent.

Frequency Table in Five Groups: Class IV

This is shown in Table 26. The combined percentage of 42.1 per cent in groups 4 and 5 is an index of good performance as also shown by the absence of students in group 1: very poor category.

Table 26

Class IV: Three Subjects – Performance

	Frequency	*Per cent*	*Valid per cent*	*Cumulative per cent*
Group 2	9	11.8	11.8	11.8
Group 3	35	46.1	46.1	57.9
Group 4	18	23.7	23.7	81.6
Group 5	14	18.4	18.4	100.0
Total	76	100.0	100.0	

Gender-wise Distribution in Five Categories: Class IV

Table 27 show that the percentage of girls coming under the top two categories (groups 4 and 5 – good and very good performance) is 47.6 per cent, evidence of their superior performance compared to the achievement of boys whose percentage in the top two categories combined, is 35.3. There is not a single boy or girl in group 1 (very poor performance) as already mentioned above under 2.

Table 27

Students' Gender Class IV – Three Subjects Performance (90) Cross Tabulation

		Class IV – Three Subjects Performance (90)				*Total*
		Group 2	*Group 3*	*Group 4*	*Group 5*	
Boys	Count	4	18	8	4	34
	% within Students' Gender	11.8%	52.9%	23.5%	11.8%	100.0%
Girls	Count	5	17	10	10	42
	% within Students' Gender	11.9%	40.5%	23.8%	23.8%	100.0%
Total	Count	9	35	18	14	76
	% within Students' Gender	11.8%	46.1%	23.7%	18.4%	100.0%

The Contingency Coefficient (C) of 0.2 (0.16 rounded) in Table 28 shows very low relationship or association between gender and performance of students in class IV. It may be said that the two variables are independent to a great extent.

Table 28

Symmetric Measures

	Value	*Approx. Sig.*
Nominal by Nominal Contingency Coefficient	0.165	0.549
N of Valid Cases		76

a. Not assuming the null hypothesis.
b. Using the asymptotic standard error assuming the null hypothesis.

The graph in Figure 7 reflects the better performance of girls as already stated under 2.

Figure 7

Graph Showing Performance of Boys and Girls

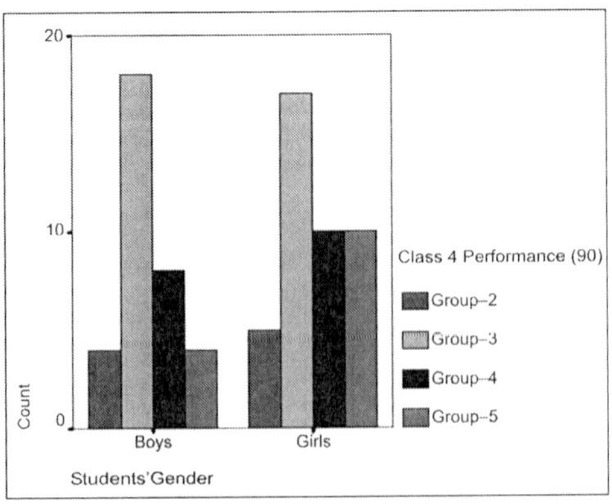

School-wise Distribution of Students in Five Groups: Class IV

As shown in Table 29 there is not a single student in group 1: Very poor performance category in any of the five schools which was mentioned earlier also. There are only four students in Sitanagaram school, but their performance is quite good with two students coming under the group 4 category (Good) and two under group 5 category (Very Good).

Table 29

Class IV School – Three Subjects Performance (90) Cross Tabulation

School		*Class IV – Three Subjects Performance (90)*				*Total*
		Group 2	*Group 3*	*Group 4*	*Group 5*	
Government Elementary School, Siddhapuram	Count	6	16	7	1	30
	% within School	20.0%	53.3%	23.3%	3.3%	100.0%
SA UP School, Bitragunta	Count	1	5	3	5	14
	% within School	7.1%	35.7%	21.4%	35.7%	100.0%
Government UP School, Sitanagaram	Count	0	0	2	2	4
	% within School	0%	0%	50.0%	50.0%	100.0%
SA Elementary School, Stuartpuram	Count	1	5	0	5	11
	% within School	9.1%	45.5%	0%	45.5%	100.0%
S Bose Government Pr School, Lingala	Count	1	9	6	1	17
	% within School	5.9%	52.9%	35.3%	5.9%	100.0%
Total	Count	9	35	18	14	76
	% within School	11.8%	46.1%	23.7%	18.4%	100.0%

Out of the remaining four schools, Salvation Army School, Bitragunta comes first in performance with 57.1 per cent (21.4% + 35.7%) of students in the top two categories (groups 4 and 5). On close analysis of group 4 and group 5 cells pertaining to Stuartpuram school and Lingala school (45.5% and 41.2% students respectively in groups 4 and 5 combined), the performances of students in these two schools are nearly equal, with the Stuartpuram school having an edge over Lingala school.

Table 30 shows the value of contingency coefficient as 0.4. This shows moderately high relationship between school and performance of students. The achievement of students depends to some extent on the schools which they attend, other things being equal.

Table 30

Symmetric Measures

	Value	*Approx. Sig.*
Nominal by Nominal Contingency Coefficient	0.493	0.018
N of Valid Cases	76	

a. Not assuming the null hypothesis.
b. Using the asymptotic standard error assuming the null hypothesis.

The graph as shown in Figure 8 gives the picture of performance when the number of students is considered. But the real picture considering the percentage of students has been described under 7.

Figure 8

Performance of Five Schools

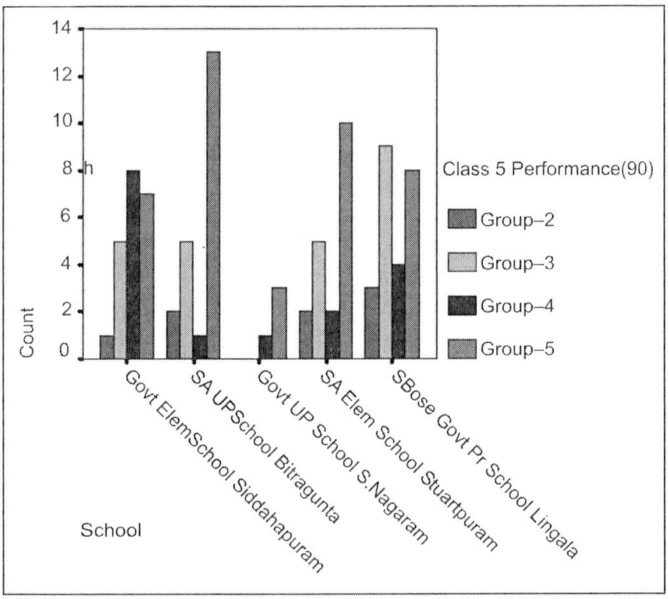

Comparison of Performance in Three Subjects

As per Table 31, the best performance of students among the three subjects is seen to be Telugu with 23.6 marks out of 30, that is, 78.6 per cent. The performance in the other two subjects (EVS and Maths) is average with 13.5 out of 30 for EVS which is 45 per cent and with 11.5 for maths which comes to 38.3 per cent only.

Table 31

Class IV Summary of Performance in Three Subjects – Case Summaries – Comparison

	Telugu (Marks 30)	*EVS (Marks 30)*	*Maths (Marks 30)*
Total N	76	76	76
Mean	23.55	13.48	11.53
Median	25.00	11.40	11.40
Sum	1790	1024	876
Minimum	8	4	4
Maximum	39	29	25
Range	31	25	21
Standard Deviation	6.455	6.725	4.003
Kurtosis	–0.179	–0.721	1.246
Skewness	–0.634	0.738	0.709

Summary of Class IV Performance

The overall performance of 76 students in the three subjects put together may be termed average or moderately good since the Mean is 48.6 out of 90 which comes to nearly 54 per cent and there are no students in group 1 category. The performance of girls is better than that of boys. Regarding schools, Salvation Army School, Bitragunta comes first. There is moderately high relationship between schools and students' performance but very little relationship exists between gender of students and their performance.

Class V

Class V: Performance of Students in Three Subjects

The achievement of 89 students in class V in the five schools considering the total of three subjects (90) in Telugu, EVS and Mathematics and also considering separate performance in each of tho three subjects are presented here.

Descriptive Statistics: Class V

Discussion of Results

According to Table 32 the Mean Score of 89 students out of total 90 in 3 subjects, is 56.1 which is 62.3 per cent which shows good performance.

This is much better than the mean for class 1: 45.6 per cent and the mean for class 2: 42.3 per cent, class 3: 62.6 per cent and class 4: 54.0 per cent.

Table 32

Class V: Descriptive Statistics – Three Subjects (90 Marks)

Class V: Three Subjects Total Descriptive Statistics									
	Statistic								
	N	*Range*	*Minimum*	*Maximum*	*Sum*	*Mean*	*Std. Deviation*	*Skewness*	*Kur tosis*
Total Tel, Evs, Maths	89	69	19	87	4995	56.13	17.610	–.440	–.762
Valid N (list-wise)	89	—	—	—	—	—	—	—	—

The range of scores for minimum 19 and the maximum 87 shows the widespread dispersion of scores – but a much better picture when compared to other classes.

Frequency Table – Groups: Class V

The frequencies shown in Table 33 is also an evidence for the much better performance of class V students, where it shows increasing percentage of students in the groups 3 and 5. Notable is the increase in percentage of students from group 4 to 5 (19.6%).

Table 33

Class 5: Three Subjects – Performance

Class V: Performance (90)				
	Frequency	*Per cent*	*Valid Per cent*	*Cumulative Per cent*
Group–2	8	9.0	9.0	9.0
Group–3	24	27.0	27.0	36.0
Group–4	16	18.0	18.0	53.9
Group–5	41	46.1	46.1	100.0
Total	89	100.0	100.0	

Gender-wise Distribution in Five Categories: Class V

Table 34 shows the better performance of girls: 67.5 per cent in group 4 (17.5%) and group 5 (50.0%) together compared to 61.3 per cent of boys in groups 4 and 5.

Table 34

Students' Gender Class V – Three Subjects – Performance Cross Tabulation

		Students' Gender Class V: Performance (90) Cross tabulation				
		Class V: Performance (90)				Total
		Group 2	Group 3	Group 4	Group 5	
Boys	Count	4	15	9	21	49
	% within Students' Gender	8.2%	30.6%	18.4%	42.9%	100.0%
Girls	Count	4	9	7	20	40
	% within Students' Gender	10.0%	22.5%	17.5%	50.0%	100.0%
Total	Count	8	24	16	41	89
	% within Students' Gender	9.0%	27.0%	18.0%	46.1%	100.0%

Relation between Gender and Performance

The value of contingency coefficient 0.01, shows no relation or association between gender and achievement in the total of three subjects (90 marks). The achievement of class V students is to a great extend independent of whether they are boys or girls.

Table 35

Symmetric Measures

		Value	Approx. Sig.
Nominal by Nominal	Contingency Coefficient	.099	.832
N of Valid Cases	89		

a Not assuming the null hypothesis.
b Using the asymptotic standard error assuming the null hypothesis.

School-wise Distribution of Students in Five Groups: Class V

There are only four students in Government DNT School, Sitanagaram, but their performance is good – all four in groups 4 and 5 whereas only 50 per cent of the students in Government Primary DNT School, Lingala belong to groups 4 and 5. Regarding the other remaining schools, notable is the performance of Government Elementary school, Siddhapuram, which comes with 71.4 per cent. Regarding other remaining schools, notable is the performance of Siddhapuram, which comes first with 71.4 per cent of students in groups 4 and 5 put together. The performance of other two schools is fairly good. (66.7%)

Table 36

School Class V Performance Cross Tabulation

School Class V Performance (90) Cross Tabulation						
School		*Class 5 Performance (90)*				*Total*
		Group 2	*Group 3*	*Group 4*	*Group 5*	
Gov-Elem School, Siddhapuram	Count	1	5	8	7	21
	% within School	4.8%	23.8%	38.1%	33.3%	100.0%
SA UP School, Bitragunta	Count	2	5	1	13	21
	% within School	9.5%	23.8%	4.8%	61.9%	100.0%
Govt UP Schools S. Nagaram	Count	0	0	1	3	4
	% within School	0%	0%	25.0%	75.0%	100.0%
SA Elem School, Stuartpuram	Count	2	5	2	10	19
	% within School	10.5%	26.3%	10.5%	52.6%	100.0%
SBose Govt Pr School, Lingala	Count	3	9	4	8	24
	% within School	12.5%	37.5%	16.7%	33.3%	100.0%
Total	Count	8	24	16	41	89
	% within School	9.0%	27.0%	18.0%	46.1%	100.0%

Contingency Coefficient (C)

The value of C, 0.4 in Table 37, shows moderately low relation or association between schools and performance of students. Other things being equal, the achievement of students of class V depends to some extent on the schools they attend.

Table 37

Symmetric Measures

		Value	*Approx. Sig.*
Nominal by Nominal	Contingency Coefficient	0.374	0.270
N of Valid Cases	89		

a Not assuming the null hypothesis.
b Using the asymptotic standard error assuming the null hypothesis.

The graph as in Figure 9 gives a visual picture of the data shown in Table 36.

Figure 9

Graph of Performance School-wise

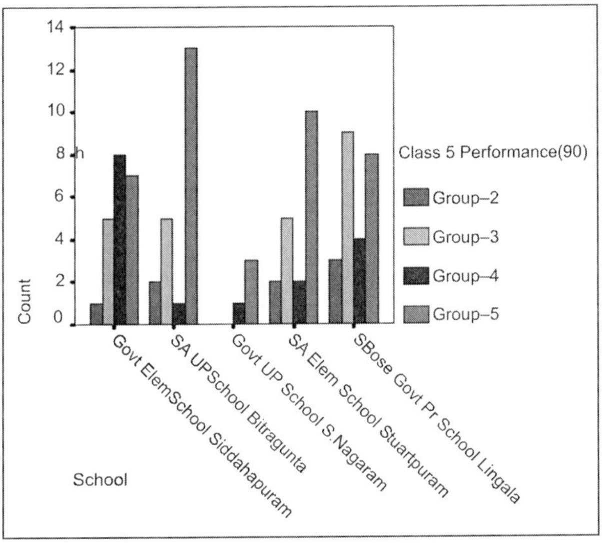

Comparison of Performance in Three Subjects: Class V

Table 38 shows that the performance of students in Telugu and Mathematics is quite good; a mean of 20.7 out of 30 in Telugu which is 69.0 *per cent* and a Mean of 19.3 in Mathematics which is 64.3 *per cent*. The performance in Environmental Science is poor in comparison. Mean of 15.5 which comes to 51.7 *per cent* only.

Table 38

Subjects Comparison

	Class V: Three Subjects Comparison		
	Telugu Marks-(30)	*EnvSc Marks-(30)*	*Maths Marks-(30)*
N	89	89	89
Mean	20.67	15.53	19.93
Median	20.57	15.60	20.57
Sum	1839	1382	1773
Minimum	8	5	6
Maximum	30	29	30
Range	22	24	24
Std. Deviation	6.262	5.950	6.967
Kurtosis	–.780	–.439	–1.008
Skewness	–.362	.190	–.305

Summary of Class V Students' Performance

The Mean achievement in the total (90 marks) of three subjects (Telugu, EVS and Mathematics is 56.1 with 62.3%) much higher than the mean achievement of class 4 students (54.0%). The performance of students does not depend on the schools which they attend, shown by the contingency coefficient of 0.4. In individual subjects, the performance in Telugu is very good (68.9%) and the achievement in Mathematics (66.4%) is good and the achievement in EVS is 51.8 per cent.

Performance of Students' Attitude

The following tables and graphs show the clear picture of the attitude of the children studying in the selected five DNT schools towards their education. As already stated in the previous section, the attitude and behaviour scales of the 100 selected DNT students in all the schools has been presented here. The total marks for the attitude and behaviour of each student in each class in the five schools are 10 points. The overall perceptions, behaviour and attitudes of the students is shown by the values of descriptive statistics in Table 39.

The negative behaviour and perception of 100 students in the DNT selected schools is 14 per cent. There are a good number of students (25%) who have positive behaviour and attitude towards their education; 64 per cent of the DNT students have more positive behaviour and attitude in the schools. The graph as in Figure 10 shows the clear picture of the DNT students' behaviour and attitude in the schools.

Table 39

Students' Attitude

Attitude Groups				
	Frequency	*Per cent*	*Valid Per cent*	*Cumulative Per cent*
Negative	14	14.0	14.0	14.0
Positive	22	22.0	22.0	36.0
More Positive	64	64.0	64.0	100.0
Total	100	100.0	100.0	

Figure 10

Graph of Attitude Groups

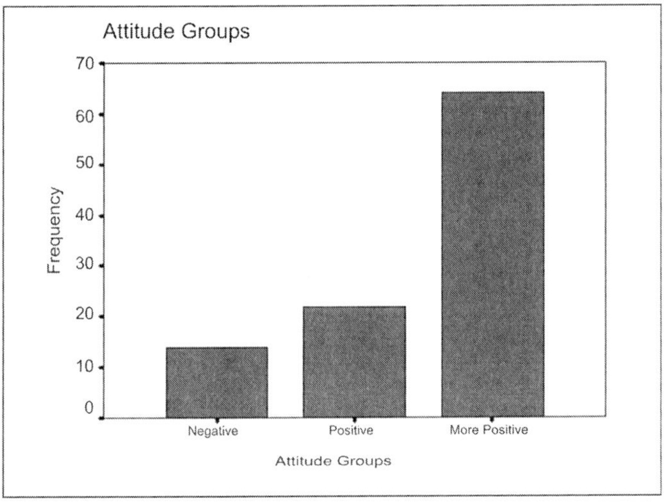

Table 40 shows that girls have better behaviour and attitude than the boys. However, both boys and girls have more positive behaviour and good qualities than negative behaviour and qualities.

Table 40

Students' Gender – Five DNT Schools – Performance

Gender Attitude Groups Cross tabulation			
	Attitude Groups		
	Negative	*Positive*	*More Positive*
Boys % within Gender	12.5%	25.0%	62.5%
Girls % within Gender	15.9%	18.2%	65.9%

Table 40 shows that there is co-relation between boys and girls in their attitudes and perception. Both have the same qualities and attitudes towards their schooling and education.

Table 41

Symmetric Measures

		Value	*Approx. Sig.*
Nominal by Nominal	Contingency Coefficient	0.087	0.680
N of Valid Cases	100		

a Not assuming the null hypothesis.
b Using the asymptotic standard error assuming the null hypothesis.

The graph in Figure 11 gives a clear picture of the gender-wise (boys and girls) behaviour and attitudes. The height of the third bar in boys and girls stands out showing more positive behaviour and attitude in the schools. This is also shown in Figure 12.

Figure 11

Graph of Gender-wise Distribution

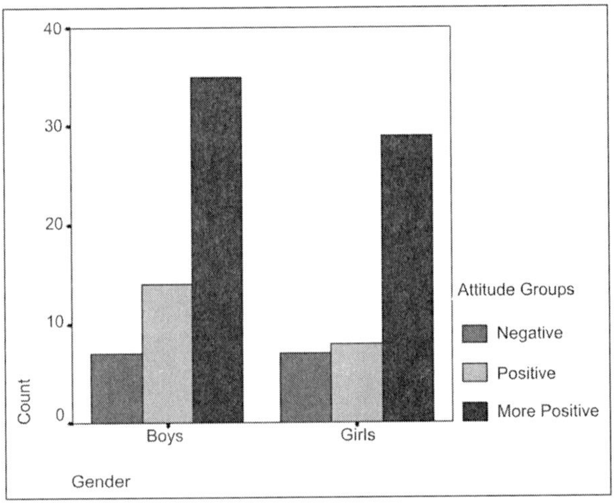

Figure 12

Attitude Groups Gender

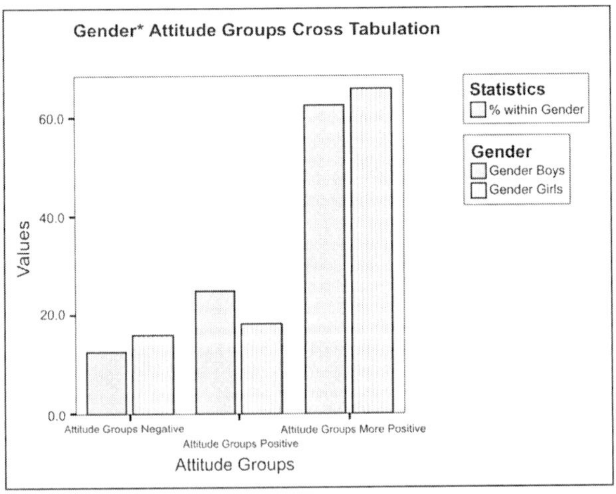

The graph shown in Figure 12 is self-explanatory. The graph shows the performance of all the students' behaviour in the DNT schools. Most of them have more positive behaviour and attitude towards their schools and education.

Table 42 shows the male/female (boys and girls) distribution of students in all the DNT schools of classes I to V with respect to their overall behaviour and attitudes towards schooling and education.

Table 42

Students Gender – Five DNT Schools – Attitudes

Gender Attitude Groups Cross Tabulation % within Gender				
	Attitude Groups			*Total*
	Negative	*Positive*	*More Positive*	
Boys	12.5%	25.0%	62.5%	100.0%
Girls	15.9%	18.2%	65.9%	100.0%
Total	14.0%	22.0%	64.0%	100.0%

Discussion: The cross table shows that 12.5 per cent boys have negative behaviour and attitude; 25 per cent of the boys have positive behaviour and attitude; 62.5 per cent of boys have more positive behaviour and attitudes in the schools. Similarly, 15.9 per cent of girls have negative behaviour, 18.2 per cent of girls have positive behaviour and the remaining 65.9 per cent of girls have more positive behaviour. The table also clearly shows that there is no gender disparity in their behaviour. Boys and girls have the same behaviour in the school and their attitude and perception of the school and education is more or less the same. The negative attitudes of some of the students reflects the poor socio-economic conditions of the parents, unattractive schools and influence of their surroundings where the children are living.

Table 43

School Attitude Groups Cross Tabulation Percent within Schools

School Attitude Groups Cross Tabulation % within School				
	Attitude Groups			*Total*
School	*Negative*	*Positive*	*More Positive*	
Gov-Elem School Siddhapuram	33.3%	37.5%	29.2%	100.0%
SA-UP School Bitragunta		14.3%	85.7%	100.0%
Govt UP School Sitanagaram		40.0%	60.0%	100.0%
SA Elem School Stuartpuram	6.5%	6.5%	87.1%	100.0%
Sbose Govt Pr School Lingala	15.4%	26.9%	57.7%	100.0%
Total	14.0%	22.0%	64.0%	100.0%

Table 43 shows the attitude of the students school-wise. Thirty-three per cent of the students have negative behaviour and qualities; 37.5 per cent of students have positive behaviour and qualities; 29.2 per cent of the students have more positive behaviour and qualities in Siddhapuram school. It means the attitude and behaviour of the students in Siddhapuram school is negative. In Bitragunta and Sitanagaram school, the students do not have any negative behaviour. The children possess more positive behaviour than the other schools. Likewise, the DNT school, Lingala also has students with negative behaviour. The students in Stuartpuram have more positive behaviour. A few students have negative behaviour in the two DNT schools, Siddhapuram and Lingala schools. However, majority of the students have more positive behaviour and attitudes towards their schooling and education.

Results and Findings

The following are the results and findings of the analysis and interpretation of the data collected from the five selected DNT schools of Andhra Pradesh. There is an average or medium performance of boys and girls in class I. The students in all the DNT schools constitute a heterogenous group (Woddars, Sugalis, Yerukulas, Yanadis, Dasaris, etc.) The students hail from poor family background. There are two categories of DNT students in class I, that is, poor performance students on the one hand, and better performance of students on the other. The performance of boys and girls is almost equal in the three subjects – Telugu, Mathematics and EVS. However, when compared to the boys, the performance of girls are better. The students of DNT schools at Sitanagaram and Bitragunta performed better than the remaining students in three other DNT schools. The performance of the students of Stuartpuram school is the lowest. The performance of boys and girls in Telugu and Mathematics subjects are better. The achievement of the primary class students in EVS is very poor. This clearly shows the link between the DNT settlement surroundings, schools and also the socio-economic conditions of the parents on the academic achievement of their children.

The performance of the students in class II is poor when compared to the performance of class I students. Further, there is a wide disparity in the students' performance in class II. Some students have very low achievement while others have high achievement level. The overall performance of class II students is poor in Telugu, Mathematics and EVS. The performance of girls in class II is better than the boys. The performance of the students in Stuartpuram is very low. The performance of the students in Siddhapuram is better. The achievement levels of the students in all DNT schools in Mathematics and Telugu is better. But, their performance in EVS is poor.

The students' performance in class III is better than class I and II. The percentage of the achievement levels of the students has increased in class III. The performance of girls is better than the boys in classes II and III. The performance of the Sitanagaram school is better. The performance of Bitragunta school is also better when compared to the other three schools. The performance of Stuartpuram and Lingala schools are very poor. The performance of students in Telugu and Mathematics is good. Their performance in Environmental Science is poor. Class III students' achievement is better than class I and II students.

The performance of class IV students is much better than classes I, II and III. Girls performed better than the boys in all the classes. In class IV the performance of all students in DNT schools are good. Out of the five schools, the DNT School, Bitragunta, performed better. The performance of the Lingala DNT school is poor. The performance of students in class 4 is better in Telugu. The performance of the students in Mathematics and EVS is average. The overall performance of girls are better than boys in class IV.

Good performance is shown by all the DNT school children in class V when compared to classes I to IV. Their performance in Telugu, EVS and Mathematics is better than classes I, II, III and IV. There is an increase in the performance of students in class V. The performance of girl students is also better in class V. The performance of all the DTN schools is better in class V. The performance of students in Mathematics and Telugu is good.

The attitude and behaviour of the students in the DNT schools are more positive towards their education. Among all the categories of children, the girls are more positive than the boys. There is a small per cent of children having negative attitudes and behaviour (14%). There is also a negative attitude and behaviour of children in the higher classes (classes 4 and 5). The students of Stuartpuram have more positive attitudes. The students in Siddhapuram and Lingala schools have more negative attitudes and behaviour in the schools. This clearly shows the relationship between their surroundings, settlements where they are living, the school conditions, parental background, the poor socio-economic conditions of parents and the poor performance of teachers in the DNT schools.

Notes

1. Clive Opie (ed.), *Doing Educational Research: A Guide for First Time Researchers*, Vistaar Publications, New Delhi, 2004.
2. NCERT, Sixth Survey of Educational Research, Vol. 1, 1993–2000, National Council of Educational Research and Training, New Delhi, 2006.
3. Nicola Bruce, Richard Kemp and Rosemary Snelgar, *SPSS for Psychologists: A Guide to Data Analysis using SPSS for Windows (Versions 9, 10, 11)*, Second Edition, Lawrence Erlbaum Associates, Publishers, Mahwah, New Jersey, London, 2003.
4. Sabita Patnayak, *Handbook of Research Methodology for CTE and IASE Faculty*, Unpublished Report, Regional Institute of Education, Bhopal, 1999.

6

Implications

Introduction

Education has an acculturating role. It refines sensitivities, activities and perceptions that contribute to national cohesion, scientific temper and independence of mind and spirit, thus furthering the goals of socialism, secularism and democracy enshrined in our Constitution. Education is an essential factor for national development. Today, it is regarded as a national activity. It is regarded as a powerful instrument of social, economic, political and cultural changes. The role of education is to impart knowledge, develop skills and inculcate right type of attitudes, values and interests. The Kothari Commission suggested that education should relate to the life, needs and aspirations of the people. It has to increase productivity, achieve social and national integration, step up the process of modernisation and develop social and moral values among the citizens. It is observed that the destiny of India is now shaped in the classrooms. Martin Luther, the German social reformer has rightly said that the progress and prosperity of a nation depends not on the abundant of its revenues or on the strength of its fortifications, but in many people's education, enlightenment and character. Education is a basic right of all citizens. The 93rd Constitutional Amendment has made primary education a basic right to the children of 6 to 14 years of age. The Government of India and the State governments are taking steps to fulfil this right.

It is a fact that education is an essential programme for economic growth, development of the society. Education is an investment and a human capital. It enhances individual's well-being. Literacy is proved to be a key variable for the development of the society and success of democracy. Illiterate people tend to have low self-esteem and low social status. Because of their illiteracy they cannot reap the fruits of democracy. Education is of value not only for the person who acquires it, but also for others. Widespread education helps to resolve social problems like poverty, ignorance, illiteracy, diseases, population growth and environmental degradation. To march towards bright future the only hope rests with educational persons. Mahatma Gandhi was of the opinion that education is the basic tool for the development of consciousness and reconstruction of society. Modern educationists believe that every individual is endowed with certain innate abilities or potentialities and these are to be brought out to achieve a harmonious development. The purpose of education is to promote the development of a well-integrated person capable of exercising such responsibilities in the society as his powers allow. Education has to make the individual physically strong, intellectually alert, emotionally stable, culturally sound and socially efficient. According to National Policy on Education, 1986, education has to produce self-aroused, more productive, more capital and more thinking type of citizens. It is not the imitative mind that is to be developed, but it is creative mind that is to be developed. The National Curriculum Framework 2005 emphasised that the basic concerns of education is to enable children to make sense of life and develop their potential, to define and pursue and recognise the right of others to do the same.

There are three important components in the educative process. These are the teacher, the pupil and the subject matter. The teacher is the main dynamic force in the system of education. He is the director of the teaching-learning process. The second important component is the pupil. To educate the pupil is the ultimate objective of the instructional process. In this context, the child's abilities, capabilities, capacities and his psychological aspects are to be taken into account. Today, there is a shift from epistemic approach to reconstructionist approach, from teacher control and subject centred approach to that of child-centred approach. The present emphasis is on the adoption of child-centred, activity oriented and competency based teaching-learning process. 'The child is the starting point, the centre and the end. His growth and his development is the ideal of education', felt John Dewey. The third important component is the subject matter or the content of education known as curriculum. It is the path of the realisation of objectives of education. In the words of Jawaharlal Nehru, 'Education has mainly two aspects, the cultural aspect which makes a person grow and the productive aspect which makes a person do things'. Both are essential. The school plays a major role in monitoring the ideas, habits and attitudes of the children in order to produce well-balanced personalities.

The present day school has to perform a number of functions. It has to teach seven 'Rs' – Reading, Writing, Arithmetic, Recreation, Rights, Responsibilities and Relationships. It has to transmit the cultural heritage of the previous generation to the present generation, conserve the culture and advance culture. The school has to recognise the individual differences, provide opportunities for the full development of the children, kindle the minds of the students and develop a passion for social justice.

It is an inescapable fact that in countries around the globe, during the past decades, notable efforts were made to universalise primary education. This is due to a variety of causes. Millions of children have no access to primary schooling. Millions of children fail to complete basic education. Millions satisfy the attendance requirements but do not acquire essential knowledge and skills. Thus, millions comprise poor, rural and remote population, nomads, pastoralists, denotified tribes, indigenous people and girls. The disadvantaged population groups are the victims of multiple handicaps due to various reasons such as (1) they do not have access to basic education infrastructure like schools, teachers and books, (2) the content of education imparted through the curriculum is not fulfilling their specific learning needs, (3) the nature of curriculum transaction on schools is not conductive to their learning styles, (4) the model of schooling and education presented to the disadvantaged is alien to the cultural needs of these groups. The school itself is against the interests of the disadvantaged. The educationally disadvantaged population groups fail to see any point and purpose in education. They remain outside the school, dropout of it or fail to achieve the desirable learning levels. It is with this background the present study 'A Study of factors affecting Students' Achievements in the Primary Schools of Denotified Tribal Settlements in Andhra Pradesh' has been taken up.

Denotified Tribes and Social Context of Education

Denotified Tribes form a large group of population in the Indian society. Due to several historical, economic, political and social reasons, the DNTs remained educationally, socially, politically and economically backward. According to 2001 census reports, the total population of DNTs in India is more than thirteen crore. They were treated as habitual 'criminal' offenders before Independence by the British Government. Even today, they are victims of mob lynching, arson, public and police atrocities. After 65 years of Independence, 99 per cent of the DNTs are illiterates and they have less chances of getting quality education. Education is a fundamental right in our Constitution as well as a universal human right. This remained a dream for an overwhelming majority of India's DNTs. The situation of the DNTs is perceived lower in status in our minutely stratified society. The fate of much India's DNTs is that of dejection, lack of status, unfulfilled aspirations, ignorance and illiteracy. Though the DNTs constitute a major segment of the Indian population, there are marked inter-state and regional variations in terms of their population. The DNTs are spread over the entire country but are most heavily concentrated in Gujarat, Orissa (Odisha), Bihar, Madhya Pradesh, Maharashtra, Karnataka, Rajasthan, West Bengal, Tamil Nadu, UP, Andhra Pradesh, Punjab and other states.

Andhra Pradesh is one of the states having the highest proportion of DNTs (59 sects/communities with 6% population). From a sociological point of view, apart from their increasing visibility in social life, the most significant contemporary fact concerning the DNTs is their growing political, cultural assertion and identity formation as habitual offenders. Large sections of the DNTs experience social discrimination and stigma particularly those located in the tradition bound and socio-economically backward states/regions. The DNTs inhabited the plains, mountainous and other isolated regions. They remained outside of Hindu civilisation. They were classified under different communities. Some of them are included in the list of Scheduled Tribes and others are in the list of Scheduled Castes and still others are in the list of Backward Classes. However, there are no complete census and survey statistics regarding the denotified, nomadic and semi-nomadic tribes in the country. Only rough population estimates on the basis of the sample surveys and growth rates of population have been done so far, with regard to these neglected and isolated population. Constitutional protection has to be guaranteed to them on similar lines as given to SC/STs by creating a separate Third Schedule – Denotified Tribes. They may be called as Scheduled Denotified and Nomadic tribes. They may be included in the Ninth Schedule as an independent list.

The DNTs are living in separate localities and outskirts of the villages. These places are called Settlements or Tandas. But, so far there are no settlement/tanda development schemes provided either by the State or the Central Governments. Facilities like infrastructure, roads, electricity, drinking water, sanitation is not available to them in their dwelling places. Like SC/STs, the government should provide provisions and budgetary allocation in the eleventh sub-plan to the DNTs for the construction of roads, providing electricity, drinking water facility and sanitation in their places. They are living as squatters. Many of these communities have no permanent houses. They are generally found only in the outskirts of the villages. Housing scheme like Indira Awas Yojana may be sanctioned to them.

Current Educational Situation of the Denotified Tribes

What is the contemporary educational status of the Denotified Tribes? According to 1991 census, there are 59 sects of Denotified Tribes in Andhra Pradesh. As per the earlier Tribal Cultural Research & Training Institute (TCR & TI) survey there are 52 communities. Among the districts, Telangana, Coastal Andhra and Rayalaseema have the largest number of DNTs. Of the total tribal population, 39 per cent of the population belong to Sugali community spread dominantly in Warangal, Nalgonda, Khammam, Mahabub Nagar and Nizamabad districts. Around 9 per cent population each comprise Yanadi and Yerukula communities dominant in Nellore, Chittoor, Prakasam,

Guntur, Anantapur, Krishna, Kurnool and Nellore. The Yanadis are inhabited more in Nellore district. The Woddars are largely inhabited in Kurnool and Anantapur districts.

The problems faced by the DNT children in their education can be classified under five areas, viz. economic factors, social factors, cultural factors, school factors and administrative factors. Poverty of parents, lack of parental demand, child labour, lack of early childcare education (ECE) facilities, migration, seasonal occupations are some of the economic factors, which stand in the way of the education of these children. Illiteracy of the parents, early marriages, community loyalties, lack of awareness, social stigma are some of the problems, which retard the educational development of the DNT children. There are a large number of school factors and administrative factors which hamper their educational development. Some of these problems are: lack of access, incomplete schools, teacher absenteeism, poor quality of teaching, unserviceable curriculum, unsuitable working hours, etc. are some of the school factors which stand in the way of the educational development of the DNT children. Lack of coordination among different managements, delays in supplies of textbooks, uniforms and other school incentives, weak inspectorate, lack of enrolment campaigns, lack of community control, lack of incentives for better performance of schools are some of the administrative factors which are standing in the way of education of the DNT children. The DNTs education scenario can be explained under the following areas that is – administrative structure, access, quality, participation, economic and education development, attitudes, awareness, aspirations, teachers' administration, innovative approaches, policies, etc.

Using the example of the DNTs of Andhra Pradesh, the present study reflects upon the issues related to the education among the DNTs in India. A few aspects can be brought to light through the present study. A gulf prevails between the DNTs and modern education system leading to their marginalisation. Here, an attempt is made to examine why this is so. Another being that while education may be accessed with greater sedentarisation, (implicit in the development strategies employed by the States) DNTs have a self-perception and way of life which makes them less inclined to low wage employment – often the consequence of sedentarisation for the majority of the DNTs. They are not simply passive bystanders to the development rhetoric, rather they involute and negotiate with the powers that be and adopt a maximising strategy through vote bank circumstances. Here a few questions arise: first, what kind of education should one envision for the children of the DNTs? Perhaps, one that recognises them and includes them, one that is not entirely detached to livelihood means, etc. As importantly, how should education be imparted to the children of DNTs? Through regular teacher student interactions, or coupling it with innovations in

Information and Communication Technology (ICT), radio, TV, etc.? or laying greater stress on orality and experiential knowledge as witnessed in alternative education experiments? The government should think of an educational programme that bridges the gap between knowledge and livelihood and a comprehensive educational support system that has potential of delivering their livelihoods. It is difficult for the DNTs to send their children to regular schools because their livelihood makes it necessary for them to keep moving. These groups include people who move from village to village in search of employment. They move seasonally in search of paid work in towns and cities. Therefore, special mobile schools, ashram schools, residential schools should be opened for the children of these communities. The DNT children must have an easy access to an equal opportunity for education. Recruitment of teachers to these schools may be done by adhering to the standards of excellence at par with other schools. The facilities and infrastructure in the DNT schools must be of national standard. The DNT children should be provided access to the general schools so that they can have a social co-education. To encourage primary education among them, more hostel facilities should be provided.

State Provisions for the Education of DNT Children

The State commitment to the education of denotified, nomadic and semi-nomadic communities' children is contained in Article 15(4), 45 and 46 of the Indian Constitution. Article 45 declares State's endeavour to provide free and compulsory education for all children until they complete the age of 14 years. Both Central and State Governments took up the responsibility of making special educational provisions. The Backward Classes Enquiry Committee (1955) under Kaka Kalelkar had recommended certain measures for the upliftment of the DNTs. However, no serious attempts had been made by the State or Central governments to implement these measures. Excepting a few, most of them still remain socially isolated. The educational standards amongst the DNTs are much lower than those of the rest of the tribes/communities. The reasons are: many of the parents of the children belonging to DNT who have been to the police stations and faced criminal charges find it difficult to admit their children to normal schools as the other communities find some pretext or the other to keep them out. As a consequence, most of the students, particularly girls belonging to DNTs, are unable to pursue education at the primary level. It was felt that the scheme of education should be such that their children should acquire vitality, energy, resourcefulness and skill. They should make use of their innate abilities in adventure, romance and achievement. Therefore, in the first two Five-Year Plans, the focus was on basic education, residential schools, the basic facility of schools especially in remote and tribal areas and also providing scholarships and books. The scope of enabling interventions expanded considerably after the Fourth

Five-Year Plan. During the period from First Five-Year Plan to Fourth Five-Year Plan, efforts were made to set up schools, educational centres, Sanskar Kendras, Balwadis and Ashram schools. Scholarships was disbursed to school-going students. These schools do not have the vocational training programmes.

School Participation of DNT Children

The studies carried out so far and the reports of the various Commissions and Committees of SC/STs do not show the educational progress and a clear census data of the DNTs. The educational progress of the DNTs is rather slow and uneven. The only sources of data that are available are the old census reports (1901, 1911, 1931, 1941, 1961), etc. and a few reports of the Commissioner and Commission for SC/STs. However, it is the fact that the literacy level among the DNTs in India in general and in Andhra Pradesh in particular is very low. There is zero per cent literacy among the DNT girl children. Though State and Central Governments have done little for the education of DNTs still there is a long way to go so far as the educational progress of the DNTs are concerned. The field study reveals the fact that there is very poor attendance and enrolment of children in the DNT settlement schools in the age of 5–14 years. The government schemes and programmes do not have any positive impact in the DNT schools. There is high dropout rate among the DNT children at the primary stage itself. The impact of poor attendance and high dropout rates of DNT children is visible in low completion rates of their enrolment and retention at the elementary school level. Marked educational disparities also exist within each category of the DNTs. The enrolment ratios in the settlement schools are very low. School attendance rates of the DNT children is very poor. Therefore, a proper census data of the school participation of DNT children in different states needs to be urgently carried out for determining the exact literacy rates, educational progress, problems, school attendance of children in the 5–14 years age, the dropout rates, percentage of enrolment, etc. needs to be brought to light to understand the stark reality of their education. Often both physically and socially isolated from majority communities, the DNTs have lower enrolment and achievement rates and higher dropout rates than the general population, Scheduled Castes and Tribes. The study in the five selected DNT schools in four districts in Andhra Pradesh reveals the fact that there is high absenteeism among the DNT who are enrolled. Absenteeism is higher in grades 1 to 5. Very young children and those old enough to help with household work are less likely to attend the school regularly. Migration, engaging children in work for money, non-residential teachers, sibling care, illiteracy of parents, labour work, contract work, child labour, psychological barriers, seasonal occupation are some of the specific problems of the tribal children in the DNT settlements. Illiteracy is rampant among the Denotified Tribes. According to a rough estimate given by a government official, about 10 per cent of the DNTs in Andhra Pradesh did have basic education. Only 2 per cent of the population were matriculated and only 15 per cent population only can write their names. Their problems are aggravated because they are living in poverty-stricken conditions for generations together. Therefore, the government has to set up quality schools, Ashram and residential schools, hostel facilities for these children. In the present DNT schools, teachers are not paid their salaries on time, appointed on contract basis and lack motivation. Illiteracy is so high that it is even difficult to draw teachers from these communities with minimum qualifications.

Educational Inequality among the DNTs

Nomadic, semi-nomadic and DNTs in India are at the bottom of the educational and developmental pyramid. This needs to be recognised. Owing to increased pressure for survival, scarcity of land and the forces of globalisation and development, the DNTs are sidelined across the country. This is aggravated by the fact that governments do not try to understand their needs in education, infrastructure and political representation. Most of the DNTs are labourers. They go to different places in search of occupations. Child labour practices are more in these communities. So they continue to remain out of school. However, it is also important to note that there is growing demand and aspiration for education among the DNT tribes (Yerukula, Sugali, Yanadi, Woddars, etc.). The situation regarding school attendance, school completion and dropout in primary and middle school levels is unsatisfactory. There is also unevenness in educational participation levels due to the reason that many of the DNTs are not included in the list of Scheduled Tribes (Woddara, Dommara, Rellis, etc.). It is also clear that a large number of DNT children are struggling to attain equitable educational access. Even equal educational opportunity in elementary education has not been achieved in terms of access and survival. The goal of equality of opportunity in education among the DNTs seems to be remote. They live under the conditions of acute poverty, displacement, forced migration in search of livelihood, poverty – all these factors act as fundamental deterrents to educational access and attainment. Hunger, ill-health, malnourishment are widely prevalent among the DNT children. Mid-day meal schemes has proved to be an important incentive for the children to attend the school. This should be implemented very seriously. Quality and nutritious food has to be provided for these children. Incentives for the food supply persons/contractors should be paid regularly as well. Special provisions needs to be made for the girl children's education to prevent the possibilities of forced labour.

Similarly, girl children of these communities need to be retained in their traditional crafts so as to find market for their crafts through government channels.

Constraints in Educational Opportunities to Children

The children of the DNTs differ in certain qualities from the students of plain and urban areas. The special qualities of these children are: (1) enjoys complete freedom/do not like restrictions, (2) do not grab opportunity but accept if provided, (3) not a leader but a follower, (4) slow learner because of lack of opportunities, (5) he/she can also learn like others, (6) disadvantaged because of lack of opportunities, (7) possess inferiority complex, (8) not speaker of words but a doer of deeds, (9) heeds to only those which are useful to him, (10) independent but not under others' direction, (11) very disciplined, (12) more self-respecting, (13) very plain and comes to do any activity if convinced, (14) opportunities are not given due to vested interests, (15) education required to be need-based, (16) education through productive activities, (17) needs vocation based education, (18) requires activities to draw out innate potentialities, (19) lacks distributive justice, (20) not less in IQ than others, (21) participates in physical activities, (22) likes to learn through imitation rather than instruction, and (23) very bold. The DNT children are very clean, articulate, honest, unite and good sports persons. However, there is a psychological impact on the children's minds when parents are taken by the police and kept in remand or in jails. There is also psychological impact on these children when the general public and school teachers abuse them (sometimes) as they come from the DNT families/settlements. Often the DNT children face a number of problems in their living surroundings such as frequent quarrels, abuse, harassment by police and the other public. The parents also use children for the preparation of illicit liquor. The children often accompany the parents to distant places for their nefarious activities. They are well versed to the code language used by their parents. Generally children are involved in petty trade and poultry work. Therefore, there is an urgent need to mainstream the social and cultural illiterates of the indigenous society children. Therefore, (1) education which is a fundamental right for children up to 14 years should be provided to the children of these communities and (2) special schools need to be set up in the DNT settlements (colonies). Parents should be encouraged to make their children attend the schools regularly. Teachers of these schools should take the responsibility for ensuring the safety and dignity of the DNT children and (3) using of the children for the nefarious activities must be stopped.

Schools

Each DNT settlement has a school. The DNT schools do not have hostels. The DNT schools are not residential schools. Some of the DNT schools are managed by the private missionaries (Stuartpuram settlement managed by the Salvation Army). This is meant to serve as an alternative to otherwise inferior mobile schools. However, the general feeling of the DNTs is that residence in hostels implies their isolation from their tradition, society and knowledge. The DNT children take the profession of their parents from the age of 8–10 years. This leads to child labour. The hostels and the schools isolate the children from the other children in the schools and succeed in bringing the divide between DNT children and the children of their communities. Thus, the hostels, residential schools though viewed as a good thing by many, this will result in a three-step alienation of these children. They will be distanced from the native children as well as their own kin groups and way of life. Parents hesitate to send their children particularly girls to these schools and hostels which further reduce the chances of DNTs right to education. In the DNT settlements, hardly any women are educated. Most of the children in the settlements lack proper motivation for study. The current scenario is that the DNT parents put their sons in hostels. They prefer that they find secure government jobs. The girl children are married at an early stage and are dropouts of the schools.

Today in all the DNT settlements, there are no proper schooling facilities. There are no proper school buildings. The existing schools were constructed during the British period. These schools do not attract the parents to send their wards to the schools. In one room, multiple classes are held. A few of them are preferring to send children to the neighbouring places. Some of the DNT schools have single teachers. There is rampant teacher absenteeism. The schools lack basic infrastructural facilities. Schools do not have toilets. Teachers are transferred frequently. These schools do not have proper equipment such as furniture, blackboards, modules, kit materials, etc. Teaching is very poor. The schools are incomplete. Schools do not have kitchens and electricity. The classrooms are unattractive. The teachers are unqualified. No proper housing facilities exist for the teachers who stay in the DNT colonies. Non-tribal teachers have a negative feelings about the DNT children. Being mobile from anywhere for six months to a year, DNT children rarely get an opportunity to attend the regular schools. There are virtually no educational institutions that have developed a system to cater to the educational needs of children on the move. They have neither their schools or hostels for housing them while their parents go in search of work. In the rare event that they do get access to education, the education itself has little or no relevance to their livelihoods. Lack of proper school buildings, lack of separate rooms for different classes, lack of teachers for each class, lack of sufficient teachers, lack of drinking water, electricity, toilets, compound wall, kitchen, etc. and lack of school health programme is seriously hampering the education of the DNT children.

In terms of development, the most pertinent aspect is education. The enrolment of nomadic/DNT children is not increasing in schools but retention rates are also not satisfactory. Poverty, seasonal migration, parental apathy, domestic insecurity, unattractive format of education and social ridicule are main hindrances in the spread of education. Some voluntary agencies have attempted non-formal education methods but their scope has been limited. The ideal solution for the DNT/nomadic children is ashram schools. In the State like Andhra Pradesh, the State Government is supporting a large number of ashram schools run by private institutions. But the quality of education is poor, as most of the ashram schools are run with political and economic motives. A large number of pseudo-DNTs also take advantage of the ashram schools. Educational efforts, from within the DNT communities, need to be made on a massive scale so that at least the next generation is put on a sound developmental path.

School Quality

Provision of schools within easy access has been relatively poor for the DNT children when compared to the general population. The settlement schools are located in far-flung places and in thick forests. Due to the geographical locations, the children are unable to attend the schools. The denotified tribal families usually live in separately segregated habitations. Their residential patterns had an impact for the physical and social access to schools. The schools in the settlements have only up to primary level. There is a need to upgrade the schools up to secondary and higher secondary levels. The DNTs have to send their children for a distance of more than 20 kms or in some cases they go to other village schools to pursue the secondary and collegiate education. DNT schools located in the settlements rank at the bottom in terms of quality, infrastructural facilities and human resources. There is an urgent need to improve the status of the schools (upgradation of DNT schools as junior colleges, English medium residential or ashram schools). In these schools, there is no provisions/rooms for serving the mid-day meals. There are no separate hostels for girls. Teachers do not have the basic facilities like tables and chairs. Timely medical check-ups and medical kit facilities are lacking. The Government should provide additional funds to improve the school quality. Therefore, the government should take active steps to provide quality basic education in the DNT schools. Most of these communities are illiterates and first generation learners. They have less chances of getting quality education in the present set-up of schools. The schooling pattern available at present should be changed totally. A new pattern of education has to be introduced in the existing schools. Adequate special provisions and budgetary allocations must be made. Special coaching centres should be encouraged by giving aids for setting up of special coaching in the schools for various examinations. Qualified and experienced teachers must be invited to give special training for these children.

Teachers

Keeping the DNT children systematically out of schools through harassment means that there will not be any competition from the next generations of these communities for government jobs. The children of the DNTs are not welcome at the municipal schools of their 'Settlement' areas. The DNT children are harassed and persecuted by the children of higher castes in the public schools. The teachers also harass and abuse the DNT children. The teachers do not check the bullying faced by the DNT children by the higher caste children. The teachers give harsh treatment to these children in the schools. It is reportedly learnt that they were made to sit separately in the classrooms by the teachers, as a result of which there is a widespread inclination in the community to keep the children out of schools and train them in traditional skills to fend for themselves in future. Therefore, the children living in the 'Settlement' areas are encouraged to work on the traditional occupations with their parents in order to restrain their children from such harassments at schools. It is also observed that the teachers refrain the children from mingling with the children of other communities.

Educational Schemes and Incentives

The incentives earmarked for the DNT schools are not properly distributed in the schools. The children studying in the schools are not receiving their scholarships, uniforms, textbooks, notebooks, school grant, mid-day meals and other incentives in time. Even if the schools received the incentives, the DNT children are not able to get them from the school authorities. In the DNT schools, scholarships and stipends are provided by the State Government to support the children to continue and complete their education. However, there is a great delay in dispatching scholarships. The government scholarships have never reached to the DNT children studying in the remote schools. In order to provide the facilities in the elementary schooling of the children of DNT communities, mobile schools and libraries should be set up at the locations of their stay so that no child remains without access to education. School administrations are known to have refused admission to the children belonging to DNTs owing to the stigma attached to them. An Act of preventing atrocity to the DNT children in the schools must include this aspect so that social discrimination in the schools can be stopped. Scholarships should be provided to DNT students from primary level to higher education to bring them into the mainstream of society. Separate book banks for DNT children should be established. The government should launch vocational training programmes for the DNT children. There should be special training programmes to develop leadership qualities among its youth so that they can act as focal point of dissemination of knowledge in their respective areas of activities. Serious efforts should be made to develop traditional skills among these children as this can ensure a sustainable source of income for them. The government should make efforts to preserve the cultural heritage/handicrafts of the DNT communities through their education. Some of the communities have developed over a period of time, through their experience and expertise in artisanship and handicrafts. Various handicraft items made by them are very popular in the country. There is a great demand of these items in the international market too. But due to the poor financial conditions, they cannot improve their production capacity. The government should come forward and encourage their children, giving them assistance for their handicraft work. Special measures/packages of education must be designed by the government in this regard. Some of the DNTs possess wonderful knowledge about herbs and medicines. Therefore, their expertise can be utilised in the collection and development of herbs and medicinal plants which are in great demand in the country and outside. The government should prepare a road map on the educational reforms for the DNT children. The road map should focus on the specific educational reforms, utilisation of government funds, curriculum, training and school health programmes. Access to education, hostels, school grant and mid-day meal schemes also should be highlighted. Serious problems such as inefficiency of the teachers, management, mismanagement of funds, nepotism and corruption should be strictly dealt with. The standards of educational facilities in these schools have to be increased.

Language

It has been recognised that education is more effective when imparted in the mother tongue at the primary level, by the community members or bilingual teachers. While this has been integrated in the educational structure of the DNT communities the quality of education and teacher motivation is so poor that most of the children do not even qualify for admission or encouraged to speak their home language at primary or secondary schools. Though the Government of Andhra Pradesh has prepared bilingual textbooks, posters, dictionaries, glossaries, kits, materials and bridge inventories in tribal languages they are hardly of any use for the teachers working in the tribal schools. There is an urgent need for the training of teachers who are working in the DNT schools to encourage the children to speak their mother tongue and also the teachers should learn children's language for the effective communication in the classroom. The Constitutional Provision of Article 350A recognised the importance of the minority languages. Children must be educated in their home language at the primary level. Loss of a language means the loss of a certain way of knowing the world. Experiences of schooling of the DNT children in Andhra Pradesh have revealed the displacement of Yerukulas, Yanadis, Sugalis, Boyas, Woddars, Dasaris and other DNT tribes. Therefore, the government should take active measures to introduce the mother tongue (Banjara, Yerukula, Yanadi, Boyas, etc.) in primary education in DNT Settlement (village) schools under Sarva Shiksha Abhiyan (SSA) under Article 29(1) and 350 A of the Constitution of India and inclusion of Yerukula and Banja tribal languages in the 8th Schedule of the Constitution. Similarly, other DNT languages also needs to be considered.

Curriculum

DNT children are imaginative participants in the process of defining their space, having the capacity to inhabit their own conceptual world whilst mediating and participating in that of adults. Which areas of the landscape/knowledge do the DNTs and their children attach meaning to, and how does their knowledge/skills relate to their own search for relaxation, play and excitement? Indeed, the DNTs have the rich folklore and art in their society. They take the central position in performing them in their villages regularly. Story-telling, dances, puppetry, folk songs, music, community gathering – all these activities in their society seems to contribute a lot for their children's fertile imagination and effective learning. In taking into consideration their culture-specific curriculum, the present work hopes to ascertain the impact that restricted movements of many of the DNT communities could have on their education, their physical and cultural well-being and extent to freedom, and natural aesthetics. This can certainly have a positive impact on their culture, creation and transmission. This suggests a particular way of learning that is sensitive to the life conditions and situations existing in their colonies or villages. Integration of games, sports, music, cultural activities should be introduced in the present schools and in the school curriculum of DNT children. Virtually no value is attached to the sophisticated skills, knowledge systems and complex institutional structures of the DNTs which should be 'at the centre of every analysis of the continuous failure, with regard to the DNTs and of the Universal Project of Education'. There is a virtual absence of focus in research on the nature of association between formal education and their traditional knowledge.

The depth of knowledge the DNT possess of their regions, forests, flora and fauna and the thick forests is unmatched. But so far, they have not been able to explore it. The parents and children of the DNT communities have abundance of knowledge about the locally available resources, herbs, medicinal plants, etc. The local business communities extract medicinal herbs collected by these communities. Further, children show acrobatic feats and perform their exceptional skills in towns, markets, bazaars by performing their feats. The children present cultural shows to the public in order to make a living. Among the children of the DNT communities, there are very good sport persons, musicians, painters and dancers also. They possess variety of skills. There is an urgent need to tap these skills performed by them by incorporating their culture in the present educational system. Education of the DNT communities must be rooted to their development process. Their education must result in a change for their betterment. Their schools must create an atmosphere of the innate understanding of their social reality of their lives and, in particular, they should be able to examine how best they wish to be and can be educated and empowered. While to err is implicit in the pedagogy, there is a need to examine why the past educational modules have not succeeded. There is a need to adopt better approaches which specifically focus on teacher training and child support programmes for the children of DNTs. The use of speech, drawings, stories, songs and photography in order to encourage the children to construct accounts of their lives in their own terms must be generated. An examination of their textbooks, as well as the folklore, material culture, symbols, etc. that adults and children use to communicate their experiences and interpretations of their knowledge, landscape, cultural expressions and problems is urgently needed. The cognitive processes associated with life management must be examined. A study of the developmental paradigm and the continued marginalisation of the DNT children must be undertaken. What is also needed is to examine the government and non-government schemes initiated for their development, linguistic marginalisation and the structural and infrastructural problems connected with their education and poverty. The larger goal of the development of the DNTs, their right to education and dignity should be explored by addressing the issue of power relations with a sensitive approach to issues of mutual perceptions. It is hoped that a set of recommendations by the government may emerge to influence the policy aimed at the development of the DNT children in their education.

Home, School and Community

Harmonious relation between school, home and community plays a very important role in improving the educational levels among DNT communities. Home atmosphere forms an important variable, influencing in the child's educational achievement. The child needs encouragement and assistance from family members for coping up with the demands coming from the schooling process. Community support, on the other hand, goes a long way, in helping the teachers to perform their duties. Community involvement is essential for enrolling the children of the community and take interest in the functioning of the school with community involvement, the teachers will be more alert and focused in performing their job. Parents' associations and Village

Education Committees (VECs) are the bodies that are expected to bridge the gap between school, parents and the village. Effective functioning of these linkages or further activating these linkages is urgently required. This becomes crucial, considering the unique problems faced by the denotified communities.

Among denotified communities, family life is frequently interrupted because of the culture of crime. Though very few families are indulging in criminal activities, the stigma attached to the community and the branding that goes with the community label are still haunting the denotified communities. Due to perceived lack of opportunities, parents do not have enthusiasm in enrolling their children in schools. Generally, the educated from denotified communities are discriminated in employment. Because of economic compulsions, parents regularly depend upon children to assist them, sometimes even in illegal activities. The attraction of making quick money lures the parents towards crime. Male members in some families are on the move, both for legitimate and criminal activities. Police harassment of parents, deeply affects the psyche of children. Children who come to schools in a disturbed state of mind, cannot concentrate on studies. On the whole, childhood in denotified communities is not a cherished experience. Children coming from families without proper environment lack interest in studies. The best possible solution is to remove the children from home atmosphere, by shifting them to residential institution. Denotified communities face several problems on social and economic fronts. Wherever the members are, their past haunts them. Efforts have been made to reform the communities by Missionaries and social reformers. Some success has been achieved. But social reforms alone cannot solve the problem, without sustainable economic rehabilitation. The community is divided. Those who are well off, are trying to give better education to their children in private schools. Others are indifferent. By and large, villagers hardly take interest in school affairs. More awareness needs to be created in the community about the importance of educating the children. The schools existing in the villages of denotified communities are in a bad shape. Inadequate staffing, lack of proper buildings, teaching aids and other infrastructure form the major handicaps. Such schools cannot serve the cause of denotified communities facing their own unique problems. Thus, on all the three fronts, i.e. the home, community and school, there are inherent drawbacks to be tackled urgently, for ensuring effective linkage between them.

Action Points

- Highlighting the home atmosphere through case studies.
- Presentation of the positive and negative aspects of community interest and involvement.
- Projecting the advantages of residential institution in enhancing enrolment, reduction of dropouts and bettering the performance.

- Orienting the teachers towards the problems of denotified communities.
- Exploring avenues for community participation.
- Highlight the psychological trauma of children whose parents are in police custody.
- Identification of the socio-economic features of parents sending their children to convents and English medium schools.
- Case studies of educated (high achievers) for projecting them as role models.
- Overall assessment of the contribution made by Missionaries, NGOs and government efforts.
- Case studies of children drawn into crime, for projecting the under currents.

Recommendations

The settlements are misnomer and, therefore, there is a need to use the names of modern villages rather than using the terms like settlements. Thirty years back the villagers of Denotified communities wished to have protection from the clutches of the police and public. They were harassed, humiliated and belted by the police. It was a vicious circle for them. Today, in the DNT colonies, English medium schools are preferred. It proves the fact that there is an ocean of difference in their life between 30 years ago when reform work was started, and the present-day conditions.

In the primary schools of Denotified Tribal Settlements in Andhra Pradesh the students face many discriminating and psychological problems. The children of Denotified Communities cannot be compared with general students. Even though the DNT settlements are now made free colonies, they are not free from the stigma. Still the public uses the word 'settlement' for these colonies. The Tribal Welfare Department should rename these colonies with patriotic historic personalities, etc.

In Denotified villages, schools should have proper buildings. Each class should have a separate room. Each classroom should have its own teacher. Then only can the teachers concentrate on the children. Headmaster is the leader and he is the sole personality in the school to mould the personality of the students, guide the teachers and maintain good rapport with the parents and community people. He is the person concerned in associating himself with the government officials. Therefore, he should be a path-finder. He takes care of the maintenance of the status of the school, upgrading it and taking care of the quality of education in the school. He should work hard day and night for the achievement of the school and give proper directions to the school personnel. People or the community look at him as an exemplary person. He should have the authority to take voluntary workers in the absence of teachers.

Every school should have a compound wall. Other rooms like kitchen and dining hall should be provided in the school. Sanitation is very important and every child should evince interest in the health and hygienic problems. The teachers and headmaster should take care of the school and children. Medical check-ups are very important. The headmaster should arrange the medical check-ups both for the teachers and for the students. Sometimes the students may have high temperature and they frequently abstain from the school. In such a situation, the teachers should take keen interest and find out the causes of their absence. At least minimum medicines with medical kit is a must. It is expected from the teaching staff to visit the homes of the students who are absent from the schools to find out the causes and motivate them to attend the school. The school should attract the students. This is by means of creating opportunities for the articulation of students, their originality and creativity. A student should not get the impression that school is not attractive and has a negative effect on their personality.

The facilities which are given to the primitive tribals, need to be provided for the schools in the DNT areas. The school buildings should have proper lighting and ventilation. Scholarship and other incentives should be given to the students. Though merit is not the only criteria, elimination of competition will go a long way for the improvement of the schools. In other words, ashram schools are preferable in areas where DNT schools prevail. In addition to the Denotified settlements, there are some hamlets in other districts where the DNTs exist. For instance, Gollakuppam of Chittoor district, Pulivendala of Cuddapah district, Madhira of Kumbum district; Lakkavaram of West Godavari district and two small villages Pullota and Tallota of Srikakulam districts. These hamlets and the surrounding areas should have ashram schools where other backward classes or dalit students can also be admitted in these schools.

Government should show priority-based education in the areas where the denotified tribes are stigmatised. If alternative jobs are not provided to the womenfolk and the youth, they indulge in the culture of crime and the children imbibe the same culture. For such children, audio-visual lessons should be providod. The headmasters must be provided with additional amount of money to deal with the day-to-day problems of the settlements. Government programmes like CLIP, CLAP (Childerns' Learning Improvement Programme, Childerns' Learning Acceleration Programme) in Andhra Pradesh are essential for these children. Play materials will also be an additional attraction to the students. Psychological factors hamper their interest when their parents are taken to the police station. In such a situation, the teachers should inspire them, solace them and explain them briefly about the conditions of their past history. However, unity is found among all the students. Sometimes they may be dull in academic subjects but they are active in other fields. In such a situation, they should be given special training in vocational courses. Teachers should give remedial coaching for such students. Headmaster and teachers of the schools in the Denotified areas should visit the homes of the students. They should know the reasons for the dropouts and persuade them to attend the school by convincing the parents and the students. When police ill-treats the students, the teachers should explain them and safeguard them. Gradually, they are required to give them moral lessons. At that moment, the teachers are models for them. The teachers should encourage them in games and sports. The students realise the interest of the teachers and gradually a change can be brought in their attitude. Maximum attention by the teachers towards the child will definitely have an impact on the minds of the parents.

Pertaining to the language of the DNTs, the children are familiar with the code home language used by the parents. If the medium in the schools is the same, it will be more advantageous for the students to converse in the same language with the teachers. Home language will reduce the gap between the teachers and children to some extent. The community should also take proper interest in the DNT schools. Parents and village elders should attend the village committee meetings regularly. Sometimes, they can also spare money for the progress of the institution. If they attend these meetings regularly, then there is scope for them to find out the causes for the dropout of their children. Sometimes the children go to the fields with their parents, protect the siblings, rear pigs, goats, sheep, milching animals. The parents and children should realise the fact that education will pave the way for their future. The village elders should persuade the Mandal Revenue Officers (MROs) and other educational functionaries of that area to attend some of these meetings. Community should have an interest in the school as well as the society, where they are living. They should watch the teachers who come from outside to devote their time for the children of the village. The school should take proper interest in the social and cultural activities and in the celebration of the national festivals. The involvement of community and parental participation is very essential. Their assistance in financial matters will help the school. Another factor is the education of girl children. There is discrimination in upbringing of male and female children. Among the Yerukula community marriageable age for a girl is 17 years. Today, child marriages are taking place in these areas. If the village elders understand the problem, then there will be scope for curbing these prevailing social evils.

Another important factor is that parents are not accessible to the children. Children have their demands, their own emotions. Unless they are satisfied they cannot be in their normal self. In the broken homes or when the father is absent, it is very difficult for the children to adjust and go to school regularly. Father's absence, ill-treatment by the police, treating of the womenfolk when they are in remand are factors which affect the mind of the child. The atmosphere prevailing in the school is quite different from that of the home.

The general atmosphere with regard to education in all the settlements is almost the same. All the settlements should have a pre-primary school with training facilities so as to enable the children to join in the State-run schools. As members of the denotified tribes, they would like to have jobs which give them immediate remuneration and relief. Employment in labour intensives industrial establishments should be created for them by absorbing them in large numbers. This might give them immense satisfaction and confidence. This will make parents realise the importance of education of their children. If parents are benefitted financially, then they will not force their children to go for labour contract work, child labour, rearing of domestic animals, etc. If teachers are able to educate the Denotified society, then automatically the importance of eradicating the child marriage, and the punishments given to them by the people in case of chastity and other things will be clear. The panchayat will decide what type of punishment is required for those people. Such type of incidents leave an impression on the minds of the students. To improve the education of the children of the DNTs, the whole atmosphere should be changed. For the overall betterment, the public, the community, the parents, the teachers and the government should work like a team and improve their situation. There should be a committee at the state level to improve all the aspects of the so-called 'Settlements'. Government officials, representatives of the DNT families, researchers, social workers should form the committee. The psychological and sociological factors of the DNT communities should be understood by one and all. Electronic media should also help these villages in such a way so as to enable them to become free citizens. Thus, the schools will come up to the expectations.

Conclusion

The present position seems to be not quite encouraging in the development and the overall conditions of the DNTs colonies, and the overall socio-economic and cultural conditions of the DNT in their settlements. Even now a few families are committing crimes in all the settlements. This can be attributed to the poverty of these people. The government should come forward to provide them with alternative means of livelihood. Though the government is taking some immediate rehabilitation measures such as providing them buffaloes, rickshaws, provision shops, loans, etc. these measures can hardly be a permanent solution. However, the following few observations are made below with a view to improve the rehabilitation development programmes for the welfare of these DNTs of Andhra Pradesh.

1. The DNTs should be provided with enough land and bank loans to make them self-sufficient.
2. Small scale industries such as basket-making, weaving, mat-making, brick-making, and the like, should be encouraged.
3. Dairy farming, piggery, poultry are useful schemes for their economic development. The government has to provide financial assistance on loan-cum-subsidy basis.
4. Arrangements should be made with banks to sanction loans to the DNTs who are interested in setting up of small business such as soda shops, tea-stalls, provision stores or fancy stores, etc.
5. They may be given employment such as constables, peons, bus conductors, etc. Such a step if taken, would not only provide them with a respectable livelihood but also take them away from the atmosphere of the settlement.
6. Stolen property dealers, corrupt police officials, investors in crime and greedy advocates should be strictly dealt with.
7. Industries may be established in the DNT settlements on the waste lands so that a large number of people will get employment opportunities.
8. Educational facilities as they exist today are not adequate. A few more schools, (English medium) colleges, Industrial Training Institutes (ITIs) and a university may be established and all these schools (up to junior-Degree stages) should be provided with the necessary infrastructural facilities.
9. Regular water supply should be provided for the DNT settlement lands so as to enable them to irrigate their lands. They should not lose interest in cultivation.
10. The state government should provide the DNTs with certain measures for the welfare of the DNTs such as: (1) Provision of suitable land for cultivation, (2) Setting up Upper Primary Schools for education, (3) Starting handloom, weaving centres as cottage industries, (4) Setting up co-operative societies for supplying credit and other necessaries of the life, (5) Opening of dispensaries, (6) Construction of *pucca* houses for habitation, and (7) Imparting training for the inmates of industrial agricultural settlements, etc. These facilities were not provided by the government. The government should immediately take up these measures to improve their conditions.
11. Woddars, Dasaris, Dommaras, Nakkalas and others have different connotations in different districts. For example the Woddars are called as Gollas, Yera Gollas, Katheras, Dasaris, etc. Unfortunately,

these communities are not in the list of Scheduled Tribes. Hence, they are losing the opportunities for reservation both in educational institutions and in jobs. Unemployed people are found in all the settlements. So, it is suggested that the government should take measures in giving them the status of Scheduled Tribes. For this purpose, they have gone even to the court. So far no justice has been given to them. The Human Right Commission, The National Commission for DNT and Semi-Nomadic Tribes, Ministry of Social Justice and Empowerment, should help them in getting the required social justice to these communities.

12. The water facilities available in the DNT colonies/settlements are not adequate. They should be provided with sufficient water facilities to encourage them to grow the cash and commercial crops. For example, the water tank in Siddhapuram DNT colony became dysfunctional. If it functions well it is useful for 20 villages of surrounding areas.
13. At present, all villages of DNT communities are plagued by the evil of illicit liquor. Lack of employment makes them take to this practice. Self-employment opportunities should be provided for the women of the DNT communities.
14. The stigma of their being ‘criminals’ constrained them more glaringly, as people always suspect a person who has spent some time in the DNT settlements colonies. No doubt, this is a serious psychological problem. To get rid of the stigma attached to them will take longer time. The terms such as ‘Criminal Tribes’, ‘Settlements’ should be removed.
15. Reformation should not be merely materialistic. They should be instilled with self-confidence and their faith in humanity should not be shaken. Rehabilitation programmes concerning these people should be entrusted to the educational institutions as part of their extension programmes or to reputed social service organisations whose approach is always humanitarian. Such people help them in the rehabilitative work. One of the main problems identified by the field experiences is about the social treatment meted out to the families of the DNT tribes. For generations together, the DNT families and their members have been labelled as criminals and have suffered dishonour and social negligence. The reasons are not far to seek here given the background of the socially despicable avocation as practiced by some of the people belonging to DNT tribes. The children and women, in particular have suffered ignominy from mainstream society. The stigma of criminality is still one of the major impediments in the smooth run of educational progress of children and youth. Children often faced a kind of social alienation in most walks of social life. Social alienation particularly in young age hampers the growth of psycho-social faculties of the children. Social practices of the mainstream society have denied

opportunities for the children coming from the so-called DNT families residing in the settlement areas. The approaches of the government often times remain impersonal and lack human element and eye on social cohesiveness in its approach. However, there can be education without even the formal modes and methods of schooling. But mere efforts on mainstream socialisation does not open a wide social canvas for the children because there is already a hostile attitude in the outside society. The school or the process of schooling in settlement areas or settlement schools may be used as instruments or tools to impart social culture, feelings of common fraternity, community approach, adjustment mentality, atmosphere of working and learning together and finally moral dynamics of social and cultural behaviour. The schools in the DNT settlement areas are to be treated or perceived from a different angle where they are expected to combine the role of an instructor, change agent, catalyst and humanism.

The main problem in the government schools or those run by private parties is that there is a general schooling atmosphere that best suits the needs of the children from the mainstream society. This kind of atmosphere need not always be congenial to the requirements of social and cultural transformation of the children who are already suffering the social stigma and are alienated. When the government is taking care to mainstream the differently-abled children through advocating their admission into ordinary schools, so that these children too will have the necessary advantage of 'feel good' factor and forget the physical constraints, the same approach may, perhaps, be extended without any reservations in the case of the children who are socially alienated. However, in the present case, efforts shall be directed towards the direction of mingling ordinary children with the children of these tribes in separate schools with residential facilities. Since the DNTs too are considered under the general item of 'tribes' by the planners and policy makers, the scope for public sanctions for the welfare of these relatively ignored tribes is limited and confined. Among the socially and economically backward classes majority of the families wish to retain some of their children at home without sending them to school. They have their own family and economic reasons for not sending their wards to centres of learning. Barring further discussion on this, the point of reference here is that children from the so-called DNT families (whether reformed or not) have a tendency of not going to school or dropping out school if already admitted, for, there is an unwritten feeling among these children that they will receive not only education, but also social humiliation from co-learners as well as teachers (sometimes). Secluded, aloof and separated they feel happier, than being insulted in the rest of the society. It is very important that the ice should be broken. So, special schools or shaping the existing schools/facilities as special schools for an ideal social integration are necessary. The need is that the children in these settlement areas may be exposed to a kind of development education where aspects of social development, mainstreaming and unhindered socialisation will combine to keep the morale of the learners on a higher pedestal. Along with prescribed and formatted curriculum, realistic or scientific knowledge, social outlook and personality development may be included in the general teaching atmosphere of the schools in settlements. Efforts are to be made to encourage ordinary students from outside the settlement to get admitted into these schools so that the dichotomy between the criminal (reformed or not) and the others may get diluted in the course of time.

Even though the Criminal Tribes Act was repealed in the post-Independence era (1952,) nobody took a keen interest in the execution of the government decision to making the settlements as free colonies. Thus, all the five settlements in Andhra Pradesh (Sitanagaram, Stuartpuram, Kapparallatippa, Siddhapuram and Lingala settlements) remained as ex-criminal settlements. The life conditions in the settlements had not changed. Out of these five colonies, Stuartpuram is under the control of the Salvation Army. The other four settlements were taken over by the government towards the end of the colonial rule. They were put under the revenue jurisdiction, and under the Social Welfare Department control. The government is the legal owner of all land and house sites in all the colonies. But in Stuartpuram, the Salvation Army is holding the key position even now. After Independence, the Madras Government appointed a committee under the chairmanship of Vepa Ramesam, ICS. The committee recommended to make all the settlements as free colonies/villages and distributed house sites to the occupants. It also recommended distribution of land to all those bonafied inhabitants who have been living there. The government notified through a G.O. in 1976 that all the DNT settlements would be considered as free colonies. Consequently, the government took control over all the lands in the DNT colonies and distributed some portion of the land in the name of local inhabitants with ownership rights. Thus, they started enjoying self-respect as the rightful owners of property on par with other members of the mainstream society.

Another important aspect concerning the DNTs is that a very small portion of them who were listed under ST category and who joined in the public employment were happy with their families. There was, thus, more clamour for public placements. The DNT families understood the importance of education, their children would definitely get good jobs. The government is also providing them some facilities including free boarding, lodging, fees, books, etc. These facilities are not being given to all the DNT families because some of them are under BC-A category. These facilities should be extended to the other DNT communities also. The parents of the children want to send their children to English medium schools or convents in the local areas. Some of the programmes that can be implemented by the government and non-governmental bodies are: (1) Designing common programmes for the people of the colonies and surrounding villages, (2) Integrated approach where the benefits would be shared by the reformed families and other families, (3) Youth exposure programmes, (4) Providing work opportunities, (5) Common health and education programmes, (6) Organisation of women groups, (7) Suitable agro-based programmes, (8) Establishment of research and reference institutes with emphasis on documentation, preservation and preparation of training modules and (9) Conduct of periodic awareness programmes and workshops, meetings on human rights issues and active interaction with the inmates, educated families, public officials, social activists and academicians.

The Denotified tribes still feel the pinch of the harassment from all the trivial and petty quarrels even at the domestic front. Their main contention is the stigma attached to them. They are unhappy with the attitude of the bureaucrats and public. The normal individuals among them are assuming their right to question which was hitherto denied to them. They are more vigorous and passionate in the act of questioning every minute aberration in their normal social life. They vociferously question all the irregularities in and outside the society. They have been unconsciously given to a staunch belief that they are morally superior to others. This is no fault of theirs. The public and the government unnecessarily involve in the routine lifestyles and problems of the DNT families. As long as this continues they cannot enjoy self-respect and human rights. Morality is more individual than social. If personal morality is socialised, we can talk of social and public morality. Without fulfilling this, any talk about the latter becomes an exercise in futility. Individual can be a moral human being when he or she is certain that their life is safe in the surrounding society and their needs are met through their hard work.

The Denotified tribes are leading a decent and dignified life. They hate their old habits. When they came out of the womb of crime and reformed themselves they had to encounter the outside institutions, social structures and individuals where elements of white collar criminality crept in. When they have tried to distance themselves from criminalisation of individuals, they were simultaneously facing the criminalisation of institutions, social structures and polity outside. While individual crime had an eagle's eye over it, the institutionalised crime had a protective cover in the democratic Indian polity.

Educational research concerning the DNT tribes has largely been deprived and neglected. Even the educational research of the SCs and STs in India has largely been descriptive, historical and empirical in nature. There is an urgent need to undertake the research grounded in critical structural and interpretative theoretical frames and draw upon conclusions from the DNT studies. Research on DNT communities must provide deeper understanding of their socio-cultural milieus, problems and educational issues concerning the DNT children. The participation of the DNT children in education is essential as is their own engagement with educational research towards an emancipatory purpose. In the education system, the syllabus may be included as per the curriculum designed by the NCF 2005 of the NCERT to meet the special educational needs of these communities. The Government of Andhra Pradesh through Tribal Welfare Department must particularly encourage the education among the DNT communities by providing all infrastructural facilities and educational needs to the DNT children.

To improve the education of the children of the DNTs, the whole atmosphere should be changed. For the overall betterment of these children, the public, the community, parents and teachers the government should work like a team and improve their situation. There should be a committee at the state level to improve all the aspects of the so-called settlements. Government officials, representatives of the DNT families, researchers, and social workers should form as members in the committee. The psychological and sociological factors of the DNT communities should be understood by one and all. Electronic media should also help these villages in such a way so as to enable them to become free citizens. Thus, the schools will come up to the expectations.

The following recommendations are suggested for the improvement of education among the DNT communities:

1. Universalisation of ICDS with secured anganwadi workers qualified to undertake pre-school education.
2. Strengthen pre-school component for Integrated Child Development Scheme (ICDS) – which is the responsibility of Women and Child Welfare Department.
3. Compulsory Elementary Education for DNT tribal children.
4. Reduction of dropout rate among nomadic, semi-nomadic and DNT children.
5. In Right to Education rules, ensure the clauses of reduction of dropout rate of NT/DNT/SNT children in settlement schools
6. Distance is actually affecting DNT children's education which is contextual for the NT/DNT/SNT communities' children (upper primary-Secondary levels).
7. Catchment area of schools – delimitation to be done and need-based assessment be done in time and time-bound manner.
8. Availability of Upper Primary and High Schools in NT/DNT/SNT colonies/villages.
9. Enhancement of scholarships for the tribal children for classes VI to XII.
10. Enhanced and simplification of norms for admission to DNT children in government, private-aided schools.
11. 25 per cent clause to be activated to ensure children from these communities to be a part of the schools and untapped capacity of the schools.

12. Girl-child friendly toilets in tribal schools.
13. Ending of Single Teacher Schools in tribal areas.
14. Qualification norms for teachers working in NT/DNT schools should adhere to RTE norms.
15. Teachers working in the DNT schools should be versatile in local languages.
16. Strengthening of District Institutes of Teacher Education (DIETs) to ensure availability of local teachers to teach in mother tongue.
17. Teacher skills need to be enhanced. Ensure teacher regularity in the DNT tribal schools and affective monitoring system in DNT schools.
18. Community participation in DNT schools and communitisation of education for NT/DNT children.
19. Nagaland model for strengthening the system of governance in tribal schools.
20. Local self-help groups, NGOs, Missionary bodies intervention/help to be extended to the education system of DNT children.
21. Right to Education deadline within six months of its notification in NT/DNT colonies.
22. School development plans for DNT schools.
23. Tribal child friendly curriculum in DNT schools.
24. In case of language without a script, the language of that state should be adopted.
25. No detention without effective implementation of continuous and comprehensive Evaluation.
26. Review of multiple standards and types of schooling in DNT settlements – no more low cost, low quality of schools for DNT children.
27. For migrant workers among the DNTs, alternative schools/tent schools/mobile schools.
28. More hostels for DNT tribal children, including basic security measures for the girls and boys to be ensured. RTE compliance to be ensured for the residential system in tribal schools.
29. Kasturba Gandhi Balika Vidyalayas for DNT girls and effective skill development norms for girl child's education in DNT colonies, safety, infrastructure norms, other programmes for the welfare of girl children, enhancing the unit cost for the development of the girl child in NT/DNT villages.
30. Safety for tribal children in Naxalite, inertial forest areas to be enhanced.
31. Banning of screaming, bullying, beating, severe punishments, no coercive conditions in schools and home atmosphere for DNT children.
32. CSIR, Kendriya Vidyalaya and Navodaya Vidyalaya schools in DNT colonies.
33. More realistic budgeting for school level programmes in tribal areas, effective mid-day meals scheme for tribal children, more fund allocation for enrolling of children in NT/DNT colonies/villages.
34. Post-elementary education for NT/DNT children.

35. Widening of Secondary Education network in tribal areas.
36. Greater thrust on quality education for the DNT tribal children in schools, more hostel facilities, very light education at the primary level and skill based, industrial, vocational training at Upper Primary, Secondary level.
37. Effective coaching facilities in tribal schools.
38. Models of other countries to be studied and adopted. Models should be affective and suitable with norms under the prevailing/existing conditions in DNT colonies.
39. Mobile, tent schools for the children of the migrant labourers among the DNT communities, and post metric scholarships for DNT children.
40. Health and nutrition for NT/DNT children.
41. Child survival and health across the ages of childhood till 18 years, including cultural and traditional practices with the causes of child marriages, denial of educational opportunities and other rights to the girl children for the DNTs need remedial action.
42. There is high level of malnutrition and forced insecurity across the NT/DNT colonies – the influence of other sections forced NT/DNTs to leave their hamlets, water scarcity for children, lack of safe drinking water, they are living in squalor amidst snakes, wild animals, their locality filled with breeding mosquitoes and factory waste, un-hygienic conditions at home front – these require due attention.
43. Prompt action in the cases of atrocities on the DNT children reported to the government authorities and the civil society.
44. Special concern for the health of girl children and nutrition of children under the category of below 6 years.
45. Unethical trials on the grown-up children of DNT communities to be discontinued.
46. Increased rate of selling of children in some of the DNT colonies, villages with false promises of bright future. Exploitation of children of DNTs through various means be put down.
47. Difficulty for the access of government services for the educated youth among the DNT communities is to be overcome through appropriate strategies.
48. Appointment of health personnel, including hospitals, nurses, doctors, Para-medical forces, etc. Mobile hospitals for the children of DNT communities.
49. Increase of State and Central Government budget for the education of the children of DNT/NT/SNT communities.
50. Life skills training for the women, youth and children in DNT villages may be organised.

Appendices

APPENDIX–I

Profile of Denotified Tribes/Communities in Andhra Pradesh

Bhatrajulu

Bhatrajulu are popularly known as Bhats. They live in Cuddapah district. They have been classified by the Government of Andhra Pradesh as a Backward Caste. They are endowed with the ability to recite ballads in poetic form. They have the ability to speak on any subject. Bhatrajulu are musicians and ballad reciters. They speak Telugu. Besides agriculture they have taken up animal husbandry, petty business and casual labour work. They encourage formal education for both boys and girls. There are very few in this community who have studied up to college level.

Boyas

Boyas are the descendants of the Boyas who had once escaped into the forests fearing that they would be caught by the local rulers/police for their tendency to steal. The Boya who lived in the hilly forest regions are called as 'Donga' Boyas. They live in Anantapur and Visakhapatnam districts. They have their own dialect called Kupia dialect. Previously, their language had no dialect. In recent times, the Christian Missionaries evolved a script for their language, making use of the Telugu alphabet. They are grouped under Group A of the Backward Classes by the Government of Andhra Pradesh. The Pedda Boyas are predominantly agricultural labourers. Since their agricultural productivity is very low, they get low wages for their agricultural work. They live in huts. Due to their poverty, some of them took up crime as a means of livelihood. Therefore, they were listed as a criminal tribe under the Criminal Tribes Act in Madras Province. The Boyas perform folk dances locally. It is called as *Kolatam*. The level of literacy among them is very low. Nowadays, the Boyas have realised the importance of education. They are encouraging their children to attend the schools. Among the Pedda Boyas formal education is not feasible for the children because of their poverty. Very few children go to school. The dropout rate of schooling children is very high due to the socio-economic backwardness and illiteracy of their parents.

Chakalis

Chakalis are a community of washermen. They are distributed throughout Andhra Pradesh. They are known by different names, i.e. Chakali, Chakla, Rajakulu, Dhobi and Madavali. Their concentration is in urban areas rather than in rural areas. Their houses are located near small tanks or streams known as *geddas*. The small tanks or streams are the main sources of water for washing clothes. As per the Report of the Backward Classes Commission of 1970, the total population of the Chakalis is 10,75,989 persons. The Chakalis speak Telugu language and different dialects depending on the area in which they live. Those living in the areas adjacent to other states, speak Tamil, Oriya, Marathi, etc. The educated people use the script of other languages also. The Chakalis are in the list of 'Backward Class' Community. Chakalis are a landless community. Washing clothes is their traditional occupation. It continues to be their primary economic activity today. Chakalis are benefitted very little by education facilities. Their children are engaged in cleaning the clothes of patients in the hospitals. Children studying in schools are not benefited by the mid-day meals programme.

Dandasis

Dandasis are traditionally employed as village watchmen. They are found in the northern coastal districts. They work as village servants. They live in East Godavari, Chittoor, Srikakulam and Cuddapah districts. The total population of the Dandasis is 5,410. They speak, read and write Oriya while communicating with their kin members. With other communities, they speak in a corrupt form of Telugu. They are classified as a Scheduled Caste. They are working as village servants. They are also engaged in cultivation, cattle rearing, agricultural labour and selling firewood. They do not have land. They work along with their children on annual payment. Child labour is more prevalent among them. The dropout rate is very high. Parents do not send their children to school because of economic reasons. Their literacy rate is very low, i.e. 10.65 per cent. They are very poor.

Dasaris

Dasaris are a Vaishnava mendicant community. They are known by different synonyms such as *Poosala Balija*, *Bukka Dasari* and *Krishna Balija* in different areas of their habitation. Dasaris are religious mendicants belonging to different classes of Sudras. They are distributed throughout Andhra Pradesh, Karnataka and Tamil Nadu. Their estimated population according to Backward Classes Commission Report was 10,000. The Dasaris speak their own dialect, *Dasari bhasha* among themselves. Telugu, Kannada and Tamil languages are used for intergroup communications depending on their habitation. They use Telugu script. The Dasaris are folk artists. They sing ballads and folktales. They are experts in repairing umbrellas, locks and keys. Some of them are astrologers and fortune-tellers. Some of them forecast the events based on the sound produced by the budbudike. Both men and women sing folk songs and participate in folk dances during socio-religious fairs and festivals. They have oral traditions regarding their origin and culture. Dasaris favour developmental programmes launched by the government like formal education. Majority of them have studied up to primary level. Those leading nomadic life have not been benefitted by the government schemes. The literacy among them is very low.

Dombs

Dombs are a Scheduled Caste in Andhra Pradesh. Domb, Dombara, Paidi or Pano are synonymous of the Dombs. They are also known as Chandalas. Their occupation is sweeping. The Census of India 1881 reports that the Doms are called as Paidis in Telugu districts. Their total population according to the 1981 census is 23,214. Oriya is their mother tongue. They are also conversant in the local language Telugu. They use Telugu script for reading and writing. The Dombs follow variety of occupations. Some of them work as labourers and village servants. The traditional occupation of their caste is weaving. They serve as musicians during the weddings of other castes. They are also employed as house-keepers, tom-tom beaters and scavengers. The Dombs are musicians. They use variety of instruments. The Dombs are considered as untouchables. They do not have free access to temples and common wells. As outcastes, their houses are placed at a distance. The Dombs are illiterates. There is hardly any educated person among them.

Dommaras

Dommaras are also known as Dommarollu and Dombaras. They constitute a community leading a nomadic way of life. The Dommaras constitute 48,612 persons in Andhra Pradesh. They live in the districts of Rayalaseema and Telangana regions. They live in Chittoor, Nayudupet, Nellore, Chilakaluripet and in Guntur. The Dommaras have their own language called Dommari which has no script. Most of them have forgotten their language. They speak, read and write Telugu. The community called Dombara is classified as a Scheduled Caste. Those who are called as Dommara are classified under Group A of Backward classes list of the State. The Dommaras are mainly a landless, seasonal, semi-nomadic community. Their livelihood is dependent on occupations such as piggery, agricultural labour, performance of skillful feats in villages and towns, comb-making and selling of beads, etc. They are engaged in petty business and trade in fancy articles and combs. Their literacy is very low. Only very few of them have formal education. Majority of the Dommaras are unable to send their boys and girls for formal education due to their economic backwardness. The dropout rate among their children is very high. Due to their illiteracy, they are frequently exploited by the money-lenders.

Jambuvulu

Jambuvulu is a Scheduled Caste in Andhra Pradesh. They live in the coastal districts of Andhra. According to the 1901 census, their total population was 22, 355. They are largely concentrated in east Godavari District (21,352 people that is 95.5 percent). They are mainly inhabited in the rural areas. Their traditional occupation is agricultural labour. They occupy the lowest rank in the social scale. The Jambuvulu are a landless community. Their main occupation is agricultural labour in which both men and women participate. Children assist their parents. Women and girl children work as domestic servants. They have folklore and folktales. Folk-songs are sung by females during socio-religious functions. They favour formal education for boys and girls. However, their literacy is very low.

Jogis

Jogi is a generic term, literally meaning devotee and a performer of 'jog'. They form the community which covers a large variety of people belonging to diverse linguistic, ethnic, cultural and regional backgrounds. The Jogis are a community of Telugu mendicants. The Jogi mendicants traditionally wear the *jangam devara* dress and go for *bitchcham* (alms). Their forefathers were experts in indigenous medical care. They had 360 varieties of herbs and shrubs. They carry with them 'virugudu visham' (an antidote for snake poisoning). The male Jogi mendicants have horizontal markings pasted on their forehead. The Jogis do not send their children to schools for education due to their poor financial position.

Konda Doras

Konda Doras are Scheduled Tribes in Andhra Pradesh. They are distributed in the agency areas of Visakhapatnam, Vizianagaram, Srikakulam and east Godavari districts. Their total population is 1,41,374. The word Konda Dora means hill chieftain. *Kubi* or *Konda* is the language of the Konda Doras. The *Kubi* language borrowed words from Oriya and Telugu. But many of them have forgotten their mother tongue *Kubi*. They are now speaking Telugu except their elders who are living in the remote villages. The traditional occupation of the Konda Dora is shifting cultivation. Most of them depend on agriculture and casual labour. Some of them also depend on fishing. The government has established ashram schools and tribal welfare hostels for their children. The literacy rate among Konda Doras is 5.97 per cent. A few boys and girls studied up to secondary and collegiate level. A very few members received university education.

Kintili Kalingas

Kalingas are also known as Kalingi and Kalingulu. The total population of the Kalingas as per 1931 census is 1,29,344. The Kalingas are agriculturists. Their mother tongue is Telugu. They are classified as category A in the Backward Class list. Cultivation is the traditional occupation of the Kalingas in Srikakulam district. The literacy rate is very poor among them. The Kalingas do not allow girl children to go to school. They dropout at the primary level itself.

Lambadis

Lambadis or Banjaras are a colourful people in Andhra Pradesh. They claim to be of Rajput caste. They are known by different names in different parts in India (such as Banjara, Brinjara, Bapari, Lamani, Lambani, Sugali, etc.). The Madras Census Report, 1891, shows that the Lambadis and Sugalis are one and the same. Lambadis move with their large droves of pack bullocks throughout the ceded districts. Before the advent of the railways in India, the Lambadis were the carriers of grain and salt in the coastal districts. They have taken to agricultural pursuits and labour construction works in Cuddapah, Kurnool, Chittor and Anantapur districts. The Lambadis have their own Lambadi language. They speak Telugu. The Lambadi girls marry at an early age as compared to boys. Literacy level among the girls is low. Their children are used in cattle rearing, trade, business, etc. The Lambadis are a wandering group with their pack bullocks. Gradually they have settled down in separate habitations known as Thandas (villages).

Malas

Malas are referred as Adi Andhras. They are a broad generic category encompassing different untouchable groups. The Malas are one of the two prominent Scheduled Castes, the other being the Madigas. Every village is invariably inhabited by the Malas. Their dwelling places are called as *Malapalli*. They play a special role in the village festivals. Some of them have converted to Christianity. The Malas are mostly illiterates. Very few of their children attend schools. Some of them studied up to the primary level. Poverty, lack of parental initiative and their socio-economic conditions are the reasons for their disinterest in education.

Madigas

Madigas are known as Jambhavanntulu and Adi Andhras. According to 1981 census, the population of the Madigas is 3,572,072. They are present in every village of Andhra Pradesh. They live in segregated hamlets called *Madigapalle*. Madigas perform many functions in Andhra Pradesh. They are story-tellers, beggars, courtesans, sweepers, musicians, temple servants, etc. Child marriage is prevalent among them. They engage in their traditional occupation of leather-work. The Madigas have realised the importance of education and many of them are sending their children to schools and colleges with government assistance. They favour formal education for boys. Boys study up to primary and secondary level. They dropout due to their nomadic life at an early stage. Girls generally do not go to school due to lack of parental support and sibling care.

Mondi Vogulas

Mondi Vogulas identify themselves as Muslims. They fashion stones into *rollu*, *esuru rollu* and *rubbu rollu* (stones). They are nomadic. They live in Bellary, Kurnool, Anantapur and Cuddapah districts. They speak corrupt Urdu among themselves. Their traditional occupation is making kitchen implements with stones. The womenfolk are experts in making mats. They collect firewood and sell them. They are landless workers. Their children are employed as casual labourers to support their families. They eke out their livelihood by working as daily wage labourers. Literacy level among Mondi Vogulas is very low. They are illiterate and educationally very backward. Generally, they stop their education at the primary level.

Muthurajas

Muthurajas are one of the ex-criminal and denotified communities in Andhra Pradesh. They are concentrated in Cuddapah, Nellore, Prakasam, Anantapur, Chittoor, Krishna, Guntur and Kurnool districts. They are the original inhabitants of the Telugu country. The total population of the community during 1968 was 7,27,585 (Backward Classes Commission Report, 1970). Telugu, Urdu, Tamil and Kannada languages are used for inter-group communication. They are mainly a landless community. They are small and marginal farmers. Some of them are professional ballad singers. Both men and women sing folk songs during the marriage and festive occasions. Men perform *kolatam* and mock fights with swords and sticks. Formal education is favourable to them. A few boys and girls studied up to graduation level. Most of them studied up to high school level only. The boys dropout from studies due to their poor economic conditions. Girls dropout from studies due to socio-economic reasons.

Nakkalas

Nakkalas are nomadic hunters. They are also traders. They are distributed in many districts of Andhra Pradesh. They are known as Guvvalollu (dove catchers), Pittalollu (bird catchers), Nakkalollu (fox hungers) and Pusallollu (bead sellers) in Telugu. They are jackal hunters, bird catchers, needle sellers and hunters. The Nakkalas speak their own dialect, '*Nakkala bhasha*' among themselves. They speak Telugu and Tamil with others. Most of them are illiterates. They know Telugu and Tamil. The Nakkalas are traditional hunters and sellers of bead necklaces. They sell bead necklaces at bus stations, railway stations, temples and markets. Nakkala women go for begging. They live upon the remnants of food from the leaf platters thrown in the dustbins. A group of Nakkalas glean food from the leaf-platters left in marriage parties and hotels. Both men and women sing variety of folk songs during their rituals. Formal education is not favourable to the Nakkalas due to their poverty.

Nirshikaris

Nirshikaris are an ex-criminal hunting community. The synonym for Nirshikari's is Pardhi in Telangana area. Nirshikari means 'hunters of water birds'. According to the Criminal Tribes Act Enquiry Committee Report of 1949, Nirshikaris were notified as a criminal tribe in Kurnool and Bellary districts. They are the same as Haranshikaris or Pardhis who are notified as a criminal tribe in Madhya Bharat under the name of Pardhis. They are a wandering tribe. They are distributed in Madras (Tamil Nadu), Bombay (Mumbai), Madhya Pradesh and Hyderabad. They live by hunting, begging, collecting and selling forest produce. They are experts in snaring birds. They are known as hunters. The community's origin is mentioned in 1961 census. Nirshikaris are concentrated in Hyderabad, Secunderabad, Kurnool, Anantapur and Rayalaseema regions. They are frequently found in Anantapur, Guntakal, Penugonda, Kadiri and Kurnool. The population of the Nirshikaris was 6,669 persons according to the Backward Classes Commission Report, 1970. They speak their own Shikari *bhasha*. It is a mixture of Parsi, Urdu, Gujarathi and Marathi. They speak Telugu and Urdu. They use Telugu script. The community is notified as a Backward Class under group A category. The education level among the Nirshikari is poor. Many of them study up to elementary school. Their children are dropouts from schools due to their poor economic conditions.

Paidis

Paidis are weavers, musicians and labourers in northern coastal districts. They are distributed in Srikakulam, Vizianagaram and Visakhapatnam districts. The total population of the Paidis is 5,647. They have their own *Paidi dialect*. They use Oriya script while communicating with their kin members. Sometimes, they use Oriya and Telugu. The *Paidi dialect* is believed to be a corrupt form of Oriya. Their language is found under classified languages. They also speak Savara dialect. They move from village to village. They are notified as a Scheduled Caste. They are agricultural labourers. Child labour is more prevalent among them. They weave cotton blankets, saris and towels. They are also involved in petty trade. The Paidis are educationally backward. Boys and girls study up to primary level. Boys and girls dropout heavily due to poor economic conditions.

Pamulas

Pamulas are also called as *Pamullollu* meaning snake in Telugu. Their traditional occupation is catching snakes and snake-charming. They are found in Rayalaseema region, in Nellore, Prakasam and Vizianagaram districts. In Telangana they are found in Mahaboobnagar and Medak districts. They speak Telugu. The Pamulas are considered as educationally Backward class/community. They were classified as a community under group A list (Backward Classes Commission, 1970). Pamulas are nomads. They wander about the villages with snakes wound on their necks. Among the Pamulas very few people are educated. Many of them are illiterate. Their nomadic way of life is a big hindrance for the proper schooling of their children. Even the parents do not favour primary education. The Pamulas are not benefitted by the developmental programmes.

Pariki Muggala

Pariki Muggalas are called as Parikilu or Muggulollu. They are experts in sorcery and black magic. They perform *bhutavydhyam* (throwing away evil spirits from the people). They live in Krishna, Guntur, West Godavari, East Godavari districts in Andhra Pradesh. They speak a dialect known as *Pariki Muggula bhasha*, which has some similarities with the *Yerukula bhasha*. They perform *burrakathalu* in ceremonial and death rites. Child labour exists in them. The literacy rate is very low among them. Their socio-economic conditions are not favourable for sending them to school. Most of their children are self-employed, children support their families.

Pitchiguntlas

Pitchiguntlas are traditional bards, folk-singers, genealogists and wandering mendicants in Andhra Pradesh. They play the *ganta* (musical bell) when they visit any house. They are mendicants. They are also herbalists and physicians. They beat the village drums, relate stories and legends. They are mainly distributed in Rayalaseema and Telangana. The Pitchiguntlas are listed in the backward communities list of the State. They have a low socio-economic status. Pitchiguntlas are agricultural labourers. They are experts in mat-weaving. They have oral traditions. Both men and women sing folk songs. They are reputed bards and folk singers of local areas. The Pitchiguntlas partly favour formal education. Most of their children work as labourers for meagre wages. Pitchiguntlas is a small Denotified community in Andhra Pradesh.

Poosalas

The community is referred to as the Poosalas owing to their occupation of selling trinkets like glass beads, bead necklaces, bangles, combs, hairpins, etc. They inhabit southern and western districts of Andhra Pradesh. The literal meaning of 'poosala' is beads. The Poosala Vandlu are itinerant traders of cosmetics and toilet materials to the local people. According to a rough estimate, their population is around 5 lakh in Andhra Pradesh. They speak their own dialect, *Poosala bhasha*. Some of them are conversant in Hindi, Urdu, Tamil and Kannada languages. The Poosalas have been listed as one of the socially and educationally Backward Classes (Backward Classes Commission Report, 1970). They move from place to place to eke out their livelihood. They are included in the list of nomadic tribes (Tribal Cultural Research and Training Institute, 1973). Poosalas are mainly a landless community. Only a few of them are holding two to three acres of dry land. Their primary education is petty business in household kitchenware and toiletries. Most of them lead a semi-nomadic life. They return to their villages periodically to look after their families and attend to their social rituals. Some are engaged as farm labourers. Some of them stage folktales to entertain the villagers on ceremonial occasions. The poosalas have oral traditions. They are specialists in folklore and folktales. They perform the *burrakathalu* on special occasions depicting the janapadas to the tune of music. The percentage of educated people among the poosala is very low. Only a few people have attained matriculation. Very few women are educated. The boys dropout from studies due to their socio-economic conditions. Girls are dropouts due to social reasons.

Reddikas

Reddikas are agricultural labourers in Andhra Pradesh. Their forefathers are believed to have migrated from Ganjam and Orissa states. The Reddikas are distributed in Srikakulam, Vizianagaram and Visakapatnam districts. They speak Telugu. Their population is between 5,000 and 10,000. The Community is notified in the list of Backward Classes under Group A category, by the State Government (Backward Classes Commission Report 1970). Agriculture is the main occupation of the Reddikas. They are receiving benefits from the government as part of weaker sections upliftment programmes. Literacy is moderate among the Reddikas.

Rellis

Rellis are indicated in the list of Scheduled Castes. They are distributed in 13 districts in Andhra Pradesh, viz. Srikakulam, Vizianagaram, Visakhapatnam, East Godavari, Nellore, Prakasam and Chittoor districts. Their total population is 76,329. Their mother tongue is a corrupt and distinct form of Oriya. They speak Telugu. They also use Telugu script. The primary occupation of Rellis is the collection and sale of leaves and fruits, seeds and grass. They also took up the professions such as sweeping and scavenging, etc. The Rellis are holding a low social status. They are also suffering from social disabilities. Formal education is unfavourable to the Relli children because of their poverty and backwardness. Very few boys and girls only go to schools. There is a high dropout rate among the children due to their poverty stricken conditions.

Woddars

Woddars are the traditional earth and stone-workers. They are distributed throughout the state. They are also referred as Vadda, Odderaja, Wuddar. The word 'odde' is said to be a corruption of the Sanskrit term, 'Oddara', the name of a country now called as Orissa. Woddars are supposed to have migrated from

Orissa state. They are the natives of the Telugu country. Quarrying stone, sinking wells, constructing tank bunds and executing other kinds of earth-work more rapidly than any other class is their occupation. They are Telugu people, who came originally from Orissa, hence their name Woddars. The Woddars call themselves as Pancha Bottulu. They are inherently tattooers in Ganjam, Visakapatnam and Godavari districts. They are classified as a Backward Class (BC Commission, 1970). The Woddars form into work-groups called gangs. They undertake earth and quarry works on contract basis. The Woddars are economically poor and socially very low. The Woddars do not favour formal education for their children.

Yatas

Yatas or Yatollu are toddy-tappers by profession. They are living in Srikakulam, Vizianagaram and Visakhapatnam districts. They were classified as a tribe under Criminal Tribes Act 1911. But this section of the community/tribe is considered and treated as a caste in Andhra Pradesh. The population of this community is projected in the census report 1970. Their total population is 83,198 (Backward Classes Commission Report, 1970). The Yatas speak Telugu. The Yatas are specialists in toddy-tapping, basket-making, mat-weaving and palmyra umbrella-making. They are also specialists in making *jelledalu* (sievers), *chetalu* (winnow) and *rekalu* (water cases). The Yatas have not yet availed fully of formal education facilities. Only a few children are going to school, dropping out due to their poverty and backwardness.

Yanadis

Yanadis are one of the largest Scheduled Tribes in Andhra Pradesh. They were a notified criminal tribe under the Criminal Tribes Act. 'Yanadi' is a corrupt form of the Sanskrit word 'anadi' which means without a beginning. Yanadis are aboriginal tribes. They are called as Anadis. The Yanadis are widely spread in the districts of Nellore, Kavali and Ongole. According to 1981 census, their total population is 3,20,444. They speak Telugu. The Yanadis are divided into two groups, Challa Yanadi and Manchi Yanadi. The Manchi Yanadi are larger in number than the Challa Yanadi, who are less civilised. Child marriage prevails among the Yanadis. The Yanadi girls get married between 12–15 years. The traditional occupation of the Yanadi was food-gathering. They practice hunting, food-gathering and casual labour. They are also engaged in secondary occupations like mat-making, fishing, crop-watching, agricultural labour and other minor occupations. The Yanadis settled in colonies are experts in making good quality mats. Boys and girls are experts in performing folk dances, singing, etc. Yanadis are traditional musicians called Yanadi Melam. They are invited for marriages, death and other ceremonies. The Yanadis are a Scheduled Tribe. Their children are entitled to free education. Educational institutions are not easily accessible for the Yanadis who are living in Villages.

Yerukulas

The name Yerukula is derived from 'eruka' which means 'prophesy' in Telugu. The women of this tribe are popularly known as Yerukasani (soothsayers) or fortune tellers. The yerukulas are a semi-nomadic tribe. They are called as 'Korcha' in the border areas of Karnataka. In the bordering areas of Tamil Nadu they are called as 'koravas' or 'koravans'. In Maharashtra, they are called as Kaikadis. However, the community calls itself as 'Kurru'. They are distributed all over the state. They are largely concentrated in Guntur, Krishna, Nellore, Prakasam, Mahaboob Nagar, Kurnool districts in Andhra Pradesh. According to 1981 census their population is 3.16 lakhs. During the British period, they were notified as a Criminal Tribe. They were under constant police surveillance. The families of Yerukulas were settled in separate colonies and settlements specially built for them at Stuartpuram, Kavali, Bitragunta, Kapparallatippa, Allur, Sitanagaram, Siddhapuram and Lingala. The Christian Missionaries established schools to educate the children of the Yerukulas in coastal areas. The population of the Yerukulas in 1971 was 1,62,560. The traditional occupation of the Yerukulas is basket and mat-making and pig-rearing. The Yerukulas favour education for their boys and girls.

Source: K.S. Singh (ed.) *People of India: Andhra Pradesh*, Vol. XIII, Part 1, 2 and 3, Anthropological Survey of India, East-West Press, New Delhi, 2003.

APPENDIX–II

Prescribed Syllabi Copy for the Children of Criminal Tribes in Settlement Schools

The syllabi prescribed for these children was elaborate and interesting. Their intention was to make them thorough in 3Rs by the time they complete the fifth standard. The elaborate syllabi taught in these schools is given below:

Space and Number Work Infant

Counting up to 20 by two's and three's and the four simple operations.

Recognising a cube, cuboid, cylinder, a cone and naming the number of surfaces.

Recognising Indian coins.

First Standard

1. Counting up to 100 by tens.
2. The four simple operations applied up to 100.
3. Addition and subtraction on slates.
4. Construction and application of multiplication tables up to 10.
5. Comparing the different surfaces in a cube and a cuboid and recognition of a square and rectangle.
6. Straight line and a curved line.
7. Drawing straight line of a given length and measuring the straight line given.
8. Measure of capacity and multiplication table.

Second Standard

1. The four simple operations up to 1,000.
2. Multiplication tables up to 16 × 12.
3. Problems involving the operations of two rules.
4. Conversion of Indian money.
5. Angles (right, acute and obtuse). Properties of a square and rectangle, scale drawing, to scale a blackboard, a room, etc.

Third Standard

1. Four simple and compound operations up to one lakh.
2. Problems involving two compound rules.
3. Tables of weights and lengths.
4. Plan of the school/house.
5. A triangle, some of its properties, a circle, etc.

Language Infant Standard

Infant Primer (by D. Ramamurti Messrs. Macmillan & Co.) Three Stories.

First Standard

1. *First reader* (by E. Marsden).
2. Eight stories (Oral, narrative).
3. Picture reading.

4. Conversation about common subjects.
5. *Third reader* (by E. Marsden).
6. Composition substance of the lessons taught or an easy lesson read out three times or a story narrated.

Second Standard

1. Reading of manuscript.
2. Letter writing.

Recitation

1. Infant Standard: story, songs.
2. First standard: 20 lines of verse.
3. Second standard: 30 lines of verse with meaning.
4. Third standard: 40 lines of verse with meaning.

Drawing Infant

A circle, an oval, a square and some forms that can be evolved out of these, a sieve, an egg, the yamy of a bird, a snail, a creeper.

First Standard

1. Some domestic articles.
2. Some leaf forms.
3. Some animals in easy form and their pets.

Second and Third Standards

1. Action drawing.

Rural Science Infants

Naming and recognising the plants and leaves of the garden and animals of the neighbourhood.

First Standard

1. The three parts of a plant and their chief uses.
2. A cat and dog compared.

Second Standard

1. Different kinds of leaves.
2. Flowers and their parts.
3. Habits of the animals of the locality.
4. Seeds and its parts.

Third Standard

1. Work of leaf.
2. Flower and root.
3. A few points relating to agriculture.
4. Value of manures.
5. Change of crop.
6. Animals, their habit and food.
7. Life of a silkworm. 8.Life of a frog.

APPENDIX–III

Sketch Maps of Criminal Tribe Settlement Schools in Madras Provinces

Map 1

Front Elevation of Government Elementary School, Siddapuram

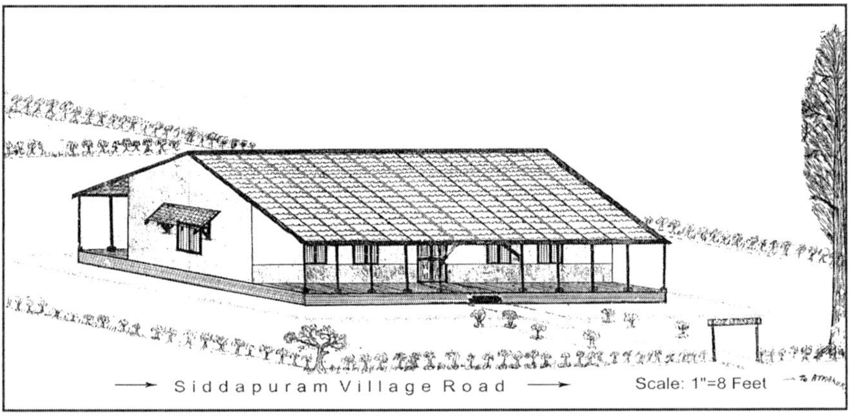

Source : Government of Madras, Home Department, G.O. No. 701, dated 10.02.1939 (State Archives, Chennai, Tamil Nadu).

Map 2

Government Elementary School, Siddapuram

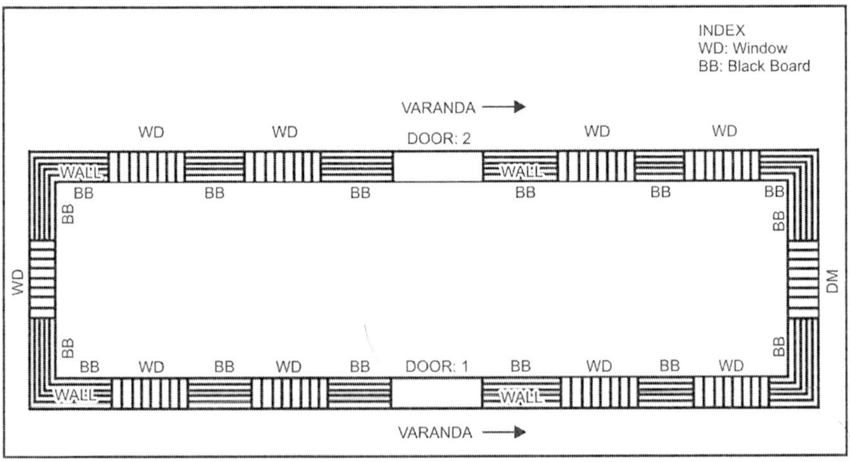

Source: Government of Madras, Home Department, G.O. No. 701, dated 10.02.1939 (State Archives, Chennai, Tamil Nadu).

Map 3

Map Showing the Villages from where the Boys and Girls attend the School

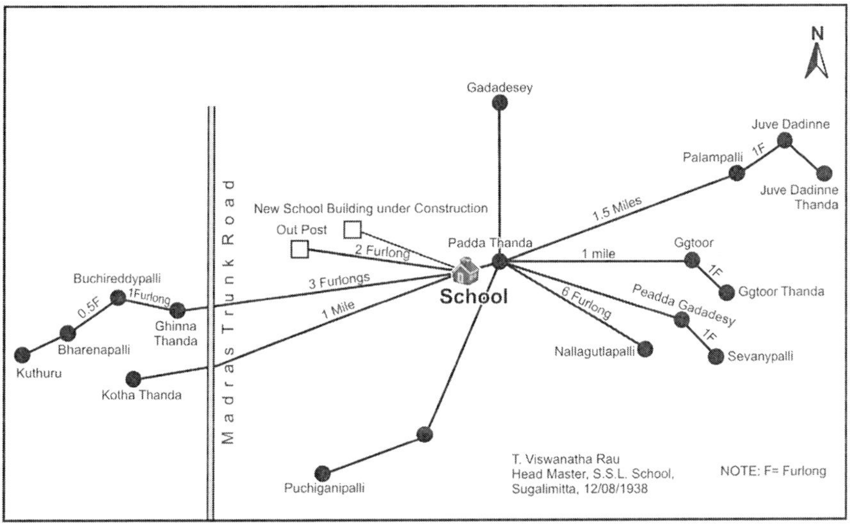

Source : Government of Madras, Home Department, G.O. No. 701, dated 10.02.1939 (State Archives, Chennai, Tamil Nadu).

Appointment of a Conductor to Promote Primary Education among the Children of Criminal Tribes in Madras Province

Note: A labour school for the benefit of the children was opened at Sugalimitta near Pungannur, Chittor District under the supervision of the District Superintendent of Police. The school was started during the year 1936. The school worked with great satisfaction. The local Police Inspector and the District Superintendent of Police took keen interest in management of the school. The school worked on satisfactory lines. A conductor was appointed to collect the young children and bring them to school. The school for children of criminal tribes was situated in the centre of the group of villages. The children were very young to walk to the school by themselves. It was reported that the parents in the slighter pretext used to send their children out to tend cattle or work in the fields. The police and others tried hard to make the school a great success. The conductor was a great help in that direction. The government had appointed the conductor on a monthly salary of ₹ 8. Thandas/settlements from which children used to attend the school were in five different directions. The conductor was instructed to go to the farthest thanda/settlement in one direction; collect the children from the thanda/settlement en route and take them to school. He had to repeat this process to fetch the children from the thanda/settlement in other four directions. Therefore another conductor was felt advantageous in making children to attend school. In view of the economic conditions, the Madras Government did not appoint another conductor. However, due to the conductor the strength of the school had gradually increased. Besides, the duty of collecting children, conductor was also utilized as an interpreter in the infant class as the children of that class were not conversant with the language of the teacher. These children used to talk in their own language. The language of the teachers working in the school was Telugu and the students were not conversant with their languages, field teachers who knew their languages were not available for appointment.

APPENDIX–IV

Condition of the Existing Schools in DNT Settlements in Andhra Pradesh and Telangana States

Government Elementry School, Siddhapuram

Government Upper Primary School, Sitanagaram

Government Elementry School, Kapparallatippa

Government Elementry School, Kapparallatippa

Salvation Army Primary School, Stuartpuram

S Bose Government Elementry School, Lingala

Glossary

adivasi	:	Earliest inhabitants (Tribes)
American baptist (telugu) mission	:	A Christian Missionary working with depressed classes in coastal districts of Andhra Pradesh.
ananda primer and ananda reader	:	Textbook prescribed for classes I to III in the DNT schools during the British period.
animal week	:	Training given by the Salvation Army managers to the DNT children to show sympathy towards animals.
boarding schools	:	Schools established by the Salvation Army for the education of DNT children in the Settlements/Thandas.
criminal tribes	:	Nomadic, semi-nomadic and Denotified Tribes
ganji	:	Porridge or watery rice or boiled rice water.
habitual offenders act	:	The Act passed by the British Government to restrict the movements of Criminal Tribes in the year 1948.
health week	:	Competitions or celebrations conducted by the Salvation Army to keep the DNT children healthy.
kanjar bhats	:	A nomadic tribe in Andhra Pradesh migrated from Bombay Presidency.
karnam	:	Village officer
kiddies	:	Small children in the DNT schools.
korachas	:	A nomadic community in Andhra Pradesh
mille	:	One year
night schools	:	Schools established by the Salvation Army for the education of Denotified Tribes during the nights in the settlements.
o passes	:	Leave Certificates granted to DNTs to go out of the settlements in search of work.

quarry work	:	Stone work or unskilled labourers working in quarries.
salvation army	:	A Christian Missionary organisation in Andhra Pradesh working on the Rehabilitation of 'Criminal' Tribes/Denotified Tribes.
settlements	:	Colonies/thandas established for the Denotified Tribes.
settlers	:	Nomadic/Denotified Tribes in a settlements/thanda.
stigma	:	Bad reputation or name.

Bibliography

Primary Sources

Archival Sources, Reports, Gazetteers, District Records, Missionary Sources and Manuals. Government orders from various departments like Judicial, Public Works (Labour), Law (General), Home and Home (Judicial) Department were collected from Tamil Nadu State Archives, Egmore, Chennai; Andhra Pradesh State Archives and Research Institute, Tarnaka, Hyderabad and National Archives, New Delhi.

Secondary Sources

Aatre, T.N., 1995. *Gaon Gada* (Marathi), Varada Prakashan, Pune.

Abraham, Susan, 1999. "Steal or I'll Call You a Thief 'Criminal' Tribes of India", *Economic and Political Weekly*, 3 July, pp. 1751–1753.

Ahmed, A., 1984. *Education of the Scheduled Tribes: Some Aspects of Inequality*, NIEPA, New Delhi.

Aiyappan, A., 1948. Report on the Socio-Economic Conditions of the Aboriginal Tribes of the Province of Madras, Superintendent, Government Press, Madras.

All India Punarvasit Jatis (Denotified Tribes Federation), Report of the All India Denotified Communities Seminar held on 31 March, 1 and 2 April 1963 at Udyogsala Press, Kingsway, Delhi.

Ambasht, N.K., 1971. "The Policy of Tribal Education", *Vanyajati*, Vol. XVII, No. 1.

Ambasht, N.K., 2001. *Tribal Education: Problems and Issues*, Venkatesh Prakashan, New Delhi.

Ananda, G., 1988. *Ashram Schools*, Concept Publishers, New Delhi.

Ananda, G., 1994. Ashram Schools in Andhra Pradesh: A Case Study of Chenchus of Nallamalai Hills, Commonwealth Publishers, New Delhi.

Ananda, G., 2000. *Educating Tribals*, Commonwealth Publishers, New Delhi.

Ananthakrishnan, M.V., *Educating Nomadic Children: An Experiment with the Convergence of Technologies*, IIT, Mumbai, nd.

Ananthakrishnan, M.V. and Ramamritham, K., 2005. "From Real to Media Anchors: Experiments with the Anchored Instruction of Nomadic Children", Paper presented in 14th AMIC Conference, Beijing, July.

Annamalai, E., 2001. *Managing Multilingualism in India: Political and Linguistic Manifestation*, Sage, New Delhi.

Antrolikar, K.B., 1950. Antrolikar Committee Report. Report of the Ex-Criminal Tribes Rehabilitation Committee, November 1950, Government Central Press, Bombay, 1951.

Apte, J.S., 1960. "Talwada Ashram School: An Experiment in Tribal Education", *Vanjayati*, Vol. 8, No. 2.

Ashirvad, N., 1992. "Glimpses of Tribal Development in Andhra Pradesh", *Man and Life*, Vol. 18, Nos. 3–4, July–December, pp. 175–182.

Bairathi, S., 1991. *Tribal Culture, Economy and Health*, Rawat, Jaipur.

Bargava, B.S., 1949. *Criminal Tribes*, Bhargava Printing Works, Lucknow.

Besant, Annie, 1916. *Social Service, New India Political Pamphlets, Presidential Address delivered at the Anniversary of the Narasapur Progressive Union on 28 June 28*, Commonwealth Office, Adayar, Madras, 1916.

Beteille, A., 1983. "The Backward Classes and the New Social Order", in Beteille, A. *The Ideal of Natural Inequality and Other Essays*, Oxford University Press, New Delhi, pp.78–121.

Bhowmick, P.K., 1963. *The Lodhas of West Bengal: A Socio-Economic Study*, Punthi Pustak, Calcutta.

Bhowmick, P.K., 1999. *Tribal Literacy in West Bengal*. R.N. Bhattacharya Publications, Kolkata.

Bokil, Milind, 'Bhatakya Vimuktanchi Loksankhya Nemki Kiti', (Marathi), *Saptahik Sakal*, Pune, 21 October 1995.

Bokil, Milind, "Facing Exclusion: The Nomadic Communities in Western India", Paper Presented at the Asia-Pacific Conference of IFSW, Brisbane, 26–29 September 1995.

Bokil, Milind, 2002. "De-notified and Nomadic Tribes: A Perspective", *Economic and Political Weekly*, 37(2), 1–8, 12 January 2002, pp. 1–8.

Bokil, Milind, "Denotified and Nomadic Tribes: A Perspective", *Economic and Political Weekly*, 12 January 2002, p. 148.

Bose, Kumar, Nirmal, "Integration of Tribes in Andhra Pradesh", *Man in India*, Vol. 44, April–June 1964, No. 2, pp. 97–104.

Budhan, 1998. *The DNT–RAG, Newsletter*, October, November, Baroda.

Capotorti, F., 1979. *Study of the Rights of Persons Belonging to Ethnic, Religious and Linguistic Minorities*, United Nations, New York.

Chalam, K.S., 1993. *Educational Policy for Human Resources Development*, Rawat, Jaipur.

Chalam, K.S., 2007. *Caste-based Reservations and Human Development in India*, Sage Publications, New Delhi.

Chattopadhyay, K.P., 1953. "Tribal Education", *Man in India*, Vol. 33, No. 1, p. 3.

Chaturvedi, M.G. and Mohale B., 1976. *Position of Languages in School Curriculum in India*, NCERT, New Delhi.

Chenchu Raju, C., 1969. "The Banjaras of Andhra Pradesh", *Tribal*, Vol. 7, Nos. 1 and 2.

Chenchu Raju, C., 1981. *Stuartpuram Girijan Settlement: A Rehabilitation Centre for Ex-Convicts*, Government Press, Hyderabad.

Cohen, L., and Manion, L., 1993. *Multicultural Classrooms*, Croom and Helm, London.

Cohen, W., Emmeline, 1949. *English Social Services Methods and Growth*, George Allen and Unwin Ltd., London.

Coombes, J.W., 1908. *The Juvenile Criminal in South India*, Lawrence Asylum Press, Madras.

Dandekar, Ajay, 2007. "Forgotten by Present, Denotified Tribes Awaits Justice", *The Economic Times*, dated 16 October.

Das Gupta, Biman, K., and Danda, Ajit, K., 1984. *Tribal Education in India*, Anthropological Survey of India, Ministry of Education and Culture, Government of India, Calcutta, 1984.

Das, A.R., Naidu, R.V.K., and Sreedhar, N., 2003. "Who Joins Ashram Schools? A Study of Ashram Schools in Karnataka", *Anthropologist*, Vol. 5, No. 3.

Das, Amarnath, R., Naidu, Vijaya Krishna, R., and Sreedhar, N., 2003. "Ashram Schools and the Education of Tribal Children: A Sociological Study in Karnataka", *Man and Life*, Vol. 29, Nos. 1–2.

Daswani, C.J., 1993. Tribal Study Synthesis Report (Summary of Significant Findings). NCERT, New Delhi.

De Souza, Alba, Forum on Flexible Education, Reaching Nomadic Populations in Africa, Garissa, Kenya, 2006 (Unpublished Report), Government of India, Ministry of Social Justice and Empowerment, New Delhi.

Deshpande, S.H., 2000. *Kahi Arthik Samajik (Marathi)*, Mouj Prakashan, Mumbai.

Devy, G.N., 1998. *The Branded Tribes of India*, PUCL Bulletin, September.

Devy, G.N., 2002. *Painted Words: An Anthology of Tribal Literature*, Penguin Books, New Delhi.

Devy, G.N., 2006. *A Nomad Called Thief: Reflections on Adivasi Silence*, Orient Longman, Hyderabad.

Dhavalikar, M.K., 1985. *The First Farmer in the Deccan*, Ravish Publishers, Pune.

D'Souza, Dilip, 2001. *Branded by Law: Looking at India's Denotified Tribes*, Penguin Books, New Delhi.

Dreze, J. and Sen, Amastya (eds), 1995. *India: Economic Development and Social Opportunity*, Oxford University Press, New Delhi.

Dreze, Jean and Sen, Amartya, 1995. "Basic Education as a Political Issue", *Journal of Educational Planning and Administration*, Vol. IX, No. 1, January, pp. 1–26.

Dubnick, M.J., 1998. "Educating Nomads: Narratives and the Future of Civic Education", www.newark.rutgers.edu/~dubnick/contact.html.

Dutt, Bahar, 2003. "The Forgotten People: Bawarias of Rajasthan", Proceedings of the Public Hearing, Muktidhara, Rajasthan, August.

Dyer, Caroline, 2010. Education and Social (in) Justice for Mobile Groups: Re-framing Rights and Educational Inclusion for Indian Pastoralist Children, *Routledge Educational Review*, Vol. 62, Issue 3.

Edwards, Vic., 1984. "Language Issues in School", in Craft, M., (ed.), *Education and Cultural Pluralism*, Falmer Press, London.

Fleras, A., and Elliot, J.L., 1982. *Multiculturalism in Canada*, Nelson, Canada.

Furer-Haimendorf, C.V., 1989. *Tribes of India: The Struggle for Survival*, Oxford University Press, London.

Gadgil, M. and Guha, R., 1996. *This Fissured Land*, Oxford University Press, New Delhi.

Gaikwad, Laxman, 1987. *Uchalya* (Marathi), Shrividya Prakashan, Pune.

Gandhi, Malli, "Status of Education Among the Denotified Tribes of Andhra Pradesh: A Case Study of Siddhapuram and Stuartpuram Settlements", *Primary Teacher*, NCERT, New Delhi.

Gandhi, Malli, 2005. "A Study of Factors Affecting Students, Achievements in Primary Schools of Denotified Tribal Settlements in Andhra Pradesh", Unpublished Report, ERIC, NCERT, New Delhi.

Gandhi, Malli, 1999. An Investigation Into the Problems Associated with the Literacy of Scheduled Tribe Children in Tribal Schools of Vizianagaram District, Andhra Pradesh, Unpublished PAC Report, RIE, Mysore.

Gandhi, Malli, 2006. Development of Audio Scripts on Socio-Cultural Aspects of the Scheduled Tribe Groups of Andhra Pradesh, Unpublished PAC Report, RIE, Mysore, March.

Gandhi, Malli, 2006. *Development of Denotified Tribes: Policy and Practice*, Sarup and Sons, New Delhi.

Gandhi, Malli, 2005. Preparation of Glossary of Savara Tribal Dialect Equivalent to the Terms used in Telugu and Environmental Science Textbooks at Primary Stage in Andhra Pradesh, Unpublished PAC Report, RIE, Mysore, March.

Gandhi, Malli, 2004. Report on the Training Programme for TTI/DIET Faculty on Monitoring of Learning Achievement in Tribal Schools of Andhra Pradesh, Unpublished PAC Report.

Gasti, Bhimrao, 1987. *Berad* (Marathi), Popular Prakashan, Belgaum.

Ghatage, B.S., 2006. *Nomadic Tribes and Social Work in India*, Shruti Publications, Jaipur.

Ghatak, N.K., 2002. Phanse-Pardhi of Maharashtra, *Man and Life*, Vol. 28, Nos. 3–4, July–December.

Government of Andhra Pradesh, 1954. Administration Report of the Harijan Welfare Department of the Work done for the Amelioration of the Condition of the Eligible Communities for the Year 1952–53, Government Press, Hyderabad.

Government of Andhra Pradesh, 1964. The Report on the Tribes of Andhra Pradesh, Tribal Cultural Research and Training Institute, 1958, Government Press, Hyderabad.

Government of Andhra Pradesh, 1965. Report of the 7th Conference for Scheduled Tribes and Tribal Areas, 1964, Guntur, Government Press, Hyderabad.

Government of Andhra Pradesh, 1966. Andhra Pradesh State Administration Report – 1961–65, Vol. 1, Government Press, Hyderabad.

Government of Andhra Pradesh, 1970. Report of the Backward Classes Commission, Hyderabad (TCRTI).

Government of India, 1990. The Report of the Commissioner for Schedules Castes and Scheduled Tribes Twenty Ninth Report 1987–89. GOI, New Delhi.

Government of India, 1948. Report of the Criminal Tribes Enquiry Committee, United Provinces of India, Government Central Press, Allahabad.

Government of India, 1959. Report of the Study Team on Social Welfare and Welfare of Backward Classes, Vol. 1, Government Press, New Delhi.

Government of India, 1961. Census of India, Vol. 1, Part 6C, (ii), New Delhi.

Government of India, 1962. Report of the Scheduled Areas and Scheduled Tribes Commission, Vol. I, Government of India, New Delhi.

Government of India, 1966. Education and National Development: Report of the Education Commission: 1964–1966, NCERT, New Delhi.

Government of India, 1967. Ministry of Law, The Constitution of India, New Delhi.

Government of India, 1975. Fifth Five Year Plan, Planning Commission, New Delhi.

Government of India, 1978. *The Gazetteer of India, Vol. 4, Administration and Public Welfare,* Ministry of Education and Social Welfare, New Delhi.

Government of India, 1981. Annual Report of the Deputy Commissioner for Linguistic Minorities for the Period 1980–1981, Government of India, New Delhi.

Government of India, 1981. Census of India, Series No. I, Part IV(A), (VII), SC/ST, Government of India, New Delhi.

Government of India, 1981. Report of the Commissioner for Scheduled Castes and Scheduled Tribes from 1953 to 1980, Government Press, New Delhi.

Government of India, 1984. Annual Report of the Deputy Commissioner for Linguistic Minorities for the Period 1982–83, Government of India, New Delhi.

Government of India, 1985–86. Annual Report of the Deputy Commissioner for Linguistic Minorities in India for the Period 1985–86, Government of India, New Delhi.

Government of India, 1986. National Policy on Education, Government of India, New Delhi.

Government of India, 1987. Census of India: Series I: Households and Household Population by language Mainly Spoken in the Household, Government of India, New Delhi.

Government of India, 1988. Report of the Commissioner for Scheduled Castes and Scheduled Tribes, 20th Report, 1986–87. Government of India, New Delhi.

Government of India, 1989. Scheduled Castes and Scheduled Tribes Prevention of Atrocities Act 1989 (33 of 1989), 11 September.

Government of India, 1991. Education of Scheduled Castes and Scheduled Tribes and Other Backward Castes, 8th Five Year Plan Document, GOI, New Delhi, pp. 8–11.

Government of India, 1991. The Constitution of India, as on 1 September 1991, New Delhi.

Government of India, 1992. Programme of Action, Government of India, New Delhi.

Government of India, 1993. *Education for All: The Indian Scene*, Second Edition, Government of India, New Delhi.

Government of India, 1993. Education of Schedules Castes and Scheduled Tribes. Department of Education, MHRD, GOI, New Delhi.

Government of India, 1995. Report of the Commission on Scheduled Castes and Tribes, New Delhi.

Government of India, 1998. National Commission for Scheduled Castes and Scheduled Tribes, Fourth Report (1996–97 and 1997–98) Volume I, GOI, New Delhi.

Government of India, 1998. Selected Educational Statistics, 1995–96. New Delhi: Ministry of Human Resource Development, (MHRD), GOI.

Government of India, 1999. Fifth Report of the National Commission for Scheduled Castes and Scheduled Tribes, 1998–99, New Delhi.

Government of India, 2000. Selected Educational Statistics 1999–2000. New Delhi: MHRD, GOI.

Government of India, 2001. Census of India, Socio-Cultural Tables (C-Series). New Delhi.

Government of India, 2004. Report of the Task Group on Development of Scheduled Castes and Scheduled Tribes, New Delhi.

Government of India, B.P. Mandal, 1980. Report of the Backward Classes Commission.

Government of India, Committee on the Welfare of Scheduled Castes and Scheduled Tribes, 16th Report, Chairman: Kariya Munda, New Delhi.

Government of India, Kakasaheb Kalelkar, 1953. Report of First Backward Classes Commission, New Delhi.

Government of India, National Advisory Council, 2004. Common Minimum Programme: Recommendations on Tribal Welfare, also see www.nac.nic.in.

Government of India, National Council of Educational Research and Training, National Curriculum Framework, 2005, New Delhi, December 2005.

Government of India, NCERT, National Curriculum Framework 2005, Position Paper on Problems of Scheduled Caste and Scheduled Tribe Children, New Delhi, 2006.

Government of India, NCERT, Sixth All-India Education Survey, Vols. 1 and 2, New Delhi, 1998.

Government of India, NCERT, 1986. Fifth All-India Education Survey, Vols. 1 and 2, New Delhi.

Government of Karnataka, 1975. Karnataka Backward Classes Commission Report, Vidana Soudha, Bangalore.

Government of Madras, 1888. Reformatory Schools in Madras Presidency for the Children of Juvenile Criminals. Approving with Certain Modifications of the Draft Rules for the Regulation of the Reformatory Schools. Judicial Department, G.O. No. 2545, dated 10 December 1888.

Government of Madras, 1912. Schools for the Children of Criminal Tribes, Education And Public Health Department, G.O. No. 776, dated 24 August 1912, TNA.

Government of Madras, 1913. Schools for the Children of Criminal Tribes Education And Public Health Department, G.O. No. 2205, dated 3 November, 1913, *TNA*.

Government of Madras, 1914. Salvation Army Industrial Home for Criminal. Tribes Children. Judicial Department, G.O. No. 1490, dated 6 July 1914, Madras, TNA.

Government of Madras, 1914. Schools for Children of Criminal Tribes. Financial Department, G.O. No. 216, dated 19 March 1914, TNA.

Government of Madras, 1914. Schools for Children of Criminal Tribes. Judicial Department, dated 19 August, 1915, TNA.

Government of Madras, 1914. Schools for Children of Criminal Tribes. Judicial Department, G.O. No. 1062, dated 8 May 1914.

Government of Madras, 1914. Schools for Children of Criminal Tribes. Judicial Department, G.O. No. 460, dated 21 February 1914, Madras, TNA.

Government of Madras, 1914. Schools for Children of Criminal Tribes. Judicial Department, G.O. No. 865, dated 16 April 1914, Madras, TNA.

Government of Madras, 1914. Schools for the Children of Criminal Tribes Education And Public Health Department, G.O. No. 423, dated 18 February, 1914, TNA.

Government of Madras, 1914. Schools for the Children of Criminal Tribes Educational Department, G.O. No. 1533, dated 11 July 1914, TNA.

Government of Madras, 1914. Schools for the Children of Criminal Tribes Educational Department, G.O. No. 2565, dated 21 November 1914, TNA.

Government of Madras, 1914. Schools for the Children of Criminal Tribes, Educational Department, G.O. No. 780, dated 4 July 1914, TNA.

Government of Madras, 1915. Criminal Settlement Schools Managed by Salvation Army. Judicial Department, Government Memorandum No. 2255A–2, dated 19 August 1915, Madras, TNA.

Government of Madras, 1915. Industrial Schools for the Children of Criminal Tribes. Judicial Department, G.O. No. 2968, dated 3 December 1915, Madras, TNA.

Government of Madras, 1917. Note Showing the Progress Made in the settlement of Criminal Tribes in Madras Presidency upto September 1916, Government Press, Madras, 1917.

Government of Madras, 1928. Madras Criminal Tribes Manual, 1927, Criminal Tribes Act VI of 1924, brought upto 31 March 1927, Government Press, Madras, 1928.

Government of Madras, 1931. Annual Administration Reports of Nellore Girls School for the years 1925 to 1930, Government Press, Madras.

Government of Madras, 1932. Administration Report on Kallar Reclamation, Madura and Ramnad Districts for 1931, Government Press, Madras, 1932.

Government of Madras, 1939. Report on Criminal Tribes, Kallar and Korava Reclamation and settlements, Administration Report for the year 1938, Government Press, Madras.

Government of Madras, 1939. Schools for Children of Criminal Tribes Home Department, G.O. No. 3953, dated 20 July 1939.

Government of Madras, 1950. Administration Report on Kallar Reclamation, Korava Reclamation, Yanadi Reclamation (Criminal Tribes) and Settlements for 1947–1948, Government Press, Madras, 1949.

Government of Madras, 1953. Administration Report on Habitual Offenders Settlements for 1951–52, Government Press, Madras.

Government of Madras, 1954. Administration Report on Kallar Reclamation, Koravar Reclamation, Criminal Tribes Settlement, Yanadi and Sugali Reclamation from 1949 to 1952, Government Press, Madras, 1953.

Government of Madras, 1956. Administration Report of the Harijan Welfare Department for the year 1954–55, Government Press, Madras.

Government of Madras, Criminal Tribe Settlements, Aziznagar, Annual Report, 1930–31, Public Works and Labour Department, G.O. No. 1794L., 15 July 1931, Government Press, Madras, 1932.

Government of Madras, Note Showing the Progress Made in the settlement of Criminal Tribes in Madras Presidency upto January 1926, Government Press, Madras, 1927.

Government of Madras, Proceedings of Board of Revenue (Land Revenue), Forest Mis. No. 882, dated 10 June 1911, and No. 1062, Judicial, 8 May 1914, Madras, TNA.

Government of Tamil Nadu, Enhancement of Charges to the BCs, MBCs and Denotified Community Hostel Boarders with Effect from 1 April 2005 – Orders Issued G.O. (MS), No. 41, dated 13 May 2004.

Government of Tamil Nadu, Welfare of Backward Classes/Most Backward Classes/Denotified Communities Education – Hostels – Part II Schemes for 2005–2006.

Govinda, R., and Varghese, N.V., 1993. Quality of Primary Schooling in India: A Case Study of Madhya Pradesh, International Institute for Educational Planning, UNESCO, Paris and National University of Educational Planning and Administration (NUEPA), New Delhi.

Gupta, J.P., 1955. Rehabilitation Work Among Ex-Criminal Tribes in India, in *Social Welfare in India: Foreword by Jawaharlal Nehru,* The Planning Commission, Government of India, pp. 242–248, New Delhi.

Gupta, Mithilesh, 1964. Rehabilitation of Criminal Tribes, *The Eastern Anthropologist,* Vol. XVII, No. 1, January–April 1964.

Haikerwal, Bejoy Shanker, 1934. *Economic and Social Aspects of Crime in India,* George Allen and Unwin Ltd., London.

Hellmuth, J. (ed.), 1970. *Disadvantaged Child,* Compensatory Education: A National Debate, Vol. 3, Brunner/Mazel, Inc., New York.

Hemalatha, T., 1989. *Tribal Education*, Himanshu Publishers, Udaipur.

Heredia, Rudolf, C., 1992. *Tribal Education for Community Development: A Study of Schooling in the Talasari Mission Area*, Concept Publishing Company, New Delhi.

Heredia, Rudolf, C., 1996, "Teaching as a Subversive Activity: Pedagogies for Change", *New Frontiers in Education,* Vol. 26, No. 3, July–September.

Heredia, Rudolf, C., 2007. Denotified and Nomadic Tribes: The Challenge of Free and Equal Citizenship, *Occasional Paper Series,* Department of Sociology, University of Pune.

Homans, Roger, "Separate Schools" in Lynch, J., et al., 1992. *Education and Cultural Pluralism*, Falmer Press, London.

Jalaludin, A.K., et al., 1991. *Basic Education and National Development: The Indian Scheme* (UNICEF), New Delhi.

Jeffcoate, R., 1982. *Ethnic Minorities and Education,* Open University Press, Milton Keynes.

Jhingran, D., 2005. *Language Disadvantage,* APH Publications, New Delhi.

Joshi, V., 1998. *Tribal Situation in India: Issues in Development*, Rawat, Jaipur.

Kailash, 1993. *Tribal Education and Occupation: Dynamics of Impact and Changes,* Manak Publications, New Delhi.

Kangas, T.S., 1999. Education of the Minorities in J. Fishman (ed.), *Handbook of Language and Ethnic Identity*, Oxford University Press, New York.

Kapoor, Richa, 2010. *People as Change Makers, Essential Services: Community Based Management for Right to Education*, Oxfam India, Working Papers Series, June.

Krishna Iyer, L.A., 1939. *The Travancore Tribes and Castes,* Vol. 2, Government Press, Trivandrum.

Krishnakumar, Asha, 2004. A 'Primitive' Perspective, *Frontline,* Vol. 21, Issue 22, 23 October–5 November.

Krishnan, P.S., 2011. "Contradiction Between India's National Aspirations and Neglect of Constitutionally-mandated Rights of Scheduled Castes, Scheduled Tribes and Backward Classes: Can Indian Society and Teachers Take the Challenge to Bridge the Gap?" *Gijubhai Badekha Memorial Lecture,* NCERT, New Delhi.

Kumar, Mukul, 2004. "Relationship of Caste and Crime in Colonial India", A Discourse Analysis, *Economic and Political Weekly*, 6 March 2004, pp. 1078–1087.

Kumar, Pankaj, 2006. "Changing Dimensions of Tribal Education", *Third Concept*, April.

Kumar, Vijaya and Reddy, Narayana, 1988. Towards Tribal Development: A Case Study of the Chenchus in Andhra Pradesh, *Man and Life*, Vol. 14, No. 3–4, July–December, pp. 179–185.

Kundu, M., 1994. *Tribal Education: New Perspectives*, Gyan Publishing House, New Delhi.

Kurien, John, 1983. *Elementary Education in India: Myth, Reality, Alternative*, Vikas Publishing House, New Delhi.

Lakshmi Narayana, Unnava, 2008. *Malapalli: Triumph of Sanga*, Translated by Ramarao (english translation), V.V.B. Sahitya Akademi, English Translation, New Delhi.

Lalitha, Vakulabharanam, 1995. *The Making of Criminal Tribes: Patterns and Transition*, New Era Publications, Madras.

Lim, Li, Ai, and Anand, Rita, "Working Paper on Confronting Discrimination, Nomadic Communities in Rajasthan and Their Human Rights to Land and Adequate Housing, Housing and Land Rights Network", Habitat International Coalition, South Asian Regional Program, Delhi (Unpublished Report).

Malakondaiah, Srirama, 2000. *Kurru Charitra (History of Yerukulas, Telugu)*, Nayagara Printers, Hyderabad.

Malhotra, K.C., and Madhav Gadgil, 1981. "Ecological Basis of the Geography, Distribution of the Dhangars: A Pastoral Community Cluster of Maharashtra", *South Asian Anthropologist, Vol. No. 2, No. 2*.

Malhotra, O.P., 1998. *Tribal Education: Impact of Education on Tribal Life and Adjustment*, Cosmo Publications, New Delhi.

Mamoria, C.B., 1965. *Social Problems and Social Disorganisation in India*, Kitab Mahal, Allahabad.

Mane, Laxman, 1997. *Upara* (An outsider), (English Version), Translated by Kamat, A.K., Sahitya Akademi, New Delhi.

Mane, Laxman, 1997. *Vimuktaya Maharashtratil Vimukta Jamati – Ek Chitra Abhyas* (Marathi), Yashwantrao Charity Pratishthan, Mumbai.

Mane, Ramkrishna, 2001. 'Bhatkya Vimuktha Jati Jamati: Ek Parshwabhoomi' (Marathi), *Hakara* (Quarterly of Maharashtra Association of Anthropological Sciences), January–June, Pune.

Mathur, N.N.G., 1994. *Tribal Education: Past, Present and Future*, Shiva Publications, Udaipur.

Mathur, P.R.G. 1992. Tribal Education in Kerala in B. Chaudhari (ed.) *Education and Literacy Programmes*, Vol. IV, Inter-India Publications, New Delhi, pp. 54–98.

McCollum, Pamela, A., and Constance, L., Walker, "Minorities in America 2000", *Education and Urban Society,* Vol. 24, No. 2, February 2000.

Merton, Robert, K., 1957. *Social Theory and Social Structure,* The Free Press, New York.

Miller, Jane, 1983. *Many Voices: Bilingualism, Culture and Education,* Routledge and Kegan Paul, London.

Misra, P.K., 1969. Rehabilitation of Nomads: A Review, *The Eastern Anthropologist,* Vol. XXII, No. 3, September–December.

Misra, P.K., and Malhotra, K.C. (ed.), 1982. Nomadic Tribes in India, Anthropological Survey of India, Calcutta.

Mittal, A.C. and Sharma, J.B., 1998. *Tribal Movement, Politics and Religion in India: Tribal Movement in India,* Vol. 1, Radha Publications, New Delhi.

Mohapatra, Subash, 2007. "Repeal the Habitual Offenders Act and Effectively Rehabilitate the Denotified Tribes", United Nations to India". *Asian Tribune,* World Institute for Asian Studies (WIAS), Vol. II, No. 48.

Moodley, A., Kogila, 1986. "Canadian Multicultural Education: Promises and Practices" in Banks, J., et al. (eds), *Multicultural Education in Western Societies,* Holt Saunders, London.

More, Dadasaheb, 1983. *Gabal,* Marathi Shrividya Prakashan, Pune.

Mudiraj, Mutrasi, 1994. Tenugollu Caste-Change of Group From 'D' to Group 'A' in the list of BCs – Report Submitted to Backward Class Commission, AP.

Nagabhushanacharulu, Chirravuru, 1967. "Nomadism in Andhra Pradesh", Paper Presented in Andhra Pradesh Nomadic Tribes Welfare Conference and Seminar, held at Guntur on 23 April 1967, Under the Presidentship of U.N. Dhebar, President of the Bharatiya Ghumanthu Jan (Nomadic Tribes) Adimjati Sevak Sangh, New Delhi.

Nair, M.K.S. 1987. *Tribal Economy in Transition,* Inter India Publications, New Delhi.

Nambissan, G.B. 2000. "Identify, Exclusion and the Education of Tribal Communities", Wazir (ed.), *Gender Gaps in Literacy and Education,* Sage, New Delhi, pp. 175–224.

Nambissan, Geetha and Batra, Poonam, 1989. "Equity and Excellence: Issues in Indian Education", *Social Scientist,* Vol. 17, No. 9 and 10.

Nambissan, Geetha, B., 1994. "Language and Schooling of Tribal Children, Issues Related to Medium of Instruction", *Economic and Political Weekly,* 15 October.

National Commission for Women (NCW), 1994. Report on Development of Female Education Among Tribal Communities, NCW, New Delhi.

National Council for Educational Research and Training (NCERT), 1999. Sixth All India Educational Survey, Main Report. NCERT, New Delhi.

National Council for Educational Research and Training (NCERT), 2002. Seventh All-India School Educational Survey. NCERT, New Delhi.

National Council for Educational Research and Training (NCERT), 2000. Fifth Survey of Educational Research. Vol. I and II. NCERT, New Delhi.

National Council of Educational Research and Training (NCERT) (n.d.) Executive Summary: Learning Achievement of Students at the end of Class V. NCERT, New Delhi.

National Council of Educational Research and Training (NCERT), National Curriculum Framework, 2005, NCERT, New Delhi.

National Curriculum Framework, 2005. Position Paper, National Focus Group on Problems of Scheduled Caste and Scheduled Tribe Children, NCERT, April 2007.

Nehru, J., 1977. "An Approach to Tribal Problems", in H.M. Mathur (ed.), *Anthropology in the Development Process,* Vikas, New Delhi.

Omvedt, Gail, 1976. Adivasis, Culture and Modes of Production in India, *Bulletin of Concerned Asian Scholars,* (12)1, pp. 15–22.

Ordonez, Victor, M., and Kasaju, K., 1997. *Basic Education for Empowerment of the Poor,* Report of a Regional Study on Literacy as a Tool for Empowerment of the Poor, UNESCO Report, Bangkok, November.

Pandey, O.D., 1988. *Tribal Education at Secondary Level,* National Psychological Corporation, Agra.

Pareek, R.N., 1977. *Tribal Culture in Flux,* B.R. Publishing Company, Delhi.

Parthasarathy, Jakka, 1988. *The Yerukula, An Ethnographic Study,* Anthropological Survey of India, MHRD, Department of Culture, Government of India.

Patel, S., 1991. *Tribal Education in India,* Mittal Publications, New Delhi.

Pati, Biswamoy, (ed.), 2010. *Adivasis in Colonial India: Survival, Resistance and Negotiation,* Orient Blackswan, Hyderabad.

Pati, R.N., and Jena, B., (eds) 1989. *Tribal Development in India,* Ashish Publishing House, New Delhi.

Patrick, Clarence, H., "The Criminal Tribes of India with Special Emphasis on the Mang Ganidi: A Preliminary Report", *Man In India,* Vol. 48, No. 3, pp. 244–257.

Pattanayak, D.P., 1981. *Multilingualism and Mother Tongue Education,* Oxford University Press, New Delhi.

Pattanayak, D.P., 1987. *Multilingualism and Multiculturalism: Britain and India,* Occasional Paper No. 6, Centre for Multicultural Education, University of London.

Pattanayak, D.P., 1990. *Multilingualism in India,* Multilingual Matters Ltd., Clevedon.

Patwardhan, A., 2000. Tribal Perspectives of Education: A Case of Adivasis in the SSP Region of the Narmada Valley, Department of Education, Delhi University, New Delhi.

Pfeffer, G., 1997. *Contemporary Studies: Tribal Studies,* Vol. II, Concept Publishing Co., New Delhi.

Prakash, D.S., Raju Suryanarayana, R.S., "Ethnographic Profile of Yerukula Tribe of Andhra Pradesh", Department of Biotechnology, Godavari Institute of Engineering and Technology, Rajahmundry, Andhra Pradesh, *Studies on Tribes and Tribals*, 2010, 8(1), pp. 41–44.

Prakash, Ved, Gautam, S.K., Bansal, I.K., Bhalla, N., 1998. *Mid-Term Assessment Survey, An Appraisal of Students' Achievement*, DPEP Core Group, NCERT, New Delhi.

Prasad Rao, D.L., Rao, V.N.V.K., Singh, K.S., and Yaseen Saheb, 2003. The Yerukulas, in *People of India, Series, Vol. XIII, Andhra Pradesh*, East-West Press, Anthropological Survey of India, Calcutta.

Radhakrishna Meena, 2007. "Urban Denotified Tribes: Competing Identities, Contested Citizenship", *Economic and Political Weekly*, 22 December.

Radhakrishna, Meena, 1989. "From Tribal Community to Working Class Consciousness: Case of Yerukula Women", *Review of Women's Studies, Economic and Political Weekly*, 29 April.

Radhakrishna, Meena, 1989. "The Criminal Tribes Act in Madras Presidency, Implications for Itinerant Communities", *The Indian Economic and Social History Review*, 26, 3.

Radhakrishna, Meena, 1992. "Surveillance and Settlements Under the Criminal Tribes Act in Madras", *The Indian Economic and Social History Review*, 29, 2.

Radhakrishna, Meena, 1997. "Missionaries and Myth Making: Salvation Army and Itinerant Communities in Madras Presidency", Research in-Progress Paper in History and Society, Centre for Contemporary Studies, Nehru Memorial Museum and Library, New Delhi.

Radhakrishna, Meena, 2000. "Colonial Construction of a 'Criminal' Tribe, Yerukulas of Madras Presidency", *Economic and Political Weekly*, 8–15 July, pp. 2553–2563.

Radhakrishna, Meena, 2001. *Dishonoured by History, Criminal Tribes and British Colonial Policy*, Orient Longman, Hyderabad.

Radhakrishna, Meena, 2007. "Civil Society's Uncivil Acts: Dancing Bear and Starving Kalandar", *Economic and Political Weekly*, 20 October.

Radhakrishna, Meena, Crime of Vigilante Justice, *Economic and Political Weekly*, 12 – 18 January 2008, Vol. XLIII, No. 2, pp. 16–19.

Radhakrishna, Meena, 2006. Of Apes and Ancestors: Evolutionary Science and Colonial Ethnography, The Indian Historical Review, Vol. XXXIII, No. 1, pp. 1–23.

Raghavayya, V., 1949. *The Problem of Criminal Tribes*, Akhil Bhartiya Adim-Jati Sevak Sangh (BASS), New Delhi.

Raghunath, Rath, 2006. "Education of Tribal Children in Kandhamal District", *Orissa Review*, May.

Rama Rao, V., 1988. "Tribal Education and the Role of the Teacher", *Man and Life*, Vol. 14, No. 1–2, January–June.

Ramaswamy, Gita, 2002. "Lambadas: Changing Cultural Patterns", *Economic and Political Weekly, 20 April.*

Rampal, A., 2002. "Texts in Context: Development of Curricula, Textbooks and Teaching Learning Materials", in R. Govinda, *India Education Report: A Profile of Basic Education,* Oxford University Press, New Delhi, pp. 153–66.

Rani, Midatala, 2009. *Problems of Tribal Education in India Issues and Prospects,* Kanishka Publishers Distributors, New Delhi.

Rao, Aparna, and Casimir Michael, J. (ed.), 2003. *Nomadism in South Asia,* Oxford University Press, New Delhi.

Rao, Mohan, K., 1999. *Tribal Development in Andhra Pradesh: Problems, Performance and Prospects,* Booklinks Corporation, Hyderabad.

Rao, S.N. (n.d.) Mobility among the Scheduled Castes of Andhra Pradesh: A Sociological Perspective, Unpublished Paper.

Rath, K.B., 1990. A Study of the Effect of Household, Community and School Factors on the Enrolment, Retention and Achievement of Scheduled Tribe Children at Primary Level, NCERT, New Delhi.

Rathod, M., 2000. "Denotified and Nomadic Tribes in Maharashtra," Vadodara, Denotified Tribes Action Group.

Raval, Indubhai, B., 1964. "A Study of Crime Among the Bhils", *Man in India,* Vol. 44, No. 3, September, pp. 221–232.

Ray, Barhardt and Harrison, Barbara, 1993. "Developing Tribal Education Strategies in Indigenous Communities, Discourse", *The Australian Journal of Educational Studies,* October.

Reddy, Viswanadha, K., 2003. "A Study of Socio-Linguistic Aspects of Kin Behaviour Among the Yerukula Tribe in Rayalaseema Region of Andhra Pradesh, *Anthropologist,* 5(2), pp. 107–112.

Road to Freedom, 2005. Report on Technical Advisory Group, DNT RAG, Bhoodan, Maharashtra.

Roy Burman, B.K., 1994. *Tribes in Perspective,* Mittal Publication, New Delhi.

Roy Burman, J.J., 2010. *Ethnography of a Denotified Tribe,* Mittal Publishers, New Delhi.

Ruhela, Satya Pal, 1968. *The Gaduliya Lohars of Rajasthan: A Study in the Sociology of Nomadism,* Impex India, New Delhi.

Sachchidanand, 1992. *Tribal India: Past and Present,* Institute of Social Research and Applied Anthropology, Kolkata.

Samavesh, 2003. Dalit, Adivasi aur School. Bhopal: Bhopal Rehabilitation.

Sastry, V.N.V.K., 1993. Chenchu Food Gatherers and Hunters of Nallamala Forests, Problems of Transition, *Man and Life,* Vol. 19, No. 1–2, January–June, pp. 83–96.

Saxena, Sadhna, and Kamal Mehendroo, 1993. "Politics of Language", *Economic and Political Weekly,* 6 November.

Shah, P.G., 1967. *Vimukta Jatis, Denotified Communities in Western India,* Gujrat Research Society, Bombay.

Shah, V.P. and Patel T., 1985. *Social Contexts of Tribal Education*, Concept Publishing Co., New Delhi.

Sharan, Awadhendra, 2003. "From Caste to Category: Colonial Knowledge Practices and the Depressed/Scheduled Castes of Bihar", *The Indian Economic and Social History Review*, 40, 3.

Sharma, Anita, 2011. "South Asian Nomads: A Literature Review, Consortium for Research on Educational Access, Transitions and Equity, Creative Pathways to Access", *Research Monograph No. 58*, January, University of Sussex, Centre for International Education.

Sharma, D.K., 1994. *Education and Socialisation among the Tribes*, Commonwealth, New Delhi.

Sharma, G.D. and Sujatha, K., 1983. *Educating Tribals: An Indepth Analysis of Ashram Schools*, NIEPA, New Delhi.

Shashi, P.S., and Varma, P.S., 1991. *Socio-History of Ex-Criminal Communities OBCs*, Sandeep Prakashan, New Delhi.

Shyamala, K., 2009. *Vanishing Nomadism: The Saga of Dommaras*, Dravidian University, Kuppam.

Shyamlal, 1987. *Education among Tribals*, Printwell Publishers, Jaipur.

Simhadri, Y.C., 1974. Institutional Factors and Tribal Criminality: An Analysis of an Yerukula Tribe in Andhra Village, *The Eastern Anthropologist*, Vol. 27, No. 1, January–March.

Simhadri, Y.C., 1979. *The Ex-Criminal Tribes of India*, National, New Delhi.

Simhadri, Y.C., 1991. *Denotified Tribes: A Sociological Analysis*, Classical Publishing Company, New Delhi.

Singh, A.K., 1995. "Drop-out from Primary Schools in Tribal India: A Case Study of the Ho in Parampancho, West Singhbhum", Ph.D. Thesis submitted to University of London, Department of International and Comparative Education.

Singh, A.K., 1995. "The Cultural Construction of Home and School Knowledge in Tribal India", *Prospects*, 25(4), pp. 735–47.

Singh, Birinder Pal, (ed.), 2010. *Criminal Tribes of Punjab: A Social-Anthropological Inquiry*, Routledge, New Delhi.

Singh, K.S. and Manoharan, S., 1993. *People of India: National Series, Vol. IX, Language and Scripts*, Anthropological Survey of India, Oxford University Press, New Delhi.

Singh, K.S., 1985. *Tribal Society in India*, Manohar Publication, New Delhi.

Sitarama Rao, 1927. Kona, Yerukulas, (Telugu), in *Andhra Bharati Monthly*, Issue No. 1–12, April 1927 to March 1928, pp. 177–180.

Somasekhar, A., 1987. "Tribal Development in Andhra Pradesh: Certain Issues", *Man and Life*, Vol. 13, Nos. 1–2, January–June, pp. 67–76.

Srivastava L.R.N., 1987. Education and of the Tribal People Economic Development, *Man and Life*, Vol. 13, Nos. 3–4, June–December, pp. 141–148.

Srivastava, L.R.N., 1992. "Development of Curriculum for Tribal Students" in Buddhadeb Chaudhari (ed.), *Tribal Transformation in India,* Vol. 14, Education and Literacy Programmes, Inter-India Publications, New Delhi.

Subba Reddy, Kethu, 1997. "Tribal Education in Andhra Pradesh, A Sociological Exploration", Unpublished Ph.D. Thesis submitted to Jawaharlal Nehru University, New Delhi.

Sudhakara Reddy, P., Raja Reddy, K., 2001. "Tribal Parents' Awareness About Educational Incentives in Andhra Pradesh", *Journal of Educational Planning and Administration,* Vol. XV, No. 3, July, pp. 377–386.

Sujatha, K., 1987. *Education of the Forgotten Children of the Forests: A Case Study of Yennadi Tribe,* Konark Publishers, New Delhi.

Sujatha, K., 1990. Education in Ashram Schools: A Case of Andhra Pradesh, *NUEPA Occasional Paper,* National University of Educational Planning and Administration, New Delhi.

Sujatha, K., 1994. *Educational Development Among Tribes: A Study of Sub-Plan Areas in Andhra Pradesh,* South Asian Publishers, New Delhi.

Sujatha, K., 1996. *Single Teacher Schools in Tribal Areas: A Study of Girijan Vidya Vikas Kendras in Andhra Pradesh,* Vikas Publishing Company, New Delhi.

Sujatha, K., 1998. *Evaluation of Quality Improvement Programmes in Education: A Study in Tribal Areas of Visakhapatnam, Andhra Pradesh,* National University of Educational Planning and Administration, New Delhi.

Sujatha, K., 1999. *Education of India Schedule Tribes: A Study of Community Schools in the District of Visakhapatnam, Andhra Pradesh,* UNESCO, International Institute for Educational Planning, Paris.

Sujatha, K., 2002. Education among Scheduled Tribes, in R. Govinda, *India Education Report: A Profile of Basic Education,* Oxford University Press, New Delhi.

Sundar, N. (forthcoming 2006). "Tribal Politics", in S. Wolpert (ed.) *Encyclopaedia of India,* Charles Scribners and Sons, New York.

Sundar, N. (n.d.), A Note on Adivasi Education, Unpublished Paper.

Sundar, N., 2004. "Teaching to Hate 'RSS' Pedagogical Programme", *Economic and Political Weekly,* 39(16), pp. 1605–1612.

Sundar, N., 2005. "Adivasi vs. Vanvasi: The Politics of Conversion and Re-conversion in Central India", In S. Saberwal, M. Hasan (eds) *Assertive Religious Identities,* Permanent Black, New Delhi.

Technical Advisory Group, Report on Nomadic and Denotified Tribes, New Delhi.

Tilak, J.B.G., 2000. Education Poverty in India, *Occasional Papers,* NUEPA, New Delhi.

Tucker, F., Booth, 1916. '*Criminocurology or the Indian Crime and What to do with Him: A Review of the Work of the Salvation Army Among the Criminal Tribes, Habituals and Released Prisoners in India*', Liddell's Printing Works, Simla.

Varghese, N.V., 1994. School Quality and Students Learning: A Study of Primary Schooling in Kerala, DPEP Baseline Study, NUEPA, New Delhi.

Vedavathy, S., 2002. Folk Medicinal Wisdom of Chittoor District, Andhra Pradesh, Indian Folklife, *A Quarterly Newsletter From National Folklore Support Centre,* Vol. 2, Issue 1, July.

Veeraiah, Palaparti, 1964. "What we did 1924–1964", *The Report of the 7th Conference for Scheduled Tribes and Tribal Areas*, Bharatiya Adimjati Sevak Sangh, November, Guntur.

Verma, R.C., 1995. *Indian Tribes Through the Ages*, Publications Division, Ministry of Information and Broadcasting, Government of India.

Wankhede, C.G. and Padma Velaskar, 1999. The Post-Matric Scholarship Scheme for SC/ST in Maharashtra and Goa: An Evaluation, Mimeo Inc., TISS, Mumbai.

Wankhede, G.G., 2001. Educational Inequalities among Maharashtra's Scheduled Castes, *Economic and Political Weekly,* Vol. XXXVI, No. 18, pp. 1553–1558.

Wells, J., 1985. "Language and Learning – As Interactional Perspective" in Wells, Gordoa and John Nichols (eds), *Language and Learning: An International Perspective*, The Falmer Press, London.

Wiles, Silvaine, 1981. "Language Issues in the Multicultural Classrooms" in Mercer, N., (ed.) *Language in School and Community*, Edward Arnold, London.

Wiles, Silvaine, 1985. "Language and Learning in Multi-Ethnic Classrooms: Strategies for Supporting Bilingual Students" in Wells, Gordon and John Nichols, (eds): *Language and Learning: An International Perspective*, The Falmer Press, London.

Xaxa, V., 1999a. "Transformation of Tribes in India: Terms of Discourse," *Economic and Political Weekly,* 34(24), pp. 1519–1524.

Xaxa, V., 1999b. "Tribes as Indigenous People of India", *Economic and Political Weekly*, 35(51), pp. 3589–95.

Xaxa, V., 2001. 'Protective Discrimination: Why Scheduled Tribes Lag Behind Scheduled Castes', *Economic and Political Weekly,* 36(29), pp. 2765–2772.

Index